T0286889

THE
ROCHDALE
DIVISION

THE
ROCHDALE
DIVISION

Conversations with Star Players, Managers
and Cult Heroes of Rochdale AFC

CHRISTOPHER FITZGERALD

First published by Pitch Publishing, 2022

Pitch Publishing
9 Donnington Park,
85 Birdham Road,
Chichester,
West Sussex,
PO20 7AJ
www.pitchpublishing.co.uk
info@pitchpublishing.co.uk

ISBN 978 1 80150 377 8

Typesetting and origination by Pitch Publishing
Printed and bound in India by Replika Press Pvt. Ltd.

Contents

In memory of club saviour

David F. Kilpatrick and

dedicated to all of those who

make Rochdale AFC mean so

much to so many.

Introduction

AS I picked my way among the throng of fellow supporters milling around the pop-up beer stall and inflatable penalty goals that had been erected outside Spotland Stadium, it truly hit home what Rochdale AFC means to me, and to all of its followers.

The festival occasion the club had put on to mark its 100 unbroken years of Football League membership took on an extra resonance. It wasn't just a nod to a sentimental milestone, it was a nod to survival, against all odds. Formed in 1907 and accepted into the Football League in 1921, never has the club been penalised for living beyond its means, nor has it ever sought to be more than the community-based hub it truly is. This is largely down to a legacy of like-mindedness.

Occupying that grey area of geographical identity between Greater Manchester and Lancashire, and living in a deep, enveloping shadow of football behemoths on all sides, Rochdale has always offered something different to the extravagant norm.

In a world of haves and have nots, football is seen as an anomaly. At the top end of the spectrum, many clubs, let alone the players who pull on their shirts, have lost most of the roots which bound them to their communities. Lifelong fans can no longer afford the ticket prices to go to games. This has never been an issue for Rochdale AFC. It has always been an inclusive place, where ageing supporters have easily been able to bring the next generation, hoping they too will catch the bug and continue the legacy.

The centenary event in August 2021 was a celebration of strength and durability. For a small club such as Rochdale AFC,

100 unbroken years in the Football League is quite remarkable. In that time, the club has survived league re-elections, mismanagement by celebrity chairmen, an attempted hostile takeover and a global pandemic.

However, those 100 years have also brought with them little in the way of success on the field.

In fact, for so long had Rochdale AFC occupied the fourth tier of English football – from 1921 to 1969 and then 1974 to 2010 – that the division was unofficially named after it. 'The Rochdale Division'; the bestowment wasn't meant as a compliment.

When I began supporting the club in 1988, as an eight-year-old boy, the gates were little over 1,000 and the players on the pitch were not the athletes who take to the field today. The latter was not unusual; it was typical of British football as a whole – but a revolution was coming that would leave Rochdale even further behind football's elite.

By the late 1980s, English football was beginning to unravel. Since the glory of the World Cup win in 1966, the game had become mired by hooliganism. The 'working man's sport' seemed to mirror the plight of the working classes in Thatcher's Britain. Grounds were crumbling and unsafe, facilities were poor; admission prices were rising. The product on the park was a far cry from the days of Bobby Moore, Geoff Hurst and Bobby Charlton.

Football's reinvention came at a critical – in fact literally terminal – time for the game. A series of separate disasters, at Heysel, Bradford and Hillsborough, resulted in the tragic deaths of hundreds of fans. These off-the-pitch events forced clubs and authorities to drag the game into the modern world, and turn it from a relic of a bygone age into a world-leading example of a premier entertainment event.

New stadia emerged from the crumbling terraces in towns and cities across the country. Shiny, plastic, all-seated, family-friendly places. They were safe, comfortable, easier to police.

Meanwhile, media magnate Rupert Murdoch took a gamble with his newly launched satellite television service and started to invest unprecedented sums of money into the elite end of the game. This, coupled with the rebrand of the European Cup to the Champions League, brought the promise of pots of gold at the end of the goal line.

English football was quick to exploit the potential. A new Premier League marketed itself aggressively, attracting affluent new spectators prepared to spend thousands of pounds to become a passive part of an upwardly mobile pastime.

This was great for the top clubs, but the money was slow to trickle down to Rochdale's level. Admirably, while this revolution was taking place, Rochdale refused to bite. The club stayed true to what it had always been. Other clubs overstretched themselves in order to buy a quick ticket to the big time, the inevitable outcome being that the administrators were called in and league points were docked.

But, while it is remarkable that Rochdale relied on player sales, meagre gates and the occasional benevolence of directors to get by, it is perhaps even more commendable that a string of managers during this period agreed to take on the footballing challenge that comes with austerity.

Only one man has managed to triumph against this adversity at Rochdale during the Premier League era. Keith Hill, unarguably the best to ever hold the post of manager, took an unfashionable, penurious club and made it known for flowing football and overachievement. In 2015, the club accomplished its highest-ever league finish – eighth in the third tier. Heady days indeed.

It was all achieved without a rich benefactor too, nor via the club spending beyond its means. Spotland Stadium, while having undergone some modernisation, still remained the quaint back-street sanctuary it always was, an agreeable contrary to the new generation of out-of-town identikit monstrosities other teams now call home.

Other men sought to achieve the greatness experienced by Hill, both before and after him, seeking to rid the club of its tiresome fourth-tier anchor or, latterly, to keep Rochdale at the next level. None succeeded.

The first pages of this book contain the accounts of managers who, at differing points over the past 30 years, have sought to make their own mark, each under a divergent set of circumstances.

This book is not meant to be an exhaustive or comprehensive account of the club's history during this time. It is instead a chance to explore the viewpoint of these managers, to obtain an insight that fans in the stands were never privy to. It is an attempt to understand what possessed them to manage 'little old Rochdale' in the first place and how they found the experience. Mick Docherty describes the task akin to 'batting against thunder'. This analogy sounds so fitting, conjuring a perfect image of impossibility.

I want to thank each and every one of those who contributed, not just for talking to me, but for being open and honest about a period in their career that was not always easy. Each provided a unique insight into the struggles and joys of managing a traditionally unfashionable club in the modern age. For the managers I was unable to speak to – John Hollins and Alan Buckley – I turned to former players Gareth Griffiths and Paul Connor to share their memories of what it was like to play under these men for the limited time they were in charge.

And it isn't just the managers who deserve credit for taking on the impossible. The players, too, countless numbers of them, have contributed to both Rochdale's achievements and bank balance over the past 30 years.

While the Premier League is seen by many as a detriment to lower-league football in England, it still remains the dream of almost all players to make it to the elite end of the game. But when does a player transition from being merely good enough to play and become elite? Is it all technical? Or does physicality and mentality play a part, too? What makes a player not only talented enough to play the professional game, but also intelligent enough to retain and then execute manoeuvres akin to a seasoned chess player – without the time to ponder them?

Throughout the 1980s and most of the 1990s, it was rare to see any Rochdale player demonstrate what could be termed an elite level of ability. The club was, on the whole, a destination for players who were on the downward slope of their career path, the last stop on the lower-league journeyman express.

But from the turn of the century, a not insignificant number of players went on to achieve their dreams at the top end of the game. I ask them, in their view, what they had within themselves that so many others didn't. Perhaps more importantly, I also wanted to find out just how big a role Rochdale AFC played in allowing them to fulfil their potential. The Rochdale connection, if you will. In doing so, they justify Dale's place in the food chain.

I would like to thank all of the players who agreed to speak to me and, when they did, for being engaging and open enough to bring their stories to life. Understandably, there were some periods in certain players' careers that were off limits but, thankfully, none involved Rochdale.

You will hear from Alan Reeves, a player who progressed from Rochdale when it was still very much the club most readily associated with the basement division. There are stories from Rochdale's own sons Craig Dawson and Matt Gilks, prolific strikers Rickie Lambert and Adam Le Fondre, the fleet-footed Will Buckley and Paddy McCourt, and mobile target man Glenn Murray.

While some of these players are rightly labelled as modern Rochdale AFC legends, it's not to discount the efforts and ability of others who contributed just as much to the cause but never made the top. To me, the efforts of players such as Steve Whitehall, Shaun Reid, Gary Jones, Calvin Andrew and Ian Henderson will always carry as much weight as those who secured the big-money moves, and their exploits are for the third section of this book. They are the cult heroes and their stories deserve to be heard and remembered. These are players who racked up the appearances, goals or both. The players who shed blood for the cause and left everything on the pitch, week in and week out. I ask them what it was that created a bond with the club as strong as that shared by the supporters.

In all of this, many of the same stories or events are touched upon across 30 years, told as seen through different eyes. This creates something of a Rashomon effect, but that is important. Managing or playing for Rochdale AFC seems much like supporting it. The experience is different for everyone – but the challenges and rewards are shared by all.

Timeline

**Key Rochdale AFC personnel in the timeframe
covered by this book:**

1992–2006:
Chairman: David F. Kilpatrick
Managers: Dave Sutton, Mick Docherty, Graham
Barrow, Steve Parkin, John Hollins, Paul Simpson,
Alan Buckley
Players: Shaun Reid, Alan Reeves, Steve Whitehall, Paul
Butler, Gary Jones, Paddy McCourt, Matt Gilks

2006–2018:
Chairman: Chris Dunphy
Managers: Steve Parkin, Keith Hill, Steve Eyre,
John Coleman
Players: Gary Jones, Matt Gilks, Grant Holt, Rickie
Lambert, Glenn Murray, Adam Le Fondre, Will
Buckley, Craig Dawson, Calvin Andrew, Ian Henderson

2018–2021:
Chairman: Andrew Kilpatrick
Managers: Keith Hill, Brian Barry-Murphy
Players: Ian Henderson, Calvin Andrew

Part I
The Managers

Mick Docherty

1994–1996

THE SUMMER of 1992. The formation of the FA Premier League is dominating the media headlines, but there is no such fanfare at Rochdale AFC, who are shaping up to compete in the resultant newly branded Football League Third Division. Jesting, supporters remark that the renaming of the old Fourth Division is the only way the club could ever achieve promotion.

It isn't a joke for assistant manager Mick Docherty, however. He knows clubs such as Rochdale are now to receive less money from the league and other rights deals than previously. Key players such as Mark Leonard will need to be sold to compensate. Fellow bottom-tier stablemates Aldershot and Maidstone have already gone to the wall. Gates are dwindling.

The hope of bettering the previous season's performance, which saw the club miss out on the play-off places on the final day with 67 points (Rochdale's highest achieved under three points for a win at this point), looks remote before a ball has even been kicked in anger.

Yet Docherty, along with his enigmatic manager Dave Sutton, will seek to battle against these odds and deliver something the supporters can truly celebrate for the first time since 1969, the last and only time the club has managed to escape the dreaded 'Rochdale Division'.

With the scene set, Sutton and Docherty would be the first in a line of management teams to attempt to haul 'little old Rochdale' from its namesake division during the Premier League era, an era of avarice and impecuniousness.

The son of Scotland international and former Manchester United manager Tommy Docherty, Mick knew his way around the game. As a player himself, he had demonstrated his ability as a full-back for Burnley, Manchester City and Sunderland, before injury brought an early halt to his career.

Throughout the 1980s he'd carved a niche as a coach or manager, with Sunderland, Hartlepool United and Hull among the clubs added to his CV, before he joined Rochdale as Sutton's number two in 1991. His first season in the post was the best Rochdale had had for years. A good many players from that time credit 'The Doc' for that.

Thirty years on, Docherty has lost none of his love for regimen, illustrated at his approval when I call him at exactly 10am, the pre-agreed time of our telephone chat. 'Very prompt, good man,' he says.

It was this discipline that first caused Sutton, himself fresh into the Rochdale hot seat, to seek Docherty out.

'Dave Sutton, a terrific man, who I can't speak highly enough of, approached me and asked me to be his number two,' Docherty recalls. 'I said, "I must warn you, Dave, that I am very volatile and I am very outspoken. I'm likely to say things that might upset you and upset the whole applecart." He didn't care. He said he'd seen me work on the training field at Lilleshall [National Sports Centre] and thought I'd be perfect for the job. As it turned out, we were a management team made in heaven. He was terrific as a manager because he was diplomatic and articulate, whereas I was less so – calling people out, no matter who they were and no matter what the outcome might be. Don't get me wrong, Dave wasn't a soft touch. He could fire off in the dressing room if the situation demanded it. He was a good judge of character too, and he allowed me to get on with the coaching side more or less on my own. It worked and the players responded to that.

'I wasn't given a formal contract, though. In fact, I never had one the whole time I was at Rochdale. Dave had one, but I think the board were trying to protect themselves from having to pay out too much should things go awry. I remember the chairman, David Kilpatrick, once said to me, "As long as you do the job we ask, you don't need a contract, because you won't be sacked."'

Such prudence from the late David Kilpatrick, and his firm friend Graham Morris, the club's finance director, would prove a frustration for Docherty. Yet, what the pair had achieved to keep Rochdale AFC in business, never mind in the Football League, lent much weight to their approach.

Kilpatrick first engaged with the club in 1980, in the days when league status for those finishing bottom of it was dependent on re-election by fellow members. Dale retained their place in the Fourth Division by a single vote that year. Kilpatrick certainly knew what he was getting into. The club was destitute and owed money for the stadium. Kilpatrick and Morris, together, salvaged this dire situation, thanks to Morris's own background in accountancy. Kilpatrick's own business background was a curious combination of funeral care and granite. He became Rochdale chairman in 1982, but stepped aside when comedian Tommy Cannon promised riches for the club in the mid-'80s. He stepped back in again after Cannon had left Rochdale riddled with debt, and, once more, steered the club back on to as stable a footing as could be managed. While a wealthy local businessman, Kilpatrick had nowhere near the capital possessed by the big-spending chairmen of the top division. Judiciousness was a necessity.

It was against this backdrop, and at the dawn of a new decade, that Sutton and Docherty began to deliver the first on-field hope the Rochdale supporters had experienced in what felt like an age. Despite the 1991/92 season being the best at Rochdale for more than two decades, the final-day disappointment came after a staggering collapse in form. Dale had lost five of their last six games and they took this malaise into the 1992/93 season, losing the league opener against Halifax and both legs of the League Cup against Crewe Alexandra.

'Sometimes it can take a while for that kind of disappointment to pass,' Docherty reflects. 'You see it sometimes the following season. There can be a hangover. A self-questioning of confidence and ability. We worked it out of the players, though, and results did pick up.'

A topsy-turvy season would follow, with Dale always in the hunt for a play-off spot, but then, applying grease to their own hands just when a firm grip mattered most they finished 11th, five points adrift.

'We came up just short again,' Docherty says. 'I think we needed a boost. A player or two, but it just didn't happen. We inevitably slid backwards. It was very frustrating for Dave and I.'

A lack of resources will become a recurring theme during our conversation.

'You really need to remember what football was like back then,' Docherty continues. 'We had no training ground to speak of. We were on local parks – you know, the dog shit and the public. We were begging land off the council, or schools for their gym halls. We couldn't train at Spotland because we shared the stadium with Hornets [the town's rugby league team] and there was an agreement neither team would train, to protect the pitch as much as possible.

'We then had long journeys to places such as Torquay or Exeter to play matches. Bigger clubs could fly to games, or at the very least teams could have an overnighter. We used to go down and back up in a single day most of the time. Things like that can make a difference to a result, they truly can.'

The following summer would see the establishment or arrival of some real household names in Rochdale folklore. Centre-half Alan Reeves would cement his reputation as one of the best in the lower leagues, as would his understudy Paul Butler. Goalkeeper Martin Hodge, too, would attract praise for his brick-wall, match-winning displays. Shaun Reid would demonstrate all of the qualities that a bottom-tier midfield disrupter should have, while Mark Stuart would dazzle on the wing as Steve Whitehall rattled the back of the net with regularity.

However, after being realistic play-off challengers for the past two seasons, tensions became high as the pressure to actually deliver grew. In fact, Docherty himself was sent from the dugout after Chester City were awarded a dubious penalty by Jeff Winter in one key game.

'The referee wanted to make a name for himself that day,' he recalls. 'It was an absolutely obscene penalty decision. I ranted and raved and he sent me off. So, he achieved double the notoriety. I mean, I am volatile, but I can usually keep a lid on it if I really have to, but I really couldn't that day. I was so incensed by a decision I thought was unfair. It's a decision like that which can affect whether a team makes the play-offs or not. So much was riding on it.'

Sadly, the quality of the squad still didn't translate into a play-off position. Once again, Dale were there or thereabouts for much of the season, but ultimately finished ninth, this time four points adrift.

'We had so many good players that season,' Docherty laments. 'Again, the pattern of a good start gave way to indifference. It's at this point you need to inject something new into the side – even better players. We didn't get the opportunity to do so, and so we just couldn't push on.'

The 1994/95 season would prove to be a pivotal one for Rochdale – and for Docherty himself. It would see the end of Dale's mini resurgence as promotion contenders and firmly reacquaint them with the bottom half of the division. It would also see Docherty take managerial office for himself.

There was little foreshadowing of what was to come. Rochdale did lose star goalkeeper Hodge to Plymouth in the summer, but saw off a Manchester United XI 3-2 in pre-season, beating a side containing a host of future first-team stars such as Gary Neville and David Beckham.

'I remember we actually played two games against Man United in consecutive pre-seasons,' Docherty says. 'One was for the public at Spotland and the other was behind closed doors at The Cliff. I think there was a bit of bother with the latter one because Eric Cantona played while he was banned and I don't think he should have. We played well in both games and I remember we took confidence from them into the new season. We were dominant with the group we had.'

The season began with Rochdale defeating arch rivals Bury at Gigg Lane. Then, a 4-1 demolition of Chesterfield, followed by an away point at Gillingham and a home win against Lincoln, focused minds once again on a promotion campaign.

Then came a 3-1 home defeat to Hereford, but the poor performance that day was not what sticks in the mind. It was the news that Alan Reeves had played his last game for the club, having signed for Premier League Wimbledon. The reported fee was £200,000. Vital money for the Rochdale coffers, no doubt, but the sale also proved a tangible marker for the team's decline on the pitch.

'I tried to use the sale of Alan Reeves to motivate the other players,' Docherty says. 'You know, telling them they could land a big move if they attained the same standard? Work hard and you will earn better wages and a better life for you and your family, that kind of thing. He was a massive loss to the team, though, with no shadow of a doubt. We were a player or two away from pushing on, in my opinion. Me and Dave knew what was needed, but we weren't given it.'

Some heavy defeats would follow – 6-2 at Barnet sticks in the mind – and Dale would struggle to effectively replace departed goalkeeper Hodge. Chris Clarke had stepped up to some acclaim but then suffered a nasty head injury, which led to reserve stopper Neil Dunford being thrown into the fray, before the infamous Matt Dickins joined on loan from Blackburn.

'Dicko was actually a good goalkeeper,' Docherty says. 'Problem is, goalies make mistakes. Even now, you watch the top goalies and you think, "How the fuck has he let that in?" If a goalie makes a mistake, it usually costs the team a goal. There is no hiding place for them. Dicko seemed to have a run like that. He got a lot of stick, but he was a good goalie, genuinely.'

The board finally lost patience with manager Sutton following a 1-0 defeat to bottom side Hartlepool in November. Despite delivering some of the club's most competitive seasons in a very long time, Dale fans were not completely vexed by his departure. Sutton had been perceived as having regular digs at supporters and his stock at the bank of goodwill was low. Docherty filled the position on a caretaker basis initially, and steered the side into the next round of the Auto Windscreens Shield and took four points from the next two league games.

'I asked Dave to be more forthright in the boardroom,' Docherty says. 'We had a good side but, more importantly, we had the makings of a *really* good side – certainly good enough to get out of Division Three and possibly the next division. If we had done that, then Dave becomes a manager with two promotions on his CV and me likewise as a first-team coach. We get a better life together. For that to happen, I told him he needed to become more dominant in the boardroom to get us what we needed. I think he tried that and, in doing so, he rubbed people up the wrong way and got sacked. I was astonished. As soon as he got the sack, I was leaving too. I was walking out the door with him. He says, "No, I want you to stay on." Out of courtesy and respect for him, I did as he asked. I inherited the same problems he had, though. The board, in my opinion, were not forward-looking. Despite what they said publicly, I think they were happy to stay in the division and enjoy the odd cup run, but anything more? No. We were always confident of taking the club forward, Dave and I. Our mantra to the board was always, "Don't sell the centre-halves and don't sell Reidy because they are the backbone of the side," and yet they got rid of all three eventually.'

There was much speculation at this time as to whether or not Docherty would land the job permanently. Rumours flourished that the Rochdale board had approached a host of names, including Sammy McIlroy, who was guiding Macclesfield Town to certain promotion to the Football League from the Conference, now the National League. Whatever the outcome of those conversations, the board saw fit to name Docherty permanent gaffer in the new year.

'I was aware the board were talking to other people,' Docherty says. 'It was difficult in that situation but I was keen to do as well as I could to prove my worth to anyone else who might come in. When I got the job permanently, I just carried on with what I had been doing. I already had a bond with these players as I was their coach. I was inclusive – whether they were in the team, on the bench or injured. They were all important to me. I still didn't get a bloody contract, though.'

Hindsight now may infer what happened next was a dead cat bounce, but Docherty's permanent appointment coincided with an upturn in form. Dale remained unbeaten during the next four league games and made the Northern Final of the Auto Windscreens Shield, where they met league leaders Carlisle over two legs for a chance to play at Wembley. These games are still talked about by supporters to this day. The first leg, at Brunton Park, took place amid a monsoon. Dale captain Andy Thackeray won the toss and elected to play into the howling gale. Trailing 3-0 at half-time, the decision looked a poor one. Worse, the wind dropped in the second half and Dale headed home on the back of a 4-1 defeat.

The return leg required Dale to win by three clear goals. The odds were against them.

'It was an opportunity to get some silverware on the counter,' says Docherty. 'A real opportunity for the club to attain something. Yes, the competition is a minor one, but it would still have been an achievement. When we went to Carlisle, I know conditions were horrendous, but I don't think we turned up on the night. We got them back to our place with a mountain to climb but we couldn't quite climb it. We put in a magnificent display, one of Reidy's best games for us, and we won 2-1. It wasn't enough, though. We were all disappointed and I think that led to a downturn in our league form because, after that, there was a feeling the season was over.'

This did indeed prove to be the final highlight of the 1994/95 season. Dale limped to a 15th-placed finish and Docherty was faced with preparing for his first, and only, full season in charge.

He managed to finally solve his goalkeeping dilemma with the permanent signing of Ian Gray in the summer, but had to contend with the loss of his combative midfielder Shaun Reid, who moved to Bury for a tribunal-set fee of £15,000.

'Shaun Reid was a proper player,' Docherty says. 'He was one of them where you just looked in each other's eyes and knew what the other was thinking without the need to speak. You just knew what you were going to get from him and that was 100 per cent commitment.

'I was absolutely ripping when he went to Bury. I actually tried to buy Shaun back later in the season. I asked the chairman for ten grand as that would have got him. The chairman wouldn't give it to me. I says, "Listen, Mr Chairman, he will get us into the play-offs, he will get us promoted and he will repay that ten grand many times over in doing so." But he wouldn't do it. Other than Ian, I didn't get in any of the players I wanted that summer. It was then I knew I was batting against thunder in this job.'

Docherty's internal misgivings aside, Rochdale opened the season with a 3-3 draw against Cardiff City, beat Second Division York City in the League Cup first leg and saw off Darlington in their first away fixture.

'I went with the squad I had, which, to be fair, still had terrific players in it. Paul Butler, Jason Peake, Mark Stuart, Steve Whitehall. That was a solid base. I had to motivate them, convince them, that we could be successful.'

Hopes were high when Rochdale visited Bootham Crescent to face York in the second leg of the League Cup with a 2-1 advantage, but the visiting side were trounced 5-1 after taking the match to extra time.

'It was the first time that season that I saw the players doubt themselves,' Docherty remembers. 'It didn't help that York went on to draw Manchester United in the next round. That caused a few mutters at boardroom level. Although I am told that it doesn't work like that and we would have, in fact, drawn Leicester had we won. Regardless, the result cost the club much-needed revenue.'

There appeared to be no cup hangover as Dale smashed Hartlepool 4-0 via a hat-trick from teenage sensation Jamie Taylor on the Saturday when returning to league business, the start of a run that – with a few setbacks aside – made Rochdale look like free-scoring promotion contenders once again. They dispatched Exeter City 4-2, while Docherty also takes the plaudits for overseeing an end to Rochdale's 75-year wait to win a game of football in London, Barnet being the recipients of a 4-0 hiding.

'The best away performance of this side during my whole time at the club, was that,' Docherty testifies.

The goals kept coming. Paul Moulden, who had been at the club on trial, scored a hat-trick as Dale beat Darlington 5-2 in the Auto Windscreens Shield and they followed this up with a terrific 5-3 FA Cup win against Rotherham United, who at the time were in the division above.

'We were very capable going forward,' Docherty enthuses, seemingly pleased to be reminded of some phenomenal scorelines. 'My dad used to say, when he was manager at Manchester United, "If they score three, we'll score four." I adopted that approach. I told the players, we might lose two goals, but I knew they could get three or four. So, I said to them, "As long as we win the game, that's what matters." Well, I know it might be exciting for the supporters, but it gave me the jitters during the games themselves. When I played at Burnley, Man City and Sunderland, we always had attacking players with flair, who could turn a chance into a goal. I always used to work on that theme at Rochdale. Players such as Mark Stuart, Jason Peake and Steve Whitehall really bought into that.'

Then the wheels fell off. Inexplicably. Dale simply stopped their free-scoring ways. Results became patchy as a consequence.

'We wanted to get better by buying better players,' Docherty says. 'We had to buy players who not only made us better but gave us the chance to sell them on for more money, so we could buy even better players. It was an idea pitched to the board but I was never given the opportunity. I think that was the crux of the matter. If you have a squad of 17 or 18 players and they are all fit, you have a chance of attaining something because you work together day in and day out. You create a bond. But players would be sold or players would get injured and we never got the means to adequately replace them. You aren't going to get success that way.

'Around this time, we lost Mark Stuart to injury. That was a big one. He fractured his jaw against Rotherham. I had to call Darren

Ryan into the first team, but he wasn't reliable. We would then lose players for smaller periods – Jason Peake for a couple, Ian Gray had to be rested as he had an operation in the summer – things like that. We would play games with what I would call half a team or I'd have to play players out of position.'

Rochdale had fallen to eighth in the league after the Christmas period but did manage to scrape past Darlington to set up an FA Cup third round tie with Liverpool at Anfield. It was a grand day out for this writer, who was only 15 years old in January 1996. However, after taking my seat in the historic stadium, awe gave way to dismay. A hat-trick from Stan Collymore, a first Reds goal for Jason McAteer and Ian Rush overtaking Denis Law's FA Cup scoring record made sure the day was all about Liverpool. Docherty's team on the afternoon, after a sprightly start, failed to make any kind of impact on a 7-0 scoreline.

'Initially, I was excited by the draw,' Docherty says. 'It was an opportunity for the players to show what they had against the best there was at the time. A chance to strut their stuff in among the Premier League celebrities. It was also an opportunity for the club to earn a lot of money. We earned £115,000 that day, I was told. After the game, we were in the boardroom at Anfield and former Liverpool manager Bob Paisley, one of the most bejewelled managers in the world, comes up to me and says, "Michael, it's not the world's worst disaster. You played well, especially in the first half." He was right in a fashion. Up until 40 minutes, we were only 1-0 down. We then lost two goals in quick succession to go in at half-time 3-0 down. That's game over against a team like Liverpool. At 1-0 we had a chance of sneaking something, but not 3-0. What do you say at half-time? All I could say was, "Go out and enjoy the second half." Inside, I was praying we didn't concede double figures.

'I remember Butty [Paul Butler], after the game, just shaking his head in the dressing room. He says, "Fucking hell, are they quick or are they quick? One minute they're there, the next minute they've gone." I says, "That's the top level, Paul, and that's what you have to aspire to." I knew this because I'd played there. I was fortunate enough to have played against George Best and Jimmy Greaves. It's a different ball game at the top level. Butty went on to play at that level, of course, but that game opened his eyes, I'm sure of that. It opened all of their eyes.

'There were 7,000 Rochdale fans there that day, too, and I was so grateful for the support they gave us. I just wish we could have given them more to cheer about. I also wish that many of them came to more of our regular games. What a difference that would have made to the club.'

The experience left Docherty feeling low, however.

'I remember I went home that night, went to the pub and got absolutely leathered,' he says, frankly. 'People kept coming up to me, saying, "Never mind, you'll be all right." And I was like, "Oh fuck off." That's how I felt. I was so desolate, it was untrue. I was disappointed for the players more than myself. I wanted them to make their mark that day. I was disappointed we didn't score, because we did have chances in the first half. I had to go into the club on Monday and be OK, for the players, you know? I had to stick on a smile. It was hard. I think I gave them a belated Christmas party to try to get morale back up.'

Despite the delayed festivities, things failed to improve in the league and, once again, after a promising start, Dale had fallen to 15th.

'We just couldn't unlock teams anymore,' Docherty laments. 'We didn't seem to know what to do in the opposition half. I tried to remedy it. I tried to get another forward in. I spoke to three different players but, as always, it came down to money. I eventually got Dave Lancaster in on loan, and he did all right, but the team, as a whole, just wasn't firing. I lost Ian Gray for the rest of the season, too, so got Kevin Pilkington in on loan from Man United. The poor lad cost us a few goals and I had to send him back early. Sir Alex wasn't happy with that. He hasn't spoken to me since.'

Docherty brought goalkeeper Lance Key in on loan from Sheffield Wednesday instead, but the curse continued. Perhaps the most memorable game of the season's run-in, at home to

Wigan Athletic, perfectly highlighted Dale's transition from a potent attacking force to a toothless, almost comical, outfit. From Key's air shot at Peake's back-pass to Whitehall's two missed penalties, the 2-0 defeat was enough to turn the terraces against the manager.

'At no point did I tell the players I thought it was over,' Docherty says. 'But, as each game went by, we got further away from the play-offs and closer to staying in the bottom half. I just enforced on them not to switch off, even if there was nothing left to play for. They had an end-of-season holiday booked together – a reward for getting to the FA Cup third round. They also had a job to do for me first, though. I remember Hereford, last game of the season. They beat us and made the play-offs. That was us back in November. It should have been us then, but instead we finished 15th.'

The board of directors, who had been vocal supporters of Docherty during the season, were not impressed by the post-Christmas slump and relieved the manager of his post.

'I'd gone away to the Lake District for some head space,' he says. 'I remember the club PA phoned me and asked if I was going to be in that week and, if I was, could I attend a board meeting. I knew something was up then. I came home and went along to the ground and they were all there, the directors, shaking my hand, knowing they were going to fire me. They mentioned different things. An interview I'd given to a local paper about the lack of money at the club. They said it was too pessimistic. They mentioned a lack of potential signings, saying I should have done more scouting. They questioned the players I'd opted to retain and those I chose to release. Things like that, things that were my business – the manager's business. They said I should have taken money in December when I was offered it. The money I was offered wouldn't have got us players as good as we already had, so what was the point? I had asked for some of the Liverpool money, but was told it was used to pay off an overdraft and other expenses. I disagreed with them, but what could I do? I didn't even have a contract. I think I got three weeks' wages and that was it.

'As far as I know, the objective each season was "do the best you can". That's what we did, Dave and I. I travelled up and down the country to watch the opposition. I'd work two hours in the morning training the players and then I'd jump in the car and drive to Northampton, say, or Carlisle, and watch a game there. That was the only way to gather the data you needed back then. We worked hours and hours and hours. It was no doddle. Now, you switch on a computer and it's all there for you. I'd be out of the equation right away nowadays, as you need to be IT-literate. They all talk in numbers now. I'm old-school. I have all this in my notebook, not a computer. The average person earns in a year only a fraction of what players earn in a week these days. It's obscene and I'm happy I had my time when I did. Yes, the carrot is there for untold riches if they become the best player they can, and motivation is always to be applauded, but they get it all far too early now.'

While Docherty's tenure was spent with pent-up frustration at the perceived prudence of chairman Kilpatrick and Morris, despite how things turned out, he has no regrets about taking on the Rochdale posts he held.

'I had six years at Rochdale,' he says. 'Four with Dave and two on my own. It was a wonderful time and it was spent with a lot of wonderful people. I wish I could have given them more. Truthfully, though, I felt I gave the club as much as I could with the tools at my disposal. It wasn't enough. I think I was a lot more outwardly pragmatic at the time, but, looking back now, I can see the bigger picture. The job cost me my marriage. The board of directors were terrific in basic terms, but they had no ambition, in my opinion. Whether that was down to finances or fear of the unknown is a question I don't know the answer to, but I do suspect they didn't want to push the boat out financially because of the small gate receipts coming in. It was a risk they didn't want to take. If they had, and Dave and I brought them promotion, would the gates have gone up to justify the spending? I think they would have, but they opted for little old Rochdale to stay in the "Rochdale Division".'

Graham Barrow

1996–1999

ONE NAME in Rochdale's modern history seems to suffer knocks more than most: Graham Barrow.

By Barrow's own admission he feels he achieved little during his time at the club, but he did put in place various elements that would go on to provide benefits for it in later years.

His arrival, after the eventual dissatisfaction of Mick Docherty's tenure, carried with it much hope, but instead of leaving a legacy remembered fondly, his era at the club more readily evokes talk of 'Barrowball', the derisive marque given to the football that supporters witnessed between 1996 and 1999.

Barrow took his seat behind the manager's desk at Spotland with a decent CV in his hand. His appointment by then-chairman David Kilpatrick seemed a sound one. He had previously guided Chester City back to the third tier of the English game at the first attempt and had then, with the help of Dave Whelan's capital, turned strugglers Wigan Athletic into something of a lower-league force, before being surprisingly sacked with the club sitting seventh. His reputation as a manager was growing.

'Mr Whelan was a man on a mission when he bought Wigan,' Barrow remembers. 'It was a bit of a shock when I got the sack. They were heading towards the Conference when I took over and I got them into the top half of the bottom division. We did have a decent working relationship, me and Mr Whelan, but he was in such a hurry that seventh in the league wasn't good enough for him. It's not unusual at the top level these days, but, back then, at that level, it was. I don't take it as personally now, as a few other managers after me have suffered the same fate. I was hurt at the time, because Wigan were on a roll.

'But look at it objectively. The only way a manager can get a job is if another manager loses theirs. That's how it works. So, I was sat by the phone waiting for the next call – and it came from Rochdale.'

While he wouldn't enjoy Whelan-esque financial backing at Rochdale, the hope was still there that Barrow, with his contacts, would be the man to take the club forward, to lead Dale out of the fourth tier and secure a first promotion since 1969.

'I'd achieved promotion with a small budget at Chester, so it wasn't an alien concept,' says Barrow. 'My goal, agreed with the chairman, the late David Kilpatrick, was to achieve the play-offs and improve on a season-by-season basis. Because I'd done it before with limited means, the board thought promotion was achievable with Rochdale.'

Barrow took the job as the England team inspired the nation at the European Championship over the summer of 1996, but, to the observer on the terrace at least, it appeared football wasn't 'coming home' to Rochdale. Playing the long game seemed to have been taken a little too literally by the new manager's charges.

In fact, such was the side's perceived unwieldy style during Barrow's occupancy that, on a visit to Spotland in 1998, *Independent* writer Nicholas Harling noted, 'The hosts base their game on massive clearances, long-range shots and the odd weaving run from their Spanish winger Isidro Díaz.'

But to understand Barrow's footballing philosophy is to understand the man's background. Hailing from Lancashire, Barrow spent most of his playing career at non-league teams such as his hometown club Chorley, and then Southport and Altrincham.

By his own admission, he was a powerful, no-nonsense defender, occasionally used in midfield if extra muscle was required, but he could pass a ball too.

'I came into the game the hard way, if you like,' Barrow says. 'We're going back to an era when I was a schoolboy. I came from a council estate where there were no phones. You had to walk three miles to a payphone because my dad didn't even have a car. It's not like it is nowadays. You had to muck in. I had a trial at Blackburn when I was young, but eventually ended up playing non-league for Chorley. I was in the same team as Mickey Walsh, who went on to do well at Blackpool and Everton. He made the grade quicker than me, but I did eventually get there myself.

'I almost signed for Wigan when they first got into the league, strangely enough, but that didn't materialise. There was also a trial at Everton, but that came to nothing. I transferred to Southport before my biggest move at that point, which was to Altrincham. The Conference was just starting up then and Altrincham were like the Man United of non-league at the time. They won the Conference title but, as it was at the time of the old re-election voting system, Rochdale, who finished bottom of the Fourth Division, stayed in the league by one vote [1979/80].

'I eventually turned professional at the age of 27, signing for Wigan. They had a really strong side at the time under Larry Lloyd and won promotion. I even got to play at Wembley [in the final of the Freight Rover Trophy]. Five years after joining Wigan, I found myself at Chester and that's where I became exposed to the notion of management.'

It wasn't a natural transition for Barrow, however.

'When I was a part-time footballer, I was working as a heating engineer,' he says. 'I had worked for a living, if you know what I mean? It meant I knew what could be waiting for me after I finished playing. Because I loved football so much, coaching and managing were an ideal opportunity to stay in it. They're a poor second to playing, don't get me wrong, but they kept me in the game.'

Barrow says that while the rough and tumble of non-league and lower-league football taught him to be physical, the long-ball game, while useful at times, was never his outright modus operandi.

'The long-ball thing was never intentional,' he insists. 'I had players like Alex Russell at Rochdale. Passers of the ball. I wanted to use them that way. I can say this now, because I've since worked with Premier League players, and it's clear that the top, top sportsmen have an unwavering belief in themselves. As you go down the ladder, unfortunately, that belief wavers a lot more easily. A few mistakes and a player starts to panic and the ball gets played long instead of short. Any manager will tell you, once the players get on the pitch, no matter what you've done with them during the week, their mentalities take over. Any footballer that's trained under me will tell you that my sessions are possession-based with shorter passing, but you're also trying to win a football match, aren't you?'

Barrow had to deal with personnel challenges from the outset at Rochdale, with the sale of powerful centre-half Paul Butler to Bury for £100,000.

'Two days into the job, Paul came to me and told me he was off,' Barrow says with resignation. 'That was a body blow. He was crucial to my plans going forward. He was a fantastic centre-half. Then I had another setback. I had my eye on Wigan's Colin Greenall, a tremendous player. He was captain material. The board backed me, we put in a bid, and Wigan said it was fine but we had to wait until the team returned from a pre-season tournament in the Isle of Man. He played well for them over there and, when they came back, Wigan said they were no longer prepared to sell him. Again, that was a body blow.'

Barrow did what he could. He signed a host of fresh faces which included the likes of Andy Farrell, Andy Gouck and Andy Fensome, and he also brought Mark Leonard back to Spotland. Perhaps Barrow's best signing was, however, Alan Johnson, who would go on to land the Player of the Year award.

The 1996/97 campaign got under way in earnest for Rochdale with a 2-1 defeat away at Jan Mølby's Swansea City which was, in mitigation, a traditionally difficult place for the team to go. A win was also lacking in Barrow's next five league games, only punctuated by a League Cup victory against Barnsley, who would go on to achieve promotion to the Premier League.

However, an unbeaten spell between 28 September and 2 November created a buzz around Spotland, even if the football on display lacked the silk to match.

It wasn't to last and Rochdale would eventually finish the season in 14th, with 14 wins and 16 losses.

'Despite this, I felt we did OK that year,' Barrow says. 'We got close to the play-off positions at times but, just as we seemed to get there, we couldn't kick on and I found that really frustrating.'

The 1997/98 campaign followed a similar pattern to the one previous, with Dale finishing four places worse off in 18th. Barrow lost his star defender Johnson to injury before the season had even started and his talented goalkeeper, Ian Gray, to Stockport County. Talismanic striker Steve Whitehall left for Mansfield Town, where he would bang in 25 goals for Steve Parkin's side, and was replaced by ex-Bury forward Mark Carter, who failed to replicate the lethal form he showed for the Shakers. He was joined by Wigan's Graham Lancashire.

'We never had it quite right at the top of the pitch,' Barrow concedes. 'You'll never get promoted if you don't have decent forwards. I signed Graham Lancashire but he didn't reproduce the form he had done for me previously [at Chester and Wigan]. Had we had a goalscorer that season, I'm sure we would have been up there. We had a good midfield with the likes of Gary Jones and Alex Russell, Neil Edwards was a top keeper at that level, too, so it was up top where we were short.'

Chairman Kilpatrick finally delivered the *coup de grâce* one game before the end of the 1998/99 season. With Dale finishing in 19th, Barrow had presided over three seasons of regression. By now, he had very little support left in the Spotland stands. Barrow had failed to rectify his striking problems, with new signings Michael Holt and Andy Morris showing promise but not consistency.

'I was led to believe I was going to get another crack at it,' Barrow says. 'I think you deserve that kind of time with a tight budget. That said, people were very good to me at Rochdale and three years is a lot of time, especially if you compare it to nowadays, but I just felt I was never that far away.'

While frustrated, Barrow accepts the financial constraints he worked under.

'Mid-season at a small club like Rochdale, you're not going to get the money when you need a boost,' he says. 'They back you in the summer, but don't have the finances to do so after that. I knew the position. We sold youth-team goalkeeper Stephen Bywater to West Ham United for a lot of money [rumoured to be £300,000 plus incentives] but I didn't see any of it. I was asked to play him in a [Football] League Trophy tie against Carlisle to help the sale, but he wasn't ready. The poor lad conceded a load of goals [Rochdale lost the game 6-1]. I had to take that on the chin to help the club. I was prepared to do it, though. It was part and parcel of football at the time.'

It is unfortunate for Barrow that the money from the Bywater sale didn't benefit the club until a year or so later. Kilpatrick once said that he owed then-West Ham manager Harry Redknapp a debt of thanks for playing the goalkeeper in a London derby against Arsenal in 2000. That appearance triggered a £200,000 payment to Rochdale and went some way to funding the purchases of Clive Platt and Paul Connor.

Meanwhile, Barrow had to scour the market for more affordable options, an area where he feels he lacked good fortune.

'Managing with a tight budget requires that little bit of luck,' he says. 'I had it at Chester. John Beck had gone to Preston and, because he likes to play the game a certain way, he didn't have room in his squad for players who played the game differently. They were still quality players and it meant I could sign them for free because he needed to move them on quickly. I never got that kind of luck at Rochdale.'

With Barrow gone, former Mansfield manager Steve Parkin took the hot seat. Under Parkin's stewardship, Rochdale shrugged free of their long-ball reputation and enjoyed a period of marked progression. Parkin eventually left to join Barnsley in 2001 with Dale sitting second in the division.

But what, if anything, did he have that Barrow didn't?

'Steve demonstrated that the club was only a few signings away from being decent,' Barrow says. 'He got Flickers [Dave Flitcroft] in, who I was interested in signing myself as I knew him from Chester. Steve actually phoned me when he got the job to say thanks for leaving him with the solid basis of a team.

'And that's the thing. I left Rochdale feeling I hadn't achieved a lot but I had improved certain aspects of the club and had always been careful with the budget. Neil Edwards, Keith Hill and Gary Jones are all positives [Barrow brought the man who would go on to be Rochdale's most successful manager and record appearance maker to the club]. People are always entitled to their own opinions but, while I was there and when I go back now, people at Rochdale are always fantastic with me.

'I will say, ironically, over the past four or five years I've probably felt more prepared for management than I did in my 40s. I had that early success with Chester, maybe too early, because you think you know it all and you really don't. You never stop learning in the game. Only now, in my 60s, do I feel I've accrued that kind of knowledge. The coaching courses teach you the basics but, only by doing, do you actually really learn.'

Steve Parkin

1999–2001 and 2003–2006

AS DAVE Sutton and Mick Docherty offered supporters hope of delivering a successful Rochdale side at the beginning of the 1990s, Steve Parkin did likewise at the beginning of the new millennium.

Parkin's arrival at Spotland in the summer of 1999 was unexpected. He had taken Mansfield Town to within a whisker of the fourth-tier play-off places the previous season but left his post a week later, citing the club's financial situation for his decision, which would have impacted his playing budget for the coming campaign. His availability didn't seem to make him an obvious target for the vacant post at a struggling Rochdale as far as supporters were concerned, given he looked to be a lower-league rising star. It was a pleasant surprise to many then, when it was announced Parkin, and his assistant Tony Ford, the longest-serving player in the Football League at that point, were to take over from Graham Barrow.

'First and foremost, there was a basis of a decent squad when I got to the club in 1999,' Parkin says. 'I spoke to Graham about the job and he told me he thought the players he had left behind were decent but had merely underachieved. He was right.

'It wasn't so much a case of me revolutionising the club, it was just a case of bringing a few more players in. I had a lot of help from [chairman] David Kilpatrick and the board in that regard. There was a strict wage structure in place, which reflected the gates we were getting at the time, but it was still very useful in attracting the players I wanted. I'd been working in that division for two and a half years with Mansfield, so I had a good idea of the standard and the type of players that we needed to bring in to improve us. I evolved it season by season from there, really.'

As well as adding his assistant Ford to the playing roster in 1999, Parkin brought in right-back Wayne Evans, midfielder Dave Flitcroft, winger Graeme Atkinson and forward Clive Platt, all of whom had a positive impact.

The tone was set with an opening-day victory at the much-fancied and newly promoted Cheltenham Town, with Dale then going on to briefly top the table, before falling away after Christmas. This would set the tone for the rest of that season and the next. Dale would look promising from August, but seemed to run out of gas as the season reached its final quarter. A draw away at Plymouth on the final day of the 2000/01 season, as opposed to the required win, was all that prevented Parkin taking Rochdale to the play-offs for the first time since their introduction in the 1980s.

'That hurt, that one,' Parkin says, 'We had to play a lot of games in quick succession at the end of the season because of postponements, but that's not an excuse. We'd left ourselves too much to do too late.'

The following season, Parkin vowed to go one better. He looked good for his word, too, as his side opened the league campaign with five wins and a draw. It also gave this writer his first experience of a Rochdale team performing admirably against Premier League opposition. In September 2001, Parkin's Rochdale, despite eventually losing to Fulham on penalties after a 2-2 draw, made sure the top-flight side knew they had been in a match. The League Cup tie belonged to young substitute striker Kevin Townson, who made an experienced back line look ordinary throughout as he bagged a brace.

Sadly, the game went ahead not long after news had broken of the 9/11 atrocity in New York City, where terrorists had flown commercial aeroplanes into the two towers of the World Trade Center.

'I remember it quite vividly, really,' Parkin says. 'Me and Tony [Ford] were heading back from training ahead of the game. I turned the car radio on and there were all these news bulletins about a bomb that had gone off in New York. We got back to Spotland and we had a little TV in our office. We turned it on and we saw the pictures and realised it was aeroplanes, not bombs, that had hit the World Trade Center. Me and Tony sat and watched this for ages and ages and ages. It took our mind – everyone's mind – off the game.

'In hindsight, as a mark of respect, that game shouldn't have gone ahead. But we were so far down the line in terms of arrangements that we couldn't postpone. Fulham were already in the Lancashire area and so on.

'We had to be professional and, as it turned out, it was a great game. Kev Townson was fantastic. He made a name for himself that night, but it was a team performance. We deserved to go through for sure. We were very unlucky.'

More spectacular results followed that season and, in November 2001, with Rochdale riding high in the league, the lure of second-tier football management at Barnsley took Parkin and Ford away from Rochdale and over the Pennines into South Yorkshire.

'It wasn't the right decision to go to Barnsley,' Parkin reflects. 'It was too early. Rochdale were almost top of the league at the time, just behind Plymouth. We had a great little squad, a squad that me and Tony had built. The ideal time to move on would have been at the end of the season. The squad was good enough to go up and I should have seen that through. We should have got that first promotion since 1969.'

Parkin also asserts that his departure was not financially motivated.

'The move to Barnsley wasn't about money,' he says. 'People will say that, but it wasn't. We constantly had a real problem of where to train at Rochdale. The club didn't have its own training facilities and so we were like bloody nomads, going from one ground to another, one area to another. We were always looking for decent facilities or pitches that weren't waterlogged. I'd done it for two and a half years and it had taken its toll. One thing I knew about Barnsley, because I'd been there a few times with the Rochdale reserves, is that their training facilities were fantastic. That was a big sway for me. It was still tough to leave, though. I had a great relationship with David Kilpatrick and the board and, I'll say again, it was the wrong decision.'

Parkin says he endured a turbulent 12 months in South Yorkshire.

'I wasn't given any time at Barnsley. They had a squad that was too big for starters. I think there were 46 players when I arrived. I managed to get rid of 16 of them in 12 months. The squad needed to become a manageable size. While I was doing this, the ITV Digital money stopped [the digital platform had paid £315m to screen lower-league football in 2001 but collapsed in 2002 due to lack of interest from the paying public]. That had a massive impact on the club as we had a lot of players on big wages. This became unsustainable, even with our trimming. We were relegated and the board couldn't prevent the club going into administration. The writing was on the wall for me and Tony from then on to be honest.'

It wasn't long before Parkin got back into football, however.

'I went to work with Billy Dearden at Notts County six months later,' he says. 'I had a couple of job offers prior to that but they didn't appeal. I'd been lifelong friends with Billy, so it was a pleasure to work with him. Notts, despite being in administration themselves, were a nice friendly club. I was enjoying football again.'

After Parkin's departure, Rochdale had employed three managers – John Hollins, Paul Simpson and, finally, Alan Buckley. The latter had left Dale in a precarious league position when he was dismissed in December 2003.

'I had a missed call from David Kilpatrick on my phone,' Parkin recalls. 'I knew Alan Buckley had left Rochdale, but I still wasn't sure what David wanted. I called him back and he said straightaway, "Will you come back?" I said I'd give it some thought, but, to be honest, it didn't take long. I knew most of the staff and players that were still there. I wanted to do it again.

'I went back, met the board, and they told me the club had to stay up. That was my only objective. We managed it by the skin of our teeth. Beyond that, my brief was to consolidate and get the club back to some kind of stability again. There was no further pressure other than that.'

On his return, Parkin worked hard to restore some pride to the demoralised unit left behind by Buckley and, the following season, it looked like the magic touch had returned when he guided Rochdale to a ninth-placed finish.

This was due, in part, to a particular gift he possessed. Parkin, during both of his spells at Rochdale, had an exceptional eye for a striker. Under his watch, supporters enjoyed goals from Kevin Townson, Clive Platt, Paul Connor, Grant Holt, Rickie Lambert, Chris Dagnall and Glenn Murray. Only Platt and Connor came at a significant cost, while Holt, Lambert and Murray have gone on to make Rochdale a seven-figure sum between them.

'I've not got a bad eye for a forward as a former defender, eh?' Parkin laughs. 'It goes back to my Mansfield days. I'd always watch strikers for the runs they made into the box. I wasn't so bothered about those who could crack it in from 30 yards, they tended to be one-offs. I was more concerned with how strikers got themselves free in the box, the intuition they showed, the way they beat a defender to the ball. At Mansfield, I signed Steve Whitehall from Rochdale and he got me 20-odd goals before he moved to Oldham. Then there was Tony Lormor, who gave me a decent goal return, and Lee Peacock, who I bought from Carlisle for £75,000 and the club sold for £500,000.

'I carried this on at Rochdale. During my first spell, I found Clive Platt, who would get me goals but would also create them too, which was vital to that team at the time.

'Kevin Townson didn't fulfil his potential, which is sad. He was probably managed in the wrong way after I left. He got a hefty three-year contract thrown at him and that probably wasn't the way to nurture him along and keep him hungry. He had a great eye for goal and was a natural finisher. He was very instinctive.

'Paul Connor was a real talent, too. I really felt for him because he got some nasty injuries and that held him back. He could have gone all the way. He still did the business for Rochdale, though. I enjoyed working with him. He was a really good lad.

'I saw Chris Dagnall loads of times at Tranmere. He was tenacious and quicker than he looked over 20 yards. He always created chances for himself. He wasn't the perfect finisher by any means, but still always looked likely to score.

'Glenn Murray was a raw one. He had an unorthodox running style, but he always seemed to get himself to where he could grab a goal. He went on to score for fun at Rochdale. I've met him a few times since and he always says he is grateful for the chance I gave him.

'I'd seen Grant Holt a little bit before I signed him. He, too, was very raw but effective. I knew I could bring him on. He had the right attributes to be a fantastic striker and just needed a little work. He proved a very worthwhile investment of our time.

'Rickie Lambert was even more pleasing. I'd only ever seen him play in midfield. I never thought he had the legs to play there, to be perfectly truthful. He did have a terrific shot, however. I started thinking, if he's a bit further up the pitch, he could create the kind of space in the box that he does in midfield. I sold this idea to him, I said, "I want you up front with Holty." He snapped my hand off because it meant less running for him.'

Holt and Lambert in particular formed one of the best strike partnerships to be seen at Spotland, but, sadly for Parkin, their goals were not enough to bring him the success of his first spell. The sale of both players came while the season was in flow and effectively derailed all momentum.

After a nightmare start to the 2006/2007 season, Parkin looked to have picked things up with a run of form culminating in a 5-0 win away at Darlington. It wasn't to last and Rochdale embarked on a run where they won just one of 11 games, including a 7-1 embarrassment at Lincoln City.

Parkin's demise finally came on Saturday, 16 December 2006, following a third consecutive defeat, to Hartlepool United. It was a game many supporters believe yielded Rochdale's worst display of Parkin's two reigns, despite there being heavier losses.

'You can only pull so many rabbits out of the hat, can't you?' Parkin says. 'I'd got to the stage where I was experienced enough to know a club like Rochdale has to sell players to carry on surviving and functioning. You can't keep hanging on to players when they have a value. Before you know it, the value is gone and the club is in trouble. It was hard work rebuilding teams, though. You lose a striker so you need to find another one that's going to get you 30 goals a season. Losing Rickie and Grant in quick succession really hurt. I think if I'd held on to them, we'd have been there or thereabouts. Instead we went backwards a little bit.'

Players met by this writer over the years have always had nothing but good things to say about Parkin. Paul Connor, who Parkin brought to Rochdale from Stoke City in 2001 for a club record fee of £150,000, is one of them.

'I've always said, whenever I've been asked to name the best manager I've played for, that it's Steve Parkin,' Connor enthuses. 'He was hard as nails but was a great person with it. He had an aura about him, in that he had the respect of the dressing room but was one of the lads as well. He got the balance right. He knew when to be the boss and when to have a beer with the boys. He was massively into team spirit. Perhaps it's considered a bit old-school now, but he would encourage the nights out and all that. I'd say that was his overall strength. He got the best out of the lads that way. When I first went to Rochdale, and I know the players concerned won't mind me saying this, we didn't have the greatest squad in the division in terms of raw ability, but it was the best dressing room I've ever been in. That made us better than a lot of the more technical teams out there.

'That's not to say Steve wasn't tactical. Training was never dull. He liked his teams organised. We had quality in the right areas, of course, but he signed leaders at the back and made sure we were strong defensively. Our training under Steve was always centred on being organised, strong and aggressive.

'It just seemed to click for me the minute I got to Rochdale. I put that down to Steve giving me the confidence to go and play. As long as we were all right defensively, he let the attackers play their own game and express themselves. I loved that about him.

'Second time round, Steve had to deal with financial changes at the club. He didn't have the same budget that he enjoyed first time. Quite rightly, the club cut its cloth. It takes time to build a successful squad with a small budget. He did get the time, but had to keep selling key players – so he was effectively starting from scratch each time.

'Rochdale was the most enjoyable club I've been at. I had bad luck with injuries there, but it was still a welcoming environment. A lot of that was down to Steve.'

After Parkin left Rochdale for the second time, director of youth football Keith Hill took temporary charge, with Rochdale only lying outside of the relegation zone on goal difference. What followed was perhaps the most effective transformation of a football team this writer has ever witnessed.

Having, on a caretaker basis, taken over a leaden side, Hill oversaw a period where Rochdale began to demolish teams regularly by four goals or more. Given the job permanently, with former player David Flitcroft as his assistant, Hill made sure the form continued, a dazzling 7-2 away victory at Stockport the highlight. In less than half a season he had taken Rochdale from the doldrums to finish just outside the play-offs.

How? 'I set Keith on his way with the youth team job at Rochdale,' Parkin says. 'Keith, when given the chance, injected the first team with a new self-belief and confidence. Again, you wouldn't think he had been a centre-half as a player, because he's a firm believer in attacking football. Once a group of players get a bit of confidence and they score a few goals, it builds momentum. You cannot underestimate the power of momentum in football. When you have it, you can quickly become unstoppable. I saw that happen in Keith's first spell and I was made up for him.'

Parkin concludes, 'My ten years as a manager were enough for me. I enjoyed it all except the 12 months at Barnsley, which were hard on me and my family. I see what managers have to go through these days, the press they have to deal with, the criticism. Latterly I've played the role of assistant manager. It's more of a free role, I suppose, and that suits me fine.'

* * *

John Hollins MBE is probably the most high-profile managerial appointment made by Rochdale in modern times.

His affiliation with the club was brief and, although his side fell at the penultimate hurdle, his time at Spotland can only be considered as a success.

Taking over from the departed Steve Parkin in December 2001, and relieving caretaker boss Dave Hamilton, the former Chelsea manager was tasked with keeping Rochdale in the promotion hunt until the season's end. Given he was without midfield general Gary Jones (who joined Parkin at Barnsley), the fact Hollins eventually missed out on automatic promotion by a single point is laudable.

As a player, Hollins is remembered as a talented and hardworking midfielder and made his Chelsea first-team debut at the tender of age of just 17 in 1963. He was predominantly London-based during his playing career, going on to feature at Queens Park Rangers and Arsenal before returning to Stamford Bridge in 1983. He was awarded an MBE for services to football in 1981.

Upon retiring from playing at the end of the 1983/84 season, Hollins took on a coaching role at Chelsea but, just a year later found himself as their manager, replacing John Neal. Hollins led the Stamford Bridge side to a sixth-placed finish in the top flight and saw off Manchester City to win the Full Members' Cup the following year. However, following the team's downturn in form, Hollins was sacked in March 1988 and so set up his own sports promotion company, stepping back into football management via intermittent caretaker posts over the next decade.

His return to full-time management came at Swansea City in 1998, at the time a divisional rival to Graham Barrow's Rochdale. Hollins guided the Swans to the fourth-tier title in 2000 but relegation followed quickly after, leading to his eventual dismissal.

He'd only been out of the game since September 2001 when the opportunity to manage Rochdale came along in December of that same year.

The board were looking for someone who could step straight into the existing setup and work with the backroom staff already in post. Hollins, baggage-free, fitted the bill perfectly.

One player who remembers Hollins's arrival is Gareth Griffiths. The reliable centre-back and former captain played over 200 games for Rochdale before leaving the club in 2006, where he then embarked on a career as a financial consultant.

When Hollins arrived at the end of 2001, Griffiths recalls the players were still smarting from Parkin's exit.

'I really liked Steve Parkin as a bloke and as a manager,' he says. 'From a personal point of view, I was gutted when he left, but I also understood. This is what happens to managers who have relative success at clubs on a low budget with low expectation. I always knew he would move on from Rochdale but, from a selfish point of view, the timing was rotten given how well we were doing in the league. We were flying. On reflection, I would call his departure a bittersweet moment. I was pleased for him, but, with him gone, we were all uncertain as to what was going to happen next.

'As a footballer, you have an idea, of course. When I was at Wigan I played for something like six managers in three years. Football is like a monarchy in that respect – the king is dead, long live the king. Things carry on regardless. There is always apprehension about who the next man is going to be, and whether or not he'll like the current players and so on, but, as a player, you just need to crack on with things.

'We were at an advantage in that the lads Steve had assembled were smashing in the dressing room. We all got on well and had a unity that would have helped any new manager.

'When we heard John was coming in, a few of us were surprised. He had been a very well-respected player but some of the younger lads didn't realise just how much. The senior players knew all right. His CV gained him instant respect with us. We were surprised that someone like John Hollins wanted to come to Rochdale, to be honest. It was definitely a left-field appointment.

'On top of that, John was a great guy. The lads all loved him. He brought a very calm and measured approach to the club. In comparison to Steve, his style was very different. There is more than one way to skin a cat in terms of achieving results. Both his and Steve's methods were effective – John's was a very relaxed style, whereas Steve was more intense. Both methods worked for Rochdale that season. Personally, I liked Steve's intense approach because I like structure and focused aggression, whereas I suppose the flair players preferred John's approach. I, for one, didn't mind a ruck in the dressing room. Like a storm, it clears the air. That wasn't John's style, though. He could still express his disappointment, but he was more of an arm-around-the-shoulder manager. He was a joker, too. He loved using his Cockney rhyming slang to amuse the players.'

The play-off semi-final games of 2002 were a novelty for many Dale fans, in that most had never seen the team compete beyond the final league game of a season. After a 2-2 draw away at Rushden & Diamonds in the first leg, confidence was high that Rochdale would progress to the final. However, despite a calamitous own goal from Mark Peters giving Dale the lead in the second leg, Jamaican internationals Onandi Lowe and Paul Hall put the tie out of reach. This writer doesn't mind sharing that he was close to tears that night.

'When you've been up there all season and miss out by the smallest of margins, you lose momentum,' says Griffiths. 'It doesn't matter how mentally strong you are, you lose it. We were in uncharted territory as a club, even in qualifying for the play-offs, so we had to use that as a motivator. We had to shake off the disappointment of missing out on automatic promotion very, very quickly.

'I always remember thinking John was like a grandfather figure at that time. I don't mean that in a derogatory way, just that he was very relaxed and reassuring about the whole thing. His outward emotional display was very good for the younger players. There was nobody ranting and raving in the dressing room and there was no additional pressure put on the young players. It was all very calm.

'That said, I don't think we did ourselves justice in those play-off games. We should have won that first leg. Still, the draw was half a job done, away from home. We fancied ourselves at Spotland, we really did, but we didn't turn up. When you're playing in a match, you can feel something. You know, even if you're a goal down, that you're knocking on the door and that you'll get back into it. I didn't feel that against Rushden. I don't think anybody did. For whatever reason, we were flat. I don't know if the occasion got to our younger players or what. The game itself, because of its importance, was all the motivation we should have needed. When we stepped over the white line, it all seemed to ebb away.

'I felt we limped out of the play-offs and it still saddens me to this day. People like myself, who were getting on a bit, had been lucky enough to be promoted before [Griffiths with Port Vale]. It's such an unbelievable feeling and I wanted to feel it again, I wanted the young players to feel it. It was a very subdued dressing room after that home leg and some of the senior lads realised they might just have missed their last chance at promotion and some of the younger lads worried they may never get it again.'

The dust had barely settled on the play-off disappointment when it was revealed Hollins would be leaving Rochdale. The manner of his departure has become the subject of much speculation in the years since.

On his appointment, Hollins had initially only agreed a contract until the end of the season. In May 2002, chairman David Kilpatrick claimed that his first offer of a contract extension had been rejected by Hollins. He later claimed that, after a fortnight of further negotiations, they were no further forward and, as a result, he had decided to let Hollins leave.

Hollins, on the other hand, claimed he received a fax from Rochdale informing him that the offer of a deal had been withdrawn. He would tell the BBC, 'I must say, I am very surprised by the decision. As far as I was aware we were still negotiating and I hadn't been given a date or time by which I had to respond. The chairman made me an offer and I was mulling it over with my wife in London.'

'My recollection as a player was that it felt like the club didn't do enough to keep John,' says Griffiths. 'They should have gone out of their way to keep him. Someone like John doesn't manage a club like Rochdale very often and it didn't feel as if the club realised that. They should have been thinking, "OK, we've hit the post this season, but we've got a good squad, John has a good rapport with the players, he's good PR for the club, we'll finish top three next time."

'I don't know if the decision was budgetary. I don't know if there were perhaps financial consequences of not being promoted. Maybe, on the other hand, there was a fear of being promoted the next season and not being able to invest, resulting in defeat every week. Things like that do happen at lower-league clubs.

'I've not spoken to John since, so I don't know what he was asking for, but, surely, it couldn't have been that astronomical. He would have known what the club could and could not afford. Whatever the reason, it was a sad day for the players when John left.'

A couple of years after leaving Rochdale, Hollins was appointed as Claude Anelka's assistant during the Frenchman's bizarre reign at Scottish club Raith Rovers. Anecdotal evidence has it that the Londoner initially brought some structure to Anelka's chaotic approach.

However, after just a month, Hollins had had enough. He would work with the players all week, set out the game plan for Saturday and then, on the Friday, Anelka would change everything. Unsurprisingly, he walked.

Nowadays Hollins is a media talent for hire, making the occasional football-related appearance on radio and television or among the after-dinner fraternity. Perhaps he even tells a tale or two about his time at Rochdale. Perhaps.

Paul Simpson

2002–2003

IT SHOULDN'T be this way for a Rochdale manager. The post should always be taken on amid an air of hope, not expectation.

Yet Paul Simpson, a virgin in the discipline, found himself in the bizarre situation of looking to replicate a play-off finish or better when he took on the job in the summer of 2002. He was, quite simply, a victim of his predecessors' success.

Steve Parkin had been revolutionising Rochdale steadily since 1999, shaking off the long-ball shackles that had blighted them for the previous three seasons.

This success eventually took Parkin to Barnsley in 2001, with Dale comfortably in second spot. His mantle was eventually handed to veteran gaffer John Hollins, whose instruction, from December onwards, was to keep the team on target. While he didn't quite manage that, the club only missed out on automatic promotion by a solitary point.

One of Hollins's most notable movements during his short spell as Rochdale manager was to bring in Paul Simpson the player. A quality, technically gifted attacking footballer, he stood out a mile in the fourth tier, despite his advancing years. His former team-mate Gareth Griffiths said of him, 'His left foot was a joke. It was astounding. Simpson was the best left footer I ever played with and I'd played with some decent people. What a player.'

Simpson was a product of Manchester City's youth system and had enjoyed a decent career representing clubs such as

Wolverhampton Wanderers and Derby County before making the switch to Rochdale from Blackpool.

'I was coming to the end of my contract at Blackpool and the manager at the time, Steve McMahon, said he'd had an approach from Rochdale,' Simpson remembers. 'He asked if I would be interested. I wanted to continue playing, so I met John Hollins and was very impressed with his ideas going forward. It was no problem to agree to join.

'Rochdale is obviously a small club but I was astounded by the staff and the players. The team was doing well when I joined, pushing for promotion, so I enjoyed the challenge.'

Simpson's arrival was seen as a real triumph for the club, reinforced by his goals and assists on the way to the season's checkout. Simpson even scored as Rochdale fell to Rushden & Diamonds in the play-off semi-finals and, despite the disappointment, supporters were looking forward to having him in the Hollins-led ranks for a full season the following campaign.

Then things went awry. Hollins wanted to negotiate an extension to his stay at Spotland, but his procrastination was deemed too much for then-chairman David Kilpatrick. Hollins left and Simpson stepped in as player-manager. It was a move that was welcomed by many but was nonetheless seen as risky, given Simpson's inexperience at a time when the club should have been looking to capitalise on the momentum generated over the previous years.

'We all expected John to stay, but the chairman told me the board ran out of patience with him, retracted their offer and he had left,' Simpson says. 'Coaching had always appealed to me. I had already undertaken coaching courses and was, at that time, doing my final year of a sports science degree.

'The chairman was aware of this and he asked me, at the player of the year awards, if I would speak to the board about the vacancy. I was interviewed a couple of days later and, shortly afterwards, I was told the job was mine.

'My plan had been to go into coaching at some point, but I didn't expect it so soon. I had already signed up to play at least one more season and that was my plan if John had stayed. I still wanted to play, so it was agreed I could be a player-manager.'

In Simpson's praise, the early days of his managerial reign provided this writer with some exhilarating memories – a 5-2 victory in Wrexham, a 4-3 triumph over Cambridge and a 2-1 win at Bristol Rovers (where Rochdale had to wear their hosts' third kit due to their own being held up in traffic). In each game, the man himself led by example on the pitch – his superior ability visibly inspiring his team-mates.

Despite a mauling by a rampant Manchester City over the summer, Simpson was pleased, in the main, with the squad he inherited and how they had prepared for the promotion push ahead.

'We had an excellent pre-season,' he says. 'Our planning was spot on. We had a decent team left over from the previous season and carried that momentum into the start of the next.'

There is also, of course, Simpson's main accomplishment during his time at Rochdale – leading the side to the fifth round of the FA Cup, an equal club record. The run also brought a figure reported to be around £700,000 into the coffers.

'The FA Cup was a great experience for the players, club, fans and obviously the staff, too,' Simpson recalls. 'It gave the club a huge financial windfall and it left them with money in the bank for the first time in a long time!'

The cup run proved enough for Kilpatrick to offer Simpson a new two-year deal, live on TV, ahead of the fifth-round tie against Wolves.

'I said to wait, though,' Simpson adds. 'We had too many games to concentrate on and I felt we could deal with all that later.'

But, despite this, Simpson's solitary season as Rochdale manager is regarded as a failure. Convincing cup victories over higher-league opposition in Preston North End and Coventry City were at complete odds with the befuddling league form that saw the team eventually finish 19th, with home crowds noticeably dropping off.

Those exhilarating early games gave way to something much more pedestrian and, from late September, Rochdale went into a steady decline. A 1-0 defeat to previous season's conquerors Rushden & Diamonds in November saw Rochdale drop into the bottom half of the table and they would never again break into the top section under Simpson.

Formations seemed to vary from one game to the next, with the dreaded long ball even rearing its head on more than one occasion, though this seemed to be out of desperation rather than instruction. The players began to look lost. Kevin Townson, the young protégé of Steve Parkin's era, was restricted to brief substitute appearances and, to the mystification of the Dale faithful, seemed to be on the periphery of Simpson's plans. More frustrating was the apparent stifling of gifted young winger Paddy McCourt, who had burst on to the scene the previous season with his ability to embark on dazzling, slaloming runs.

'Before I was appointed as manager at Rochdale I was aware of the reputation that Paddy was building,' says Simpson. 'My first impression was that we had an incredibly talented kid who played the game as if he was still playing at school with his mates. He could beat players for fun, was quicker running with the ball than most players were without the ball, and had wonderful balance. However, it was also clear that he had no idea of his responsibility for the work needed in a team.

'Through pre-season, it was obvious that he was going to be a good sub, as we weren't able to trust him to work in the team. I think, over the season, he had some decent games as a starter, but the matches where he came on as a sub, and ran at defenders, were his most effective.

'During my first few months as manager, there were discussions between Manchester City and Rochdale to do a deal to take Paddy there for a big fee and then loan him back to us for the season. Unfortunately for Paddy, and us, there was interference from people trying to force the deal through quickly, which annoyed Kevin Keegan, who was Man City manager at the time, and I was told the deal was off. It would have been interesting to see how Paddy could have developed given the chance at a top club that early in his career. Sadly, I don't think he had the full career a player of his ability should have had, but he has still done very well.'

Despite having to disappoint them, Simpson is adamant his players did their utmost for him.

'There is no way I would say the players let me down,' he says, adamantly. 'They showed a great attitude towards me from day one and I know they did all they could to try to win games.

'The board showed faith in me to give me the job and, although they didn't give me a lot of money to work with, they did what they could. We had some decent young players and a good set of senior players too. That said, I had to pick the teams I thought would win us games.'

Simpson instead cites a naivety with his available budget as his key error. He decided to spend the majority of it on what he thought would be three key players – Crewe centre-back Steve Macauley, Huddersfield midfielder Chris Beech and Scunthorpe winger Lee Hodges. All three had performed well at a higher level but, for one reason or another, they would only play a handful of games for Simpson's side.

'I was given £3,000 per week to add to the squad I inherited,' Simpson says. 'My idea was to use that money to bring a spine to the team. I brought in three players, hoping they would be major additions to our squad. With hindsight, this was probably wrong and I should have used the money more wisely.'

Hodges arrived at the club unfit and, while Simpson won't admit it publicly, it clearly irked him. Someone who had been a leading light in the division previously found himself shipped off to Bristol Rovers on loan and then out of Rochdale permanently. Meanwhile, Beech arrived as an obvious general for the midfield, a clear replacement for Gary Jones, who had followed Parkin to Barnsley. However, injury limited Beech's impact to disappointing cameos and another of Simpson's Rochdale vertebrae was dislodged. Macauley, like Hodges, was sent out on loan after a handful of appearances, this time to Macclesfield, who he would go on to join permanently.

'I was new to the job and got no help from the board in terms of how to do it,' Simpson says. 'It was a very steep learning curve.

'I don't think it would be right to say anything or anyone held me back, though. I made mistakes and this is all part of learning. In hindsight, I think we peaked as a group the season before, in the play-off games, and, although we did very well as a group for a long part of my season in charge, we were not well enough equipped to maintain it over the full season. The excitement of the cup took over, too, and the players struggled to reach those heights in some lesser league matches.'

It was a disappointing finish, given the previous season's fifth place, but it wasn't enough for the axe to fall cleanly. Kilpatrick's enthusiastic verbal contract offer earlier in the season was not so keenly supported by the rest of his board at the season's end and some felt that, while Simpson had something about him as a manager, he perhaps needed another, more experienced person brought in to hold his hand.

'When the season ended, the chairman said he intended to step back and so the other directors met me in his place. They said they wanted me to stay but they were going to choose an assistant to work with me.

'In the last game of the season, away at Macclesfield, we lost in the last couple of minutes. This defeat caused us to drop a number of places in the final league table. The directors said that if we had won, and stayed higher up the table, all would have been fine but, as things stood, they had to be seen to do something.

'I was told to remove either Jamie Hoyland, my assistant, or the youth coach Colin Greenall. It was ludicrous. Neither of these two were the problem. I said I was not prepared to accept those terms. I told them I would leave and that they could do what they wanted. So that's what I did.'

Simpson's spell at Rochdale hardly hindered his coaching career. In fact, it inspired him. Back-to-back promotions with Carlisle and almost getting Preston into the Premier League are fantastic achievements and perhaps vindicate Kilpatrick's foresight when giving the fledgling manager his debut shot.

'I learned a heck of a lot during my time at Spotland,' Simpson says, frankly. 'Some good things and some bad. The way some supporters turned on me, and my family, for example, was a massive eye-opener into the life of a football manager and this helped thicken my skin for the future.

'I also discovered that you can't please all of the people all of the time and so chose to do my job to the best of my ability, work as hard as I could and stick to my beliefs. Unfortunately, supporters are not party to all that goes on behind the scenes and make their assumptions based on part of the facts. As a manager, you are totally judged on results. If they are not good, like ours towards the end, then the rest normally takes care of itself.

'I learned a lot in terms of planning, coaching and setting up a team to get results, which you don't learn on any coaching course. Another huge one for me was delegation. I thought that I should do everything myself in my first job but found out by Christmas that I was burning out. It was only when I left and reflected on the season that I realised this, and took the lesson into my next job.

'Overall, managing Rochdale was a good experience, although I expect not many people will agree with that. It was a job I have no regrets about taking, but I am also glad I chose to leave when I did. It was a season which helped the club for the next few years, due to the cup money, but also helped me to move on to better things.'

* * *

Alan Buckley recalls being interviewed for the post of Rochdale manager in the club's bar, but he wasn't put off by the less-than-traditional setup because, by his own admission, he 'was desperate'.

In July 2003, the club was in another summer of upheaval. Paul Simpson had walked away after being given an ultimatum he said he found unacceptable and, once again, the board was looking for a new first-team manager.

There was change threatened at the very top, too, with David Kilpatrick stating his desire to step down as chairman – but not before ensuring a new man sat behind the manager's desk.

Former Grimsby, Walsall and West Bromwich Albion boss Buckley proved to be that individual. Rochdale got him at just the right time, too. He claims in his autobiography, *Pass and Move*, that he was at his lowest ebb after being out of football since leaving Lincoln in 2002. The then-52-year-old had a good track record at clubs with smaller budgets and, once again, the appointment seemed a sound one.

A club statement at the time bore this out, saying, 'The board of directors felt it was extremely important to appoint a manager with a wealth of experience. This is certainly something Alan Buckley will bring to the club. He has gained promotion on several occasions and his sides have a good reputation for playing attractive football.'

But, as Simpson discovered the season previous, a will to play attractive football is futile if you don't have the tools with which to achieve it.

This was certainly highlighted on the opening day of the 2003/04 campaign. The fixture compilers had been cruel to Rochdale and handed the club a curtain-raiser against newly promoted Yeovil Town at Spotland. The focus was always going to be on the visitors, given they had claimed the Conference title by 17 points the preceding season. The media interest was intense.

On a scalding August afternoon, a 2,000-strong sea of green and white swept into Rochdale to celebrate their side's first Football League game in 108 years.

There was only ever going to be one winner.

Of the many media members present on the day, *The Guardian's* Jeremy Alexander best summed up Dale's style during the 3-1 defeat when he said, 'Rochdale are more hewers of wood, taking uneasily to Buckley's wish that they should be sewers of silk.'

Dale fielded six debutants in that line up, none of whom looked fully integrated. The marquee signing of pre-season, if Rochdale ever do such a thing, was Manchester City midfielder Chris Shuker via the loan market.

But it was the club's record signing Paul Connor who was on the scoresheet that day. Brought to the club by Steve Parkin for £150,000 in 2001, he was looking to rediscover his form for Buckley.

'I remember they hit us like a brick wall,' he says. 'Yeovil were fit, strong and full of confidence. I felt, going into the game, we underestimated them. The manager didn't, but the players did. There was a bit of a, "They're just a Conference team, how good can they be?" mentality going on. It was a red-hot day I remember too, which made it difficult. In fact, it was a difficult afternoon full stop. We were taught a real lesson.'

It wasn't the opening-day defeat that tainted Buckley's love for football, however. It was the fact he refused to move to Rochdale and instead elected to make the 220-mile round trip from Grimsby every day to conduct training.

In *Pass and Move*, he says, 'I enjoyed driving, what could be the problem? It destroyed my soul … I would get up at six, shower and get in my car. I would get back home about seven, have something to eat and fall asleep. Then do it all again.'

Connor agrees that this had a detrimental effect on the squad.

'He was committed, you could never say he wasn't, but, with the travelling, he was having the odd day off,' he remembers. 'I think that was having an effect on a few of the lads. Sometimes, on a Friday, we'd just do a half-hour session. It wasn't as organised and it wasn't enough. That was down to the manager having to travel, I'm sure of it. His training sessions were good, though. His drills were all about passing.'

Buckley attempted to ease the burden on himself somewhat, by bringing former Dale assistant manager Tony Ford, who still lived locally and had been made an MBE, back to the club.

'Fordy is a great lad,' Connor says. 'For what he did in the game, for all those years he kept playing as an outfielder [until he was 42, making 931 league appearances], he had the immediate respect of everyone else. Some of us had already worked for him, too. He ended up taking a lot of the pre-season training sessions himself.'

Despite the stuttering preparation and poor opening day against Yeovil, Buckley's Rochdale did begin to pick up results, an away victory at York coming on the back of a particularly impressive performance being one of note. The manager gave homegrown goalkeeper Matt Gilks more games, and he seemed to have a faith in youngster Kevin Townson his predecessor didn't. Buckley also gave Connor more responsibility.

'Alan made me a focal point of his team, to be fair to him,' says Connor. 'It was obvious his budget was quite poor. He was having to wheel and deal. We had a lot of trialists at the club that summer. To be honest, he actually assembled a decent first 11 given the budget he had, but, if we got any injuries, the rest of the squad was quite young and inexperienced.'

Come October things began to unravel spectacularly and seven league defeats on the bounce led the support to ask serious questions about Buckley's suitability. A welcome win over arch rivals Bury arrested this dire run, but it was papering over the cracks and, just after Christmas, following a poor home defeat to York – the side Dale had played so well against away from home earlier in the season – it was all over.

'As a comparison, Steve Parkin's squad, for example, was full of experienced pros and leaders and Alan didn't sign enough of those,' Connor says. 'That's probably what did for him in the end. I can't fault him for the way he treated me, though. He gave me a few enjoyable months of playing football. I started that season really well for him before I broke my foot in training. I was out for three months and Alan got the sack during that time. I wish I'd gotten to carry on working with him because, as I say, he was a decent bloke and got me enjoying my football again.'

Keith Hill

2006–2011 and 2013–2019

IN HIS pomp, Keith Hill quipped that Rochdale AFC would one day build a statue in his honour. While on the surface that may seem like immodesty of Caesar Augustus proportions, even the briefest glance at Hill's achievements would prove that the perception of his totemic status is not misplaced. He is, quite simply and inarguably, Rochdale's most successful manager.

Since its formation in 1907, the club has only ever been promoted from the 'Rochdale Division' three times. Two of these came under Hill's reign. The club has only ever appeared at Wembley twice. Again, that's down to Hill. Of his 570 games in charge, Hill won 235 of them (41.2 per cent). He is also responsible for garnering the most points Rochdale have ever amassed in a season (82 in 2009/10) which also included 25 league wins, a record not achieved since 1927. Hill also led Dale into the fourth round of the FA Cup four times, one of which led to a fifth-round appearance. His club CV sparkles.

The average supporter could not have seen this coming, however. The gruff Boltonian played for Rochdale under both Graham Barrow and Steve Parkin. He was a no-nonsense defender very much in the mould of those managers, unafraid of a red card. The football revolutionary he would later become would have seemed unfathomable at the time.

He had sampled promotion to the Premier League as a player, with Blackburn Rovers in 1992, but would never play there, instead being transferred to Neil Warnock's Plymouth Argyle before he found his way to Rochdale.

Hill admits he hadn't really thought about becoming a coach or manager after his playing days were done, but he did at least have the foresight to do his coaching badges so that there was something to work with.

'If you asked the majority of my team-mates from my time at Blackburn or Plymouth, I don't think many of them would tell you they saw me going into coaching or management,' he says.

'When I actually first joined Rochdale as a player, under Graham Barrow, that's when I embarked on my coaching certificates. I was 27 years old at that point and I wish I'd have started even earlier, to be honest, because it gave me a different perspective of the game, you know, from a coach's or manager's point of view?

'I got my UEFA C and B licences while I was still at Rochdale and my A when I was at Cheltenham, which is where I played after I left Dale. This meant, by the time I finished playing, I already had all the qualifications I needed to go into coaching. I later got my UEFA Pro Licence, once I got the manager's job at Rochdale. I really enjoyed learning about the other side of the game and how important the tactical side is, but also the development side, too. During the course of learning all that, it made me realise it was something I really, really wanted to do, to make a big impact on player development first and foremost.'

Hill's first chance to flex his now famous coaching muscles came at Bolton Wanderers. 'I started by coaching an under-nine team,' he says. 'I really, really enjoyed that because coaching young football players with enthusiasm and the willingness and curiosity to learn was brilliant. It planted a seed with me. It started my approach to take all of those attributes from children and see if they would work with a group of older players.'

It was with Rochdale's youth academy that Hill would get to test his new theorem.

'I had a really good working relationship with Steve Parkin and Tony Ford when I had played for them,' he says. 'When the youth team coaching position came up at Rochdale, I got an interview on Steve's recommendation and that's how I got the job.

'I am never afraid to give players an opportunity if they have ability. Ability, for me, is effort. That's the number one skill. If they have the ambition, the effort and the desire, and all those other attributes I see in very young players, then I'll support those players all the time. I like to think I played just a small part in the success of the youth players who went on to achieve great things. I just opened the door for them.'

While developing young players gave Hill a certain professional fulfilment, he would soon be given the opportunity to see how his methods prospered with seasoned regulars. A run of poor results saw both Steve Parkin and Tony Ford depart Rochdale for the second time in December 2006, and Chris Dunphy, who had replaced David Kilpatrick as chairman, turned to Hill to keep their bench warm, albeit temporarily.

'Chris phoned me and asked if I would take the manager's job on a caretaker basis,' Hill recalls. 'The first thing I did was ask Steve Parkin's permission, because he'd been ever so good to me as a player and in bringing me back to the football club as a youth team coach. Once I had that, Chris promised me that I wouldn't be sacrificed if things didn't work out and I would be allowed to go back to being youth team coach.

'I was only going to take the job for as long as was necessary. Once I had these assurances, it was just a matter of planning. The first was a short-term plan, where I brought fellow former Rochdale player Gareth Griffiths in to help me. I had built up a good relationship with Gareth when I returned to the club as youth coach. That first week, I gathered the players, the same ones who had been there the week before under Steve, and we worked on how we wanted to play continuously – day in, day out. We came up with a plan to play against MK Dons, the first opponent with me in charge, and we got narrowly beaten 2-1 away from home. We played ever so well. We were still 22nd in the league, but I embraced the challenge that came with that.

'The next game was Wrexham at home and we drew two each. I had to change tactically during that one as we found ourselves 2-0 down. Then we won our next two games 4-0 against Boston and Grimsby. The things we had been working on started to click.'

At this stage, Hill looked to have tossed his own hat into the ring for the permanent job with some conviction. However, fate almost played its hand here and, if things had gone another way, Rochdale would have been deprived of their most successful manager after just three matches.

'Leading up to the Boston game, I'd had a phone call on the Thursday telling me [former Oldham boss] Andy Ritchie was going to be taking over as manager, but I was still to be in charge against Boston, as there were a few minor details that were to be ironed out,' Hill says.

'The thing with Andy didn't materialise because Chris was true to his word. Andy wanted to bring all of his own staff in and Chris didn't want to sacrifice me, so Andy changed his mind. As a result of that, I got the Grimsby game, we won 4-0, and then Chris told me the job was mine until the end of the season.

'That's when I started to form longer-term plans. Gareth Griffiths had always told me it was short-term for him and he wanted to go back to the financial business he'd set up after he finished playing. So, I turned to another ex-team-mate to be my assistant, who still remains my number one football friend to this day, Dave Flitcroft.'

And with that, the partnership that would come to be affectionately known by Dale supporters as 'Hillcroft' was born. A Morrissey and Marr for the modern football age. A Lennon and McCartney. The pair brought the football club hit after hit.

'The challenges we embraced were to overachieve, create an identity that the whole of the football world would know us for, and create an environment that the players both embraced and owned,' Hill explains.

'The first part of the journey for all of us was magnificent. We had 24 games left of the season and we won 13, drew seven and lost four. We went from 22nd to chasing the play-off positions and we nearly achieved it. We just made sure there was no wasted time. We made sure we were pre-organised and post-organised. Training intensity was all geared towards the way we wanted to play both in and out of possession. The players embraced it and they enjoyed it. Once they started owning it, they started to realise how successful they could become. We were marching into every game and there was a real fear from the opponent that they were going to get turned over because of our identity and the way we played. The opposition knew that, when they faced Rochdale, it was going to be a really tough game.'

During this dazzling period, Rochdale truly demonstrated their will and ability to blitz teams from the first whistle. Both MK Dons (5-0) and Stockport County (7-2) found this out the hard way. It truly was no-fear football.

'Myself and Flicker [Flitcroft] were as determined as the players to overachieve,' Hill says. 'The club had wallowed in League Two for decades. Even when me and Flicker were playing for the club it was known as the "Rochdale Division". We wanted to smash that to pieces. We had Gary Jones, John Doolan, Nathan Stanton, Rory McArdle and Glenn Murray in the squad, who were all real leaders. When they saw how successful we could be, with the way that we trained, the way that everyone adopted our personality – we knew, and they knew, it would carry on to the next season.'

The beginning of the following season delivered something of a grounding for supporters, however. The summer had been encouraging, especially with Hill's contract being made permanent and that too of loanee goal machine Adam Le Fondre from Stockport. Yet the opening game, away at Peterborough, brought with it a comprehensive 3-0 defeat, as did the first home league match of the season against Chester City (2-1). Hill wasn't perturbed. He knew he could deliver something special in what was Rochdale's centenary year.

'We were quite naive at first, me and Flicker, because we promised everybody promotion that season,' he reflects. 'What we quickly realised is that it's very difficult to maintain that continuity and momentum from one season ending to the next beginning. We had to really start afresh, with recruiting and retaining players, to maintain what we had achieved the previous season and take it further with promotion. We laid a plan down to the board of directors – this is what we want and this is how we are going to do it.

'We had a very good squad of players and worked very hard in pre-season. Yes, we did lose the first two games, but one of those was to Peterborough who, that season, were by far the best League Two side I have ever witnessed in my lifetime. Our first victory was MK Dons. We won 3-2 with two very late goals from Chris Dagnall and Alf [Le Fondre]. That was the turning point and it came early enough in the season.'

Hill's plan was one of patience.

'One thing we always had to do at Rochdale was to have sustainability for the season,' he says. 'We were never going to start as favourites for any season. Some of the form in that August-September time, we knew would be indifferent. But, we also knew, as long as we could hit November, December and January, when other teams had lost their enthusiasm, we would start to take advantage and our form would grow. We planned to be as successful as we possibly could be against every team, of course, but, more importantly, we aimed to take maximum advantage of those teams that were always going to be below us. We wanted to blow those teams away on a regular basis. And, if we could beat a Peterborough, or an MK Dons, then that was a bonus.'

Rochdale's form, which was especially strong from March onwards, propelled them into the play-off positions at the season's end, even though striker Glenn Murray had been sold to Brighton & Hove Albion in the winter. This was the first time Dale had achieved the feat since 2002. There, they would meet a strong Darlington side at the George Reynolds Arena, before then hosting the deciding leg of the semi-final. Thousands of Dale fans made their way north-east only to be deflated by Jason Kennedy's exquisite shot into the top corner. Chris Dagnall equalised for Dale with a deflected effort, but substitute Ian Miller headed in a free kick to snatch victory for the Quakers in the dying minutes.

Almost 10,000 supporters packed into Spotland for the return fixture. When Clark Keltie put Darlington 1-0 up from the penalty spot, it would have been easy to assume at this juncture that Rochdale had reverted to their historic type of folding just when it really mattered. Well, what followed was certainly historic.

Dale levelled when Dagnall stabbed in Adam Rundle's cross before David Perkins struck a sensational 25-yard thunderbolt to send the semi-final into extra time.

The drama wasn't yet over. Perkins was given a straight red card after a late challenge on Ricky Ravenhill, but ten-man Dale held on and forced the tie to penalties. Two iconic moments followed, but only the latter seems permanently seared into the memories of Rochdale supporters who were there that day, this writer's included.

Jason Kennedy's penalty was saved by Dale goalkeeper Tommy Lee, but it was substitute Ben Muirhead's winning kick, Dale's fifth, that sent the stadium into raptures. The image of him wheeling away having set up Rochdale's first Wembley appearance is perhaps one that is the most synonymous with Hill's tenure at the club.

'Those were magnificent moments in my life, the players' lives and the lives of everyone connected to the football club,' Hill says. 'Many managers and players strive their whole careers for a Wembley appearance. It was the pinnacle of the all-inclusive environment we had created at Rochdale. This included the board of directors, the players, all the staff and the supporters. Every one of those people knew our identity. They knew we were hard working and that we represented them. So, for us to be able to do that at Wembley, was going to be an honour.

'The play-off second leg was a magnificent achievement on the day, when we found ourselves in a position of losing 3-1 on aggregate to high-spending opposition, but then turned it around to win on penalties? Wow. The atmosphere was electric. The only atmosphere that has rivalled that at Spotland for me was the end of the Tottenham game [2018].'

As thousands upon thousands of Rochdale supporters descended upon the capital for an historic day out against Stockport County, Hill wasn't feeling as jubilant.

'We went into that play-off final with key personnel problems,' he says. 'We found ourselves very, very thin in midfield. I had no other alternative but to play [full-back] Simon Ramsden there. At the time, John Doolan was coming to the end of his career. He would've been the first name picked two seasons before, and we had lost Chris Basham and Lewis Montrose to injury, while David Perkins was suspended after he got sent off against Darlington. It made for a difficult final, but, again, one in which I would always commend the players for the courage they played with, especially in getting us 1-0 up.'

It was Rory McArdle who set Dale on their way with a header at the near post before Nathan Stanton flattened the ecstasy by diverting a cross into his own net for Stockport's equaliser. The second half definitely belonged to the Hatters and the magnificent Anthony Pilkington bulleted a header in off the crossbar to put them ahead right after the break. Liam Dickinson scored a third with a near-post strike before Dale's Adam Rundle sent a splendid volley home to restore some respectability.

'On that day, and probably throughout the course of that season, I would say that Stockport were a better pound-for-pound team than us,' reflects Hill. 'But we overachieved again to get to Wembley. Having lost Glenn Murray in January was a significant loss to us, make no mistake. The 4-3 win at Chesterfield, just before he was sold, was a classic. Murray was at the top of his game and we looked unstoppable at the time. To still narrowly miss out on promotion against an excellent Stockport side, was definitely another overachievement.'

The 2008/09 season is probably the only one where supporters may have questioned if even Hill himself could push Rochdale out of the 'Rochdale Division'. Yes, there were the usual fine results that Hill had made his trademark, a 6-1 demolition of Chester City being chief among them, but, as the season approached its zenith, and Dale still looked to be in with a shout of the automatic promotion spots, a last-minute winner at Wycombe courtesy of Adam Le Fondre looked to be the catalyst for them to do just that. It wasn't, and Dale would win just once more before the season's end, having to make do with the play-offs once again. This time the semi-finals lacked the fanfare of the previous year and a 0-0 draw followed by a 2-1 defeat against Gillingham ensured there would be no Wembley day out again.

'It's very difficult and emotional to pick players up after something like a Wembley defeat and make them go again,' says Hill. 'One thing you can't do as a manager is rest on your laurels or feel sorry for yourself. The group, the players, will respond to the way you act and behave in this situation, both to the messages you give out vocally and your body language. So, we regrouped, we said we'd go again and we also said we didn't want anyone in the dressing room who didn't want to go again, work hard or overachieve. We came up with a strapline for the season, "We are gonna run all over the opposition." We felt we had the perfect 15 players, but you're always having to look over your shoulder, especially in Rochdale's case, where there was historical debt. You're always having to sell players, but you still have to show that courage and ambition for the task ahead.

'We were well-prepared, and we did make the play-offs again, but we couldn't get to the final. I still don't know how to sum that season up, to be frank. It wasn't quite the standard of our previous season. After losing to Gillingham in the play-offs, we knew we needed a little bit of a clear-out, to be honest. We also knew we would have to recruit one or two if we were to finally achieve promotion.'

The vast majority of those attending Spotland the following season weren't around in 1969, when the club last sealed promotion from the basement tier. Generations of supporters since have craved their own season of glory to cherish. In 2009/10, Hill delivered. By Christmas Rochdale were streets ahead of the rest, sitting proudly at the top of the table like a star on a festive tree. Not only did promotion look inevitable but a first league title looked certain too.

So dominant were Dale against the opposition that Hill coined the phrase, 'We footballed them to death.'

Yet, with seven games remaining, and Dale being able to mathematically secure promotion down in Devon at Torquay, they imploded, losing 5-0. They lost the next game, too, 1-0 at home to Darlington. Supporters started to get twitchy again. The goods were finally achieved one match later, however, after a scrappy affair against Northampton Town, settled by Chris O'Grady's 23rd-minute strike. The celebrations lasted for days. Rochdale hadn't seen a promotion since man first walked on the moon. There was to be no title party, though. Dale failed to win again that season and eventually finished third behind big-spending Notts County and Bournemouth.

'It was a magnificent season and a magnificent achievement,' Hill says. 'Promotion had been our aim and we delivered it. We were expecting to go all the way and be promoted as champions. The intensity that we played at for three quarters of that season was amazing. We blew everybody away that we possibly could. There was a suggestion we limped over the line, but I don't subscribe to that. I knew the inner workings of the squad of players that we had and there was a little bit of self-protection that went on, I won't lie. We knew that players were going to leave, because their contracts were running down. They were going to go to the Championship, or they were going to go to other clubs that could pay a lot more money than we could. They had worked exceptionally hard for those opportunities.

'Once we sealed promotion, it was almost like the season had finished and that we'd all achieved what we needed to achieve on behalf of the supporters. Remember, it'd only been done once in the club's lifetime prior to this. I was really disappointed we didn't win the title, though, and I was unfair with the players at times. I remember my dad saying to me, "Don't spoil what you've achieved. These players deserve their opportunity to switch off." It was disappointing, but I understood. They were protecting their own interests. They had done everything me and Flicker had asked of them.

'Did I think we could have won the title? Yes. Do I think we were the best team in League Two that season? Yes. Did we show that over 46 games? No. We got promoted after 40 games and the players deserve a huge amount of credit for that. They stuck with it when they could have started looking after themselves at an earlier stage. I have since put my disappointment to one side, knowing we still achieved what hadn't been achieved since 1969. It took me and Flicker three seasons to do it.

'There had been suggestions that all our talk was just that, and that we were finding it difficult. Yes, we were. We had to keep finding new ways of keeping that momentum going. That season we finally did it. We footballed teams to death. The emergence of players like Craig Dawson made people take note. We got beaten to the title by a Notts County side who, on one player alone, Kasper Schmeichel, had spent the equivalent of our entire budget. Let that sink in. That's what we were competing against. So, for us to get promoted with honesty and one of the lowest budgets in League Two is testament to Chris Dunphy and the board of directors, the players that we had and the staff. We were all on the journey together and every one of them deserved to join in the celebrations when we got promoted because they all contributed.'

A first season in the third tier for 30 years led most supporters to adopt an attitude of 'enjoy the ride'. Early draws or wins were greeted with chants of 'The Dale are staying up'. This irked Hill a little, who aspired to much more than simply making up the numbers. For the first time, he made a real tactical switch to his setup.

'I'm not sure if you realised, but during the latter stages of the League Two campaign, the change had already started,' Hill explains. 'I started playing Gary Jones as a number ten and he hated it. He hated every moment of it. I remember Barnet, the last game of the season, where he came off the pitch fuming at me, and he said, "I hate this position, I can't stand it. What are you doing to me?" It was all part of us trying to design what we wanted to do in League One. We wanted to go into League One and be successful. We thought we needed an extra midfield player. We wanted a couple of defensive midfield players and one spontaneous player who could run everywhere and get on the end of things. As soon as Gary Jones took to that, he realised how successful he was going to be. He knew he could do what he wanted and that he had protection behind him. It worked a dream. With someone like Chris O'Grady playing up front, and Antony Elding playing off the left, wheeling in on to his right foot, it created a special blend. We had what we considered to be a solid base to work from.'

This solid base led to some extremely memorable results and performances as Dale ended their first season in League One in a respectable ninth place. Perhaps the stand-out game was a 2-0 victory away at Southampton, a team that contained a host of players who would go on to light up the Premier League, including former Dale hero Rickie Lambert. The stand-out moment was Gary Jones's long-range howitzer. It sent a message to the wider footballing world. Dale were no longer the team of old.

'When you consider we beat the likes of Southampton, Sheffield Wednesday, Bournemouth and Huddersfield, it was a great season,' reflects Hill. 'Again, the players bought into what we were telling them. As before, once they saw it worked, they owned it.'

Sadly, supporters had little time to relax and reflect on another historic season. Speculation had already started to circulate that Dale's management duo were being coveted by higher powers. Sheffield United and Barnsley were two names that featured more than most.

After giving assurances to the public that he was 'going nowhere', it was announced shortly after that both Hill and Flitcroft had agreed to join the Championship Tykes.

'To be completely honest with you, I could have left three or four times previous to that,' Hill admits. 'There's a perception of who I am and there's the reality of who I am. The reality is that I'm honest. With every group of players I worked with at Rochdale, there is an intimacy. We become lifelong footballing friends. We had done everything asked of us the previous season. Myself and Flicker did want to achieve what we considered the impossible dream, which was to get Rochdale into the Championship, but we knew players like Craig Dawson had been sold. We knew Scott Wiseman was going to leave. We knew that we couldn't retain Chris O'Grady and Matty Done. Other players had intimated they wanted to leave too. So, it was very difficult for us to achieve what we wanted in League One on a League Two budget. The overachieving mentality at some point needs backing with finances or you end up tripping yourself over because all your best players leave and you're left threadbare because you don't have enough time to create a layer of players who are ready to step in. A system of progression wasn't therefore evident to me and Flicker at that time.

'It was a long, drawn-out situation when we left for Barnsley and it could have been achieved a different way. There were a lot of politics, with people protecting themselves, but, because myself and Flicker had been offered a contract extension by Rochdale, it meant that Barnsley had to give them a substantial fee.

'Me and Flicker were adamant that we were Championship managers. It was the next challenge for us. People still take away from what we achieved at Barnsley, but we created there what we did at Rochdale. We cut close to £2m off the budget, retained Championship status and developed players. A lot of those players made Barnsley a lot of money, too.'

Hill's replacements, first Steve Eyre and then John Coleman, failed to keep Dale in League One and, after just two seasons, the dream was over. As fate would have it, with Coleman leading Dale into a League Two campaign the following season, Barnsley were drawn to face Hill's old club at Spotland in the League Cup.

'Taking the emotions out of it, it was a job,' Hill says. 'We were there to win. I had spent that whole summer trying my best to develop John Stones, who scored in that game. He became a significant transaction for Barnsley and now represents England. Anyway, we won, despite our goalkeeper being sent off. Rochdale gave us a good game. It was certainly an entertaining one with the number of goals in it [it finished 4-3 after extra time].'

But what did Hill think of this new-look Rochdale side?

'I didn't think our hard work had been undone,' he says. 'I just think me and Flicker weren't appreciated or respected in the manner we should have been at that particular time. I think there was a general consensus that what myself and Dave had achieved had been relatively easy and it certainly wasn't. We spent the best part of the 24 hours in each day trying to achieve the success that we did. I think that recognition and respect has come since, but, at that time, it wasn't there. I think there were too many tricks missed by Steve Eyre and John Coleman. I don't think they realised that the interconnections between everybody at the club that me and Flicker established, were integral to the success we achieved. I don't think that identity needed changing. The players still there, such as Gary Jones, were already bought into that.'

Fate once again intervened in the destiny of both Rochdale and Hill. Things didn't quite work out for Hill at Barnsley and he departed in the December, leaving the other half of Hillcroft at the wheel. Meanwhile, John Coleman was relieved of his duties at Rochdale a month later.

'Managers lose their jobs in football,' Hill says. 'It does happen, because of results, no matter how good a manager you are and John is a very good manager, as he has proven time and time again with his success, identity and recruitment at Accrington Stanley.

'I contacted Rochdale director Andrew Kelly, who has been a superb supporter of me, and asked if there would be an opportunity to be interviewed for the vacant manager's position and one thing led to another and I got the job. An experienced owner of a Championship club said to me, "You're an out of work Championship manager, why are you going back to League Two? You could be making a grave mistake here." But I really wanted to go back and recreate what I had done previously. I trusted the CEO Colin Garlick, I trusted director Paul Hazlehurst, I trusted the chairman, Chris Dunphy, and I trusted Andrew Kelly. I had a great working relationship with those four people in particular from my first experience at the football club. Knowing they were there, and trusting my own methods, I had no fear in going back.'

Hill moved quickly to make his mark, recruiting players such as Ian Henderson, who would go on to have a huge impact, and Joe Bunney, who scored the winner in a final-day victory over Plymouth Argyle, ensuring Dale finished a respectable 12th.

'There is no money at Rochdale,' Hill explains. 'That's not meant to be detrimental or disrespectful, but it's a fact. There is no footballing money. You have to generate your own income by being successful and via the sale of players. The sale of players when I went back was integral to what we did on the pitch and to our financial security. We stabilised the club after its relegation and then rebuilt it – me, Chris Beech [Hill's new number two], Tony Ellis [head of youth] and the board of directors.

'My next task, over the summer, was to recreate the identity that I had established the first time. My identity is very important. I know who I am. The players know who I am and they know what I want. It's transparent. Anyone who doesn't buy into us being all inclusive and all having the same agenda, has to go. It's not ruthless, it's common sense. You don't belong if you don't believe in what we are trying to achieve. Bobby Grant, the leading goalscorer from the previous season, was the first player to leave. He made the club a lot of money, too. He's an excellent player, Bobby, but he didn't 100 per cent fit into my identity, the way that I coach, the way that we train. So, it was important that I recruited the players who did. I told them, "We are going to be the fittest team in League Two."'

And Hill was right. Once again, a visible and immediate transformation was apparent as Rochdale romped to automatic promotion.

'We built an amazing squad of players,' he says. 'To get promoted in my first full season back, in the manner that we did, considering where we were when I took over, was an amazing achievement. Absolutely amazing.

'I don't think we beat the teams who got promoted along with us that season, Chesterfield and Scunthorpe. But, again, we beat the teams we had to. Ian Henderson was a big, big character for us. I also wouldn't underestimate what Michael Rose and Peter

Cavanagh did for that team either, in kneading the squad of players together. I signed Peter Vincenti and Oliver Lancashire, who had both been relegated with Aldershot the previous season. I knew I could get good players from relegated sides, but, let's be honest, the driving force of that season was the acquisition of Scott Hogan and the loan signing of Jack O'Connell. The latter, at 18 years old, was absolutely amazing. His performance level, for someone that inexperienced, was absolutely phenomenal. We got him back for our season in League One too – and I'm sure, if he hadn't been recalled by Brentford, we would have made the play-offs that year.

'I had Brian Barry-Murphy, too. He was coming to the end of his playing career. I said to him, "You will continue to train and be part of the first-team squad, but you will be my coach in that changing room. You will learn how to become a coach as a result, while you're still helping me to get a good read every day on how the players are acting, interacting, feeling, handling the pressure and so on." That kind of communication is key.'

Also that season, Rochdale produced one of their finest ever displays to knock Championship side Leeds United out of the FA Cup in the third round. A beautiful side-footed volley over goalkeeper Paddy Kenny from Henderson capped a wonderful performance.

'We were like the Championship side the day we played Leeds United,' Hill beams. 'I bumped into Brian McDermott the other day, who of course was manager of Leeds at the time we played them, and he still talks about that game. That was a Championship display against an elite Championship side. I've achieved two play-offs and two promotions with Rochdale, but that game is one of the proudest moments of my life. I know we've played other big sides in the cup. Against Nottingham Forest, you could say we got a fortunate penalty and rode our luck, but against Leeds we absolutely dominated. The goals that we scored too, I mean, come on. Scott Hogan and Ian Henderson that day tortured Leeds. Tortured them. It was Matty Done's first game at left-back too, because Rose was suspended, and he was brilliant.

'Peter Cavanagh was absolutely dominant in midfield, too. Every manager makes mistakes and, I tell you, mine was letting him go. I should've kept him for another season. You think players at certain ages can't play League One football and you move them on, but I should have kept him when we got promoted. No question about it. He was a brilliant player who read the game ever so well. I was searching for a Peter Cavanagh for a long time after he left. I tried it with Keith Keane and it did work, but his injury problems meant he couldn't get a run of games for us. Again, it goes back to what I said earlier. As a Rochdale manager, you are working with a jigsaw where pieces keep being taken away and you have to find another piece that fits. You can't just go out and buy the same piece. You have to look elsewhere and maybe do some work on that piece before it fits.

'This is where the development system at the club comes into play. The work done by Chris Beech and Tony Ellis there was crucial. There was a clear plan from top to bottom and bottom to top. I said to them, I want these types of players and, if you develop them, I will fast-track them into the first team. We needed a layer of players to replace those we had to sell at any given time and I couldn't always go out on the open market and get them. The work done in the academy was evident when I came back with the likes of Jamie Allen, Callum Camps and Scott Tanser. They haven't all gone on to achieve what I believe they should have in the game, but they were brilliant for me. It carried on with the likes of Aaron Morley, Andy Cannon, Daniel Adshead and Luke Matheson. There will be more to come, I guarantee it. In addition to helping the first team, they then become saleable assets for the club.'

The next three seasons back in League One were halcyon days for Rochdale, in which they achieved the highest league finish in their history. More high-profile scalps were taken along the way and Hill found new ways to adapt, such as Matty Done's devastating form as a number ten, or the return of Grant Holt for a Dale swansong.

Until early January of the 2016/17 season, Hill had found a way of playing that teams struggled to cope with. Then something happened from which the club never really seemed to recover. Striker-turned-full-back Joe Bunney was injured. For both player and club, it proved a real turning point.

'There are always key moments for a club like Rochdale with a small squad, where the loss of one or two players can destabilise you, especially when they are very difficult to replace in the short term,' Hill says. 'We managed to finish that season really well, but there was a certain period where Bunney was out with a broken metatarsal and it coincided with us propelling towards the play-offs. We had been to Barrow in the FA Cup and beaten them, and then we got beat 4-0 by Oxford. That was the turning point of our season where it almost crumbled.

'I'm going to the Oxford game with four players unavailable as a result of injury in the Barrow game. We were right up at the top end of the table at this point. It highlighted our issues in a nutshell, where we just didn't have a deep enough squad to maintain the momentum built up by a certain group of players. Our intensity was always going to take a toll on our squad with it being so shallow. That was always going to make the promotion challenge that bit harder. We almost got the job done at the end of the season, though, but we drew at Oldham. We were winning 1-0 and then I had to take Keith Keane off and they equalised. I believe that cost us the three points that would have given us a play-off place.

'It's all small margins, especially with a small budget and a small squad. If we were going to get promoted to the Championship it had to be in those first three seasons. Anything after that starts to ebb away. In addition to the players you sell, those players you've maintained, and who have stayed with you, get older and less efficient, and they are very difficult to replace. The house will implode on itself eventually. Then, you either decide to leave, which I did the first time, or you're asked to leave, which is what happened to me the second.'

Some may argue that Hill's eventual departure was a protracted affair that began in 2017/18, where a perceived lack of consistency in selection or commitment to players led to Dale's worst season in

League One under his watch. An incredible FA Cup fifth round tie against Tottenham, which Dale took to a replay at Wembley – Spurs' home while White Hart Lane was being rebuilt – couldn't quite paper over the cracks. It took a great escape, achieved in dramatic fashion on the final day of the season, thanks to Joe Thompson's strike against Charlton, for Dale to avoid relegation. The jubilation of survival, which mirrored celebrations of the same in the 1980s (albeit a division higher this time) soon gave way to post-mortems. Some supporters suggested Hill was chucking stuff at the wall at times, but his switch to five at the back actually showed how he should manage: making the most of what he had and trusting his players without overthinking things.

It's fair to say, though, that the 2018/19 season was a mess, from the signings of journeyman Aaron Wilbraham and the re-signing of former player David Perkins without any real idea how they should be used in the team, to the departure of chairman Chris Dunphy.

Hill cites the latter as finally triggering the death knell for his own time at Spotland.

'When Chris Dunphy left as chairman, it absolutely altered everything,' he says. 'Colin Garlick, the best CEO I have ever worked with, had gone to Port Vale, Andrew Kelly had gone and Bill Goodwin left also. These were key components to the club. We all had a mutual trust. Between us, we had agreed an approach similar to that of Crewe Alexandra. If we ever got relegated, it would be done in a sustainable way so that we could bounce right back, even if that meant becoming a bit of a yo-yo club until things clicked again.

'When Chris phoned me to tell me he was leaving, it was very difficult for me. From that point on, the sands were constantly shifting and it became evident very quickly that I wasn't part of the long-term plan. It was very hurtful, because I had made my mind up that I wanted Rochdale to be my career adventure. Chris trusted me enormously. He left me to run the football side of things and, as long as I didn't overspend, that was that. I never overspent. The club was financially sound. Chris left and then I was being told the club was in debt and I had to sell players. I felt isolated. The new board had their own plans and I wasn't part of them. Well, I was part of a plan to sell players in the January transfer window, you know, Harrison McGahey, Andy Cannon and Joe Rafferty, and then, once that was done, it soon became evident my time was up. Yes, we were in a poor position in the league, but my agreement with Chris was as I said, we would manage any relegation in a sustainable way. I was never sure what the new chairman, Andrew Kilpatrick, actually wanted going forward. David Bottomley became the club's new CEO and we had plenty of no-prejudice conversations about my future at the football club.

'Once the news was delivered to me that my employment with the club was being terminated, I didn't really want to know what the succession plan was. That was it for me.'

Hill left Rochdale on 4 March, 2019. It was a very sad day and didn't seem befitting for a man who had delivered a legacy to a penurious small-town outfit that will be spoken of for as long as the club exists. He didn't even get chance to give a valedictory wave. Supporter reaction was one of sorrow, although Hill had been perceived to be making more and more slights towards the fans, as pressure from the club's league position intensified.

'Everything I did at Rochdale AFC was on behalf of the supporters,' he explains. 'I know what they wanted. Did I get emotionally upset with player performances? Yes. But do I want to protect them 100 per cent from every criticism but my own? Yes. Absolutely. I had a mentality of, "Don't you dare criticise my players when I know what they're doing every week and the sacrifices they are making." Leave the criticism to me. My mantra is to always deflect. Deflect away from the player and on to me. If you want to dish some stick out, then give it to me. As long as I was creating a diversion away from that group of players, so I could continue working with that group of players, then I was happy to take the flak from a minority of people.

'All these achievements during my time were not down to me alone. Yes, I planned it and I drove it, but the players delivered it and they delivered it on behalf of those supporters. I still believe I have a strong relationship with a group of supporters who understood me. Did I get angry at them at times? Of course. It happens. But that shouldn't in any way, shape or form distort our relationship and the magnificent successes we've celebrated together. I consider Rochdale AFC to be my club. It's part of me and always will be.'

Steve Eyre

2011

IF PAUL Simpson had big shoes to fill following the departure of John Hollins, then Steve Eyre had to plug those that would have fit a fairytale giant.

Keith Hill, the director of youth football who had taken over from Steve Parkin with so little expectation in 2006, had gone on to lead Rochdale to a first Wembley appearance and, two seasons later, a first promotion since 1969.

At the end of the 2010/2011 season, he had led Dale to an equal best finish of ninth in League One.

That Hill had, just a week earlier, ruled out leaving made the blow all the more bitter when he made the move to Championship side Barnsley during a bleak June in 2011. The club felt rudderless without him, left to float down the perilous waters of a League One pre-season without its enigmatic admiral. Without wanting to sound too dramatic, the supporters sensed the club's very soul had been stolen.

Chris Dunphy was faced with his toughest decision as chairman. Appointing a successor to Rochdale's most efficacious manager was a decision he could not afford to get wrong. Hill had revolutionised the club from top to bottom. His emphasis on sports science and youth, and the infrastructure that went with this, needed to be protected.

Perhaps that is why Dunphy sought to appoint a man with a similar ethos to Hill's. Steve Eyre was approached for the job with more than two decades of coaching the juniors and reserves at Manchester City behind him.

'That's true, I was just starting my 21st year at City when I was approached to speak to the Rochdale board,' Eyre recalls. 'Management was something I wanted to do one day, yes, but this opportunity came to me out of the blue.

'I was interested, of course, flattered even, but, at that point, I only wanted to go to the initial interview for the experience. To see what it was like.

'I was up front with the City staff. I told them about the approach and went to the interview with their blessing.

'I spoke to my father [former Manchester City player Fred Eyre], I spoke to the people at City, nobody wanted me to leave, but they said I should go to have the discussion. They knew I was ambitious and they didn't want to stand in my way. In football, opportunities can be rare.

'It was very informal with Rochdale at first, but I wasn't casual. I made it clear I was up for the challenge and that the time was right for me to perhaps try something new in working with a first team.

'I was then asked to go for an official interview with the chairman and the chief executive, Colin Garlick. Quickly afterwards, I was invited for a second interview and, at that point, it started to get a bit more serious. I realised I could actually be leaving City. I was offered the Rochdale job the same evening.

'I was proud and torn at the same time. For the first time in two decades, I had to decide about my career for myself. At City, I'd been steered and led by older, more experienced people such as Alex Gibson, Jim Cassell and Paul Power but, at that moment in time, there was only one person who could decide where my career was going and that person was me. I wasn't shy in doing it, I'm a competitor after all, but leaving a club I loved after 21 years was hard, yes.'

Despite Rochdale having achieved, at that point, their joint-highest league finish the previous season, Eyre found he had inherited a host of problems when he got behind his new desk.

'Keith Hill, who is a friend of mine, had a great trust with the team, with the chairman, with the board and with the supporters,'

Eyre says. 'They were big shoes to fill, of course they were, but I'm not sure people fully appreciate the size of the task that awaited me.

'I didn't have a first-team goalkeeper, I didn't have a training ground and I didn't have any staff. Eventually, we ended up renting Stockport County's training ground, having to share with them each morning. It was a free-for-all and, at times, we were even sharing the same pitch. It was far from ideal.

'There were other challenges, too. I had a captain [Gary Jones] at 35 years old holding out for a two-year deal when the club was only offering him one year. I only had seven players to work with that were signed on. Two of them got injured on the first day of training [Joe Thompson and Brian Barry-Murphy]. We lost Craig Dawson, Matty Done and Scott Wiseman to other clubs. There was also someone at the club who wanted the manager's job and didn't get it, which was another challenge I had to handle. As a novice manager in my first job, it was a tough start.

'I had to meet it head on, though. I had chosen to do it. I arrived at Rochdale with a fanfare of well-wishers from Man City and elsewhere in the game, all of whom were saying I would be a success, which was nice, but with it came added pressure. It built the expectation from the supporters and the board.

'My biggest challenge, though, was recruitment within the budget. I have no complaints about the budget itself. It was set before I accepted the job, so I knew what it was, but I made mistakes with it. As a young manager with no scouting network support, it was tough. My signings ranged from good, to bad, to indifferent. We had a respectable youth academy in place but, at that time, there was nothing to tap into. Now, it has produced the likes of Callum Camps, Scott Tanser and Jamie Allen, but it was in its infancy when I arrived. There was nothing there to use.

'A lot of my recruits were gambles and, perhaps, too young. I had five goalkeepers on trial during pre-season. None worked out. It was a real problem position for me. It was very much fingers in the dam. You would sort one problem and another appeared.'

Of the three keepers Eyre did use for competitive games, none of Jake Kean, David Lucas or Matt Edwards made the grade.

'I honestly think I was cursed as far as goalkeepers went,' Eyre says. 'I remember we were due to play Aldershot in the League Cup and David Lucas's knee locked in match prep. I had to stick Matty Edwards in goal and ask a 17-year-old youth keeper to drive down to Aldershot with his dad, just to sit on the bench. We lost and Aldershot drew Manchester United in the next round. To say that blow was felt would be an understatement. Then there was a time, against Sheffield United, when David Lucas got knocked out cold during the game and, another occasion, against Colchester, I think, when he was violently sick in the changing room just before kick-off. I know managers have to deal with injuries and setbacks but, where goalkeepers were concerned, I was especially unlucky.'

Goalkeepers aside, Eyre's on-field signings, in all fairness, will be his legacy – the general consensus being that there was an over reliance on former City youth players, and the centre-half Neal Trotman. Trotman came to Spotland with a decent record behind him but a series of calamitous performances saw him ushered out on loan by November. There was Marc Twaddle, too. A player who had played on the left of defence or midfield in Scotland for both Partick Thistle and Falkirk, Twaddle found himself playing a seemingly alien role at centre-half for Rochdale.

Ashley Grimes and Andrew Tutte were two of the former City youngsters of note who Eyre brought to Spotland over the summer, the latter having previously played for Rochdale on loan and being part of Eyre's side that beat Chelsea in the 2008 FA Youth Cup Final.

Grimes, having been prolific during a loan spell at relegated Lincoln City the previous season, seemed a real capture for Rochdale at the time of his signing, but supporters failed to see an acceptable attitude on the pitch and his goal return wasn't what it should have been for a main striker.

'Grimes and Tutte were good players for Rochdale,' Eyre says. 'I said at the time that Tutte was a future Rochdale captain and so it proved. Grimes is a talented goalscorer. But, it's fair to say, Neal Trotman wasn't a success for me.'

Eventually, Eyre brought in Frank Bunn, a former reserve team coach at City, as his assistant, but was still far from convinced his side was ready for the challenges ahead.

'I managed to convince the team that we were ready to start the season,' Eyre confides. 'We trained very hard. We went to Spain. We beat Southport and West Brom. The team were ready in terms of organisation and fitness, but, at the front of my mind, I knew we were short on personnel.'

Things were about to get worse on that front. Having lost to Sheffield Wednesday on the opening day, Rochdale then sold Chris O'Grady, the main striker at the time, to the Owls for a reported £300,000.

'My team was planned around Gary Jones and Chris O'Grady,' Eyre admits. 'I supported Jones with his two-year contract wish. He was important to me as a first-time manager, and he was good for the club, legend that he is. Added to that, the chairman promised me no bid would prise Chris O'Grady away and that I could plan for the team with him in it.

'We were entering the final stages of the summer transfer window and I remember Mr Dunphy phoning me to say, "I know we said Chris O'Grady was Plan A, but now you need to look for a Plan B. He's going." I had to find an identical player, a focal point for the entire team, in three weeks. That phone call from the chairman left me with a dry mouth and a knot in my stomach. Even if I had months, it would have been difficult to replace Chris.'

Instead, as attacking options, Eyre ended up with Matthew Barnes-Homer on loan from Luton, who were a non-league team at the time, David Ball on loan from Peterborough, and Ahmed Benali on loan from Manchester City. Of those, only Ball looked worthy of the shirt, but he was recalled early by Posh.

Eyre had his eye on a bigger prize, however.

'With just a day remaining of the transfer window, I was swimming against the tide,' Eyre says. 'I spent the whole day offering terms back and forth with Shefki Kuqi [a free agent after leaving Newcastle United]. He was exactly the type of the player we needed. He eventually gave me an answer at 11.30pm to tell me he was signing for Oldham. It was gutting. It wasn't the only time I was scuppered late on with players either. Defenders Miguel Llera and Jean-Yves Mvoto were going to sign for me before going elsewhere for more money.'

Despite the constant setbacks, Eyre still feels he got the desired response from his players on occasion.

'We had the expected opening-day defeat at Sheffield Wednesday,' he says. 'The scoreline was fair. Then we had a galvanising draw against Huddersfield where we came back from two down. We rallied in the second half and, I still believe, if that game had gone on another five minutes we would have won it.

'That type of guts and determination was what I wanted in every game. It's what I strive to get from any player I coach or that plays under me.'

Then there were wins against Premier League outfit QPR in the League Cup, and local rivals Bury and Preston in the league. Eyre cites these performances as the best of his tenure.

'There was adversity attached to some of those games, though,' Eyre says. 'On the way back from London following the QPR win [an evening midweek fixture], the coach broke down at 3am. We didn't get back to the club until quarter to seven in the morning.

'And that Preston game, for me, really sticks in my mind. The term "a week is a long time in football" was never more apt than here. We went out of the FA Cup the previous Saturday to an 83rd-minute screamer scored by Bradford's Nahki Wells. It was a real blow. Seven days later, to the minute, Nicky Adams scored at Deepdale to give us a morale-boosting win and lift us out of the relegation zone. It summed up the topsy-turvy nature of things at the time.

'And that's the thing. I had reliable players like Andrew Tutte, Gary Jones and Jason Kennedy. On any given day we could tear teams apart, like we did Bury in the derby, 4-2. We could give it going forward, without a doubt. But when we went a goal behind, we had a fragile back line and a novice goalkeeper. We could never get a foothold in a game on a regular basis. Over time, I believe we would have done. We didn't find our identity often enough.'

Eyre was eventually sacked six months into his contract following a goalless draw with Yeovil, a game he says Rochdale should have won 8-0, but, despite this, he harbours neither grudge nor regret about his time at the club. It's also worth noting that the side didn't climb any higher up the table following his departure.

Chris Dunphy told the BBC at the time, 'We currently have a squad of 28 players, which is the biggest Rochdale Football Club's ever had by a long way – Keith's squad was about 18 or 19. We're also on the biggest budget we've ever done at Rochdale, which is not a fortune but it is a big clump.

'You add them all together and I feel that I've done everything I can as chairman to support the management team, and if we're not getting results the only thing I can do is change the management team.'

'I know what was good, I know what would have been good and I know what was bad,' Eyre says of his time at Rochdale. 'I've dissected it, I've unpicked it and I've moved on. I would have liked to have stayed longer and done better for Rochdale. It would have been slow progress, but we would have moved forward, I know it.

'The chairman was disappointed, though, as the fans wanted instant success. Taking the Rochdale job took me out of my comfort zone, but has turned me into a stronger coach with a stronger skillset in terms of what I can bring to football for the rest of my life. I don't regret taking the job. I regret losing my job, but I'm proud I did it. I felt saddened to learn my fate over the telephone and not in person, but, thankfully, that practice isn't generally commonplace in football. I only ever wish Rochdale success in the future. I still love going to watch them when I get chance.'

However, one thing that still irks Eyre is that he feels rumours had deliberately been fed to supporters concerning his ability to manage first-team players.

'I was disappointed with the rumours circulating about me,' he says. 'It was put out there that I was just some under-12s coach and that I exaggerated my credentials. I think the Rochdale supporters were unaware of my wider responsibilities at City. I was working as manager of the under-18s at the club and as a coach to the reserves. I was also overseeing the entire youth programme. Because I loved the club that much, and because I love coaching, I spread myself around all the age groups from under-12s up to the reserves. I chose to go in on a Sunday morning with the under-12s and to stay on a Thursday night to work with the under-15s. Those were my choices.

'There was a long spell when, through the working week, I coached every player from the under-tens to reserve level, always with four or five fixtures. Eighteen-hour days were normal. I won the FA Youth Cup at such a young age with great players and great staff around me. Those are my credentials. I coached the City reserves to victories over Chelsea, Arsenal, Manchester United and, of course, Rochdale, which is when Mr Dunphy became aware of me. For anyone to think Mr Dunphy didn't carry out due diligence on me is ridiculous. I know who put these rumours out there, but I have enough dignity not to start mudslinging. It was an attempt to undermine my genuine achievements and to make an already granite-like challenge even harder.'

Eyre next became a head coach on a caretaker basis in 2013 at Championship side Huddersfield Town, a club he joined at League One level not long after leaving Rochdale two years previously.

'I was lucky enough to have ended up at Huddersfield, who picked me up when I was down,' he says. 'I was welcomed immediately and, by the end of the same season I left Rochdale, I was in the semi-circle at Wembley, leaving the division through the top end of it. I believe I can stand tall and proud. Winning the play-off final at Wembley was a justified achievement for 20-plus years of coaching.'

And his spell at Rochdale hasn't dampened his enthusiasm for another crack at management one day.

'I love developing players. I'm a student of the game and try to bring that to those I coach. I wouldn't shy away from management in the future. I would like the chance again but certainly not in the short term.'

John Coleman
2012–2013

IF STEVE Eyre was an attempt by the Rochdale board to maintain the modern approach implemented by Keith Hill, John Coleman was an appointment that harked back to the Dale of old.

Here was an old-school lower-league manager who had enjoyed relative success on a minuscule budget at Accrington Stanley, and he couldn't have asked for a tougher challenge as he attempted to prevent a deflated and demoralised Rochdale squad from hurtling out of League One after just two seasons.

Following Eyre's departure in December 2011, director of youth football Chris Beech was given a chance to arrest the slump on a caretaker basis. A 5-1 defeat to Stevenage at Spotland helped put paid to that brief stint and the board knew they needed a seasoned hand to steer the wheel – and fast.

After much speculation, the club eventually announced the appointment of Coleman in January 2012, and his assistant Jimmy Bell, ending the Liverpudlian's 13-year association with Accrington.

During that time, Coleman had led the Lancashire club from the Northern Premier League First Division back into the Football League, reaching the League Two play-offs in 2011.

He left Stanley sitting tenth in League Two, just two points off the play-off places, and arrived at Spotland with Rochdale lying 23rd in League One, four points from safety.

Like Eyre before him, Coleman chose to leave his comfort zone for an altogether bigger challenge, laden with pressure.

'I made it known the first time round that I was interested in the Rochdale job, when Keith Hill first left,' Coleman says. 'There had been a bit of dialogue and I had been asked if I was genuinely interested, I said yes, but the club didn't pursue it at the time. Six or seven months later, Rochdale came back to me.

'The chairman told us he expected the club to go down, but it would be seen as a bonus if we kept the club up. They were looking more towards reshaping the club for the next season, which, to be honest, myself and Jimmy were too.'

Despite a first-game derby win over local rivals Bury, Coleman was unable to arrest the form he had inherited and Rochdale were relegated from League One.

'We did our best to keep the club up,' Coleman says adamantly. 'We won our first game against Bury, we were on a crest of a wave, but we couldn't build on it because the weather turned terrible and we didn't play for two or three weeks. After that, we just couldn't generate the momentum.'

Coleman wasn't perturbed by the challenge.

'Yes, there were lots of differences between Rochdale and Accrington,' he says. 'It's a bigger club for one. Spotland looks much more like a league ground than Accrington's Crown Ground does for a start, no disrespect to Accrington. It didn't daunt me or Jimmy at all, though. It's what we wanted.

'The hardest part was that there was a division in the camp when we arrived. That was evident from day one. We did our best to try to get that away, but it never left.

'Some players embraced our methods and some didn't. They weren't necessarily against me and Jimmy, though, they were against each other. It was always going to be a problem. We introduced a meeting before and after training in an attempt to improve the relationship, but there was a set mentality there. As far as that issue was concerned, we knew we could do our best work over the summer.'

With a pre-season to make the team his own, plus being back in the more familiar surroundings of League Two, hopes were high that Coleman would get Rochdale firing again.

'During pre-season, we went to Austria,' he says. 'We worked really hard for six days and implemented how we wanted to play during the coming season. It was bought into by the players and morale was high. We were supposed to end the trip with a match, but it got rained off. Instead, one of the players had a birthday, so I let the squad go out to celebrate, you know, for a drink. But there were too many high jinks for my liking and it soured the trip in the end. A few of the boys got into a bit of trouble and I wasn't happy. They abused my trust. I felt a lot of hard work had gone to waste.'

Coleman's strength at Stanley was that he was able to tap into Liverpool's non-league scene, in which he had been a decent striker during his playing days. His eye for a player was not in doubt, demonstrated by the fact he launched the league careers of talented footballers such as Gary Roberts and Bobby Grant.

While this worked brilliantly for Accrington, it led to Coleman being on the receiving end of criticism at Rochdale, similar to that levelled at his predecessor Eyre, in that he was only prepared to sign players he had worked with previously.

Some supporters labelled the Dale squad under Coleman as the 'Scouse Mafia' due to the fact most of his signings hailed from his hometown of Liverpool.

'I think that's a bit unfair,' Coleman says. 'Of the players I signed, I had never worked with Rhys Bennet before, or Joe Rafferty or Matty Pearson. I had never worked with Dele Adebola or George Donnelly either. I did sign some of my former players, yes. I tried to give some of them another lease of life – a last chance in the game because they'd done well for me before. I got them in on shit money and a short deal. Ian Craney, for example. It didn't pan out the way I wanted, but it wasn't an old pals' act, I just wanted to get them going again, to the benefit of them, me and Rochdale.

'I got Bobby Grant into the club for next to nothing and the club made money on him. You'll not hear any complaints about that. I'm the first to admit that not all my signings worked out, but that happens to every manager at every club.'

It was during Coleman's time as manager that Gary Jones's second spell at Rochdale came to an end. It was a poignant moment for all, given he had made more appearances for the club than any other player (531) and was the first to captain the club at Wembley.

Worse, Jones left under a cloud.

'Gary Jones went through a rocky spell and we dropped him for a game,' says Coleman. 'He was 35 years old and, naturally, we said to him in passing, "What are your long-term plans? Have you ever thought about coaching?" I wanted to bring him on to my coaching staff. I think he got the wrong end of the stick and thought that I was suggesting he was done as a player. I wasn't. Gary then asked to leave the club. We didn't ask him to. I wanted him to stay and join my staff. I had no problem with him at all. People can believe what they like.'

During the season, there was criticism from sections of the support about Coleman's methods. There was a general feeling that the free-flowing football and sportsmanship that had been built up since 2007 had given way to something more primal. Following a 3-2 home defeat to Exeter, Coleman decided to issue an open invite for fans to meet him.

'We were 3-0 down but shouldn't have been,' he says. 'We were outstanding in the game and got it back to 3-2, but couldn't equalise. It was a tremendous effort, but we got booed off the pitch. I didn't like that. Someone shouted at me from the crowd and I said, "Don't shout at me from up there, speak to me outside." It eventually led to a meet the fans event at the stadium. It was like a doctor's surgery. I was there for three and a half hours. Not one person was aggressive. Nobody left dissatisfied either. I can empathise with fans, I really can, and I enjoyed talking to each and every one of them. I was open and honest with them throughout.'

Coleman says internet message boards caused him more mischief than any supporter in the stands.

'If you read internet message boards you'll go mad,' he says. 'They're negative by nature and not representative of an entire fan base. It's the same 15 or 20 usernames that crop up. The message board I looked at would have you believe we had a disastrous spell in charge at Rochdale. Look at the stats, though. Gillingham, Rotherham, Port Vale and Bradford were promoted from League Two that season. We went to Rotherham, Gillingham and Bradford and won at all of them. We drew at Port Vale. Is that disastrous?

'The problem with message boards is that quite a few senior people at Rochdale pay attention to them. I think they're frightened of them. I also had someone in my dressing room that couldn't be trusted. They were posting things on there that were exaggerations of the truth. Some of the things posted were outright lies, too. I heard claims that myself and Jimmy turned up to training late and drunk. That really angered me. I never found out who it was, but it was very, very disappointing.

'I'm the first to admit that I made quite a few mistakes at Rochdale. I know I didn't ingratiate myself with the fans, but it sickens me when I see players and managers wave a club's scarf about when they have no affinity to that club. I wanted to wave the Rochdale scarf when I'd done something for the club – promotion or a trophy. Maybe that backfired on me. One of my problems is, I'm not from Manchester and I'm not Keith Hill. That's not my fault, but I shouldn't have pushed that down the fans' throats. I'm my own man and have a lot of belief in my own ability. I know I'm a good Football League manager. I felt I got unfair criticism, but I know I should have tried to ingratiate myself more.'

Coleman also believes he should have been more assertive with the Rochdale board.

'I should have brought in my own staff,' he says. 'I was only allowed to bring in Jimmy Bell. I should have stood firm. The training ground was unacceptable, too. I should have made that a deal breaker, but I didn't have the power at Rochdale that I had at Accrington. I believe these things ultimately weakened my position.'

Over December 2012 and into the new year, Dale went on to lose eight out of ten games, dropping from the upper echelons of League Two into mid-table. It was enough for Chris Dunphy to call time on Coleman's reign.

'The end, for me, was bizarre,' he says. 'It was January and I needed a centre-half and a left-back to help us push on. The board said it had to be a one-in-one-out policy. I got a £30,000 offer for Jason Kennedy. He didn't want to stay and had already tried to leave at the start of the season. I recommended we sell him because he was going to go for nothing in the summer. I had also arranged for Dele Adebola to move on. Ashley Grimes wanted to leave too, and Rotherham would have given us £30,000 for him. That would have got me £60,000 into my budget and three wages off the payroll. We were only four or five points outside the play-offs at this time. The board dragged their feet, though. I knew something wasn't quite right.

'I was then summoned to a board meeting and had to go through all this again. I went home, had a nap and woke up to a phone call from the chairman telling me I'd been relieved of my duties. I was really gutted. Why could they not have told me at the board meeting instead of letting me outline my plans again? It was all wrong. I told the chairman this. I thought we were about to turn a corner. I just needed those players.'

Meanwhile, Hill, like Steve Parkin before him, had found the transition from Rochdale to Barnsley an ill-fated one. He returned for a second spell at Spotland. Coleman believes Hill's sudden availability ultimately forced Chris Dunphy's hand.

'Listen, as soon as Keith Hill became available, I was a dead man walking,' Coleman says. 'I'm a realist. When he was sacked at Barnsley, and because of what he'd done previously at Rochdale, of course he was going to get pointed in that direction and, of course, Rochdale were going to look in his.

'I attach no blame to Keith Hill for going back. What does annoy me is that he was allowed to sign a load of players when I couldn't sign two. He didn't let Adebola go until near the end of the season. He didn't sell Grimes or Kennedy, so where did the money come from? The club got what they wanted, though. They got back into League One with Hill. Perhaps they would have got there a season earlier had they kept me and Jimmy, but we'll never know.'

Now Coleman is back at Accrington Stanley as manager and has established them as a League One club.

'I love Accrington Stanley and it was a big wrench to leave in the first place,' he says. 'I'm glad to be back here as I feel I got Accrington to this level. I wouldn't say they're the only club I can manage, though. I'm still ambitious. Myself and Jimmy could do a job higher up. Again, I mean no disrespect to Accrington, but we've been good to them and they've been good to us.

'Don't misconstrue my feelings towards Rochdale, either. They're a fantastic club. They're well run and do things the right way. OK, it ended a bit sourly for me, but I have no animosity towards the club. At the end of the day, it's a smashing place with good people.'

Chris Dunphy
Chairman, 2006–2018

'THE SALE of players is the only way a club like Rochdale can survive in the modern football environment,' says Chris Dunphy, wistfully. 'But when I was chairman, the club was selling on our terms and not out of desperation.'

The former chairman has been widely credited for making Rochdale AFC a beacon for what a sustainable football club should be, a reputation it has held for the past 15 years or so. Now, in retirement, he hopes this approach can be maintained by current and future custodians of the club for many years to come.

'We did have a model in place,' he says. 'For example, looking exclusively at our youth academy players, we wanted them to have a 100-game target for the first team in mind and, after that, we want them to look to move on to a higher level. It's good for the player and it's good for our club.

'While I was chairman, between 2006 and the end of 2018, the club became financially stable. In the past, we sold our players for survival. Under my watch, we only sold if it was in the interest of the player or the club. That is a big difference, believe me. I've had criticism for selling our best players in the past, but, through the youth academy, we had others ready to step up. That's why our system worked.'

As alluded to in the introduction of this book, Rochdale's most successful period came not from oil-damp cash but from astute management both on the field and in the boardroom.

'We introduced sell-on clauses to our player sales about 15 years ago,' Dunphy says. 'That way, we continue to make money over the player's career. We made over £5m from these clauses over the last decade of my chairmanship. Rickie Lambert is the best example. He went from us to Bristol Rovers, to Southampton, to Liverpool.

'We employed a two-fold clause. We tell the buying club that we want money if they achieve certain milestones, such as promotion or reaching cup finals, and then, naturally, if they sell the player on for a profit, we get a cut of that too. The money we make from these add-ons equates to more than the buying club would ever pay in an outright transfer fee.'

Not many clubs boast a lifelong supporter as chairman nowadays, but, with Dunphy, that's exactly what Rochdale had. As a boy, Dunphy would regularly walk the three miles from his home in Milnrow to Spotland to watch games. He had no idea, of course, that, many years down the line, he would be running the club.

He first joined the Rochdale board for a brief spell in 1980, returned in 1990 and became chairman in 2006. His stewardship of the club during his time as chairman attracted, for the most part, praise.

'Football has changed rapidly in the period covered by your book,' Dunphy says. 'I first joined the board in 1980. At the time, the club owed the Inland Revenue £200,000, which is a lot of money nowadays, but was even more then. On top of dealing with that, the board used to meet weekly to have a whip round to pay the players' wages. You then had a manager and an assistant manager to pay and that was it. It was all we could afford. Things were that tight.

'Although things did improve over the following years, meaning we could pay decent money for players such as Andy Flounders, Clive Platt and Paul Connor, we were never too far away from that original model.

'It was Keith Hill who showed us that, by installing an infrastructure, we could reap rewards in the long term. We went on to employ a sports scientist, fitness coaches and goalkeeping coaches. We had a massive backroom staff, but this is what allows you to bring your own players through.

'When I took over as chairman in 2006, the board was in turmoil. There was a black hole of about £400,000. I'm not exaggerating when I say administration was a realistic possibility. I didn't want us to go that way. I'm pleased that I kept this club competitive, but in an honest way. Everyone here bought into the way we went about things, including the fans. Other clubs were looking at us seriously. When I went to these chairman's conferences, people asked me how we do it. They asked how we achieved success without spending millions.

'The answer is the infrastructure. We've a great academy and, right through the club, there were professionals at every level. This is how we achieved success.'

Of course, the football club was not Dunphy's only concern. His main business, Christopher Dunphy Ecclesiastical, has installed heating systems in churches for more than 40 years. It is a testament to Dunphy's acumen that he juggled both his roles successfully.

'The fact I wasn't a full-time chairman worked well for me,' he says. 'Full-time chairmen have too much time to think. They end up interfering in everything. If you've got someone who's good at their job, you let them do it. That's what I do in my business and that's what I did at Rochdale. I know of chairmen who tell managers which players they should be picking and how they should be playing. Believe me, my football knowledge is nowhere near what the manager's is. They're the ones who are going to deliver on the pitch, not the chairmen. We make suggestions, sure, and we're here to advise, but it is the manager who runs the team.'

It's natural, then, that I ask Dunphy about the man who brought Rochdale its greatest years.

'Keith Hill is a good football manager because he is a good man manager and he is good on a budget,' Dunphy explains. 'During his first spell here, he was very outspoken about his budget and what other clubs were doing in the transfer market. During his second period, his attitude changed. He realised there is kudos in achieving success on a tight budget and in playing by the rules. It was good promotion for him and good promotion for the club.

'We don't pay big wages at Rochdale and Keith's approach was that if a player asks about the money first, he doesn't want them. Keith got the right players. He got those who turned down more money elsewhere to play the style of football we played here. They signed for football reasons in other words.

'I remember talking to Sheffield Wednesday's [then] chairman Milan Mandarić about Chris O'Grady, who we sold to them in 2011. He said he didn't want him anymore and that we could have him back. I said we couldn't afford him, that Wednesday were paying him too much money. Milan said they weren't. I told him Chris was on £1,200 a week at Rochdale, now he is on £6,000. Milan said, "You're right, I am paying him too much money."

'At Rochdale, everybody was pulling the same way. There were no superstars or prima donnas and that doesn't happen a lot elsewhere in football. Keith managed to assemble a dressing room of players who were decent off the pitch as well as on it. I'm pleased we managed to achieve that.'

Despite the past decade or so being the best in Rochdale's history, attendances at Spotland remained modest.

'I don't know why more people don't come to watch us,' Dunphy says. 'Other than the obvious Manchester clubs, look at Burnley. They get more supporters from Littleborough [part of the Metropolitan Borough of Rochdale] travelling to watch them than come to watch us. They have a history, though. They have won the cup and they have won the league. That gets handed down through generations. Rochdale have never been fashionable in that sense. There have been no real glory days for grandfathers to share with their grandchildren.

'The other thing is, over a weekend nowadays, there are eight or nine top-flight games on the television. It's easier for people to watch football without having to go out to watch it.

'When you're looking to appeal to younger people, you realise most of them enjoy playing games consoles more than real sports these days. People are now actually paying to watch people play games consoles. They're selling out cinema-sized venues in Holland at the minute. In the next 50 years, this could be the new spectator sport.

'With all that considered, I believe we have to accept these things and get on with what we've got. My business plan was to survive if nobody came through the gates. That was my focus. It was suggested that I should sell seats at a third of the price, but then you need to get three times as many supporters in to the stadium to make it work. Quite simply, it wouldn't.

'I remember when we played Fulham in the League Cup in 2001. We got about 6,000 on the gate that night and played brilliantly, despite going out on penalties. Someone came up to me in the pub afterwards, enthusing about how good we were. He said he didn't realise Rochdale could be so good. I asked him if he was coming on Saturday for the league match. He said he would rather wait until we got another big game. That sums up the attitude to me. Some spectators can be fickle folk.

'Therefore, rather than focusing on the gates, we did a commercial deal on the stadium, for example. A deal for quarter of a million pounds would keep us going longer term than a few more people on the gate.'

We then get down to business. I ask Dunphy about the other managers featured in this book and, in the interest of fairness, offer him a right to reply to everything they have said.

'I understand why managers say certain things about their dismissals,' he says. 'We're talking about their livelihood, aren't we? They've got to protect their reputation, whatever happens. The ones you cover in this book all had their own ways of doing things and that was fine. You can't stifle individuality and I wouldn't really want to.

'But, let's be honest, those who had to be dismissed were dismissed for a reason. I won't have it said that I failed to back a manager, though.

'After we parted ways with John Coleman, he was on the radio saying I wouldn't back him. He actually signed 19 players while he was here. I checked up after I heard him say that. I've backed every manager since I've been chairman. In fact, I've backed some too much on occasion.

'It's never nice telling someone they are out of a job, but that is what a strong chairman has to do when things are not working for their club. You can tell, as a chairman, when a manager has lost the team. You acquire it as an instinct. You have to act when your instinct starts tingling.

'With John Coleman, the decisive moment came when it was clear to everyone that we were desperate for a striker. We asked him about this, but he didn't have a clue where to look. The only name he came up with was a centre-half. We knew at that point we were going nowhere with John. We had to make the decision to let him go. He'd had his chance.

'There were other reasons that I won't go into here, which influenced our decision. There was a culture change at the club, shall we say? Everything came to a head at that point and a choice had to be made.

'Don't get me wrong, what he's done at Accrington is commendable. He fits in perfectly there and does a great job. It suits them, but I realised it's not where I wanted Rochdale to be.'

Dunphy also refutes that he reneged on a promise to Steve Eyre that Chris O'Grady would not be sold.

'I met with Chris not long after Keith Hill left for Barnsley,' he says. 'He told me he had made his mind up to leave for better money if an offer came in for him. Sheffield Wednesday did just that. I certainly didn't tell Steve Eyre we were keeping him, as Chris had already outlined his intentions.

'Before we appointed Steve, after Keith left, we had an unprecedented volume of applications for the manager's job. The first one I opened was from Ossie Ardiles. The second was from the manager of the Libyan national football team. We had someone who had been at Paris Saint-Germain, as well as a host of Italians. It was crazy.

'I think Steve is a very good coach but he wasn't ready to manage a football club when I employed him. I realise that now. Because of what Keith Hill had done at Rochdale, in his first managerial role, coming from that world of youth coaching, I thought Steve would do the same, what with having the same attributes. I was wrong. I can only say that through hindsight.

'We wanted Steve to succeed. He is an honest and decent lad, but I realised quite quickly that he wasn't a decision maker. He brought six goalkeepers away on the pre-season trip abroad. Far too many, but we let him get on with it. Unfortunately, he carried on in that fashion. You see, when you're in the position of manager here, with a trapdoor below you, you need to be ruthless. You can't afford to be indecisive. You can make a mistake once, but you can't keep making it.

'I think Steve will have learned that from his time here and I'm sure if he becomes a manager again, he'll be better prepared because of it.'

However, Dunphy does feel that other managers were harshly treated in the years before he became chairman.

'Before I first took over as chairman, the board wasn't run as democratically as it was during my time,' he says. 'A lot of decisions were made without the rest of the board being made aware, including me.

'Paul Simpson and John Hollins were both a victim of this. I don't think Paul Simpson was given enough support by the board at the time. The ultimatum Paul was given was decided on by people other than me. He got his own back when he got Carlisle promoted in a game against us at Spotland, mind you. He was supping champagne on the steps here. He was lapping it up and fair play to him.'

Dunphy's first dismissal as Rochdale chairman was Steve Parkin.

'With Steve, he was very reluctant to use the young players,' he says, 'I think where he went wrong was that he didn't remove Tony Ford as his number two. Tony was great when he was on the pitch as a player, but, when he finished playing, he didn't do what a number two should have been doing. I suggested Steve make Keith Hill his number two, who was youth coach at the time, but he wanted to keep Tony. I think that was his mistake.'

Parkin was dismissed after an away defeat at Hartlepool, one of the worst Rochdale performances seen at the time.

'After that defeat, Steve locked himself in the changing room so that he didn't have to speak to me,' Dunphy says. 'I still don't know how he got home that night because he didn't get on the team bus. I felt for him, given the success he had had at Rochdale previously, but, again, it was a decision that had to be made.'

Dunphy left his post as chairman in December 2018, a move that surprised everybody connected to Rochdale AFC.

'I left the board because all of the directors who had the club at heart were no longer there,' he says. 'Bill Goodwin had resigned, Paul Hazlehurst had passed away, Jim Marsh had retired due to ill health. I could not work with those who remained, as they all had their own ideas and wanted to take the club in a direction I could not agree with. I would not be a mouthpiece for someone else's decisions. I chose my words carefully, using "retire" rather than "resign", so that the transition could be as easy as possible for them, not for me, and left them to run the club as they saw fit.

'However, I did say to Andrew Kilpatrick, who replaced me as chairman, that, should the club ever need any help or advice, I would be willing to give it. I was never contacted by anyone from the club from the day I told them of my intention to leave.'

The period that followed was a tumultuous one for Rochdale, which led to Kilpatrick stepping down as chairman in 2021 and two board members being voted off by shareholders at a memorable EGM in the June of that year.

The current board is now almost entirely made up of long-term supporters again. Dunphy believes this is to the club's benefit, as is its youth academy, which he advocates has given Rochdale its strength.

'Good young players now want to come to Rochdale like they used to want to go to Crewe Alexandra,' he says. 'They know they've a real chance of making the first team. Academy director Tony Ellis does a great presentation when recruiting young players. He shows them the team sheet from the FA Cup third round in [January 2015], Rochdale v Nottingham Forest. In that squad there were six players from the youth team. We beat Forest 1-0 and it's a great selling point. In the past, the very best kids would go to City or United, now they're coming here. It will make Rochdale AFC a preferable destination for many years to come.'

Part II
The Players

Alan Reeves
1991–1994

ASK ANY Rochdale fan over the age of 35 to name a former player who personifies the term 'reliable centre-half' and the majority would give you Alan Reeves – and with good reason, too.

The floppy-haired marvel from Birkenhead was an integral part of a Spotland back line that repelled frequent bombardment in the early 1990s. Reeves was much more than a mere stopper, however. He was that rare sort of lower-league defender who looked comfortable on the ball, who could carry it forward rather than hoof it upfield, and who could contribute to an attack through consideration rather than by fluke. As a result, he quickly established himself as a fans' favourite and a consistent Player of the Year award winner.

Nonetheless, it was a bittersweet day when his assured displays – in well over 100 appearances for the Dale – led Premier League side Wimbledon to sign him in 1994 for £200,000, believed to be the largest fee Rochdale had received up to that point when considering the additional £1,000 paid for each appearance. As a spotty teenager in those days, this writer mourned the loss of the player rather than celebrated the financial windfall.

Reeves's Premier League move certainly couldn't have been forecast when he first arrived at Spotland as a blond 24-year-old from Chester City in the summer of 1991, having already been on Norwich City's books without making a single appearance.

Smiling, he tells me how growing up on the Wirral, and constant competition with his twin brother David – who himself would become a Rochdale nemesis during his years with Chesterfield and Carlisle United – shaped his footballing attitude.

'Me and my brother were Liverpool fans growing up, but we never really aspired to play for them,' Reeves says. 'We started out playing properly, I suppose, when we both signed for a club called Heswall FC in the West Cheshire League. [Former Rochdale striker] Steve Whitehall played for them, too. It was a pretty good standard, as a lot of non-league was back then. David got spotted by Sheffield Wednesday when we were both 18. He was a lot more developed than I was at that age, even though we were twins. He was six foot one and imposing; me, well, I was five foot nine and ten and a half stone wet.

'I didn't set out to be a defender, but that's the way it always seemed to be. I was always defending because David was always attacking. Even at school, I remember he picked one wall in the playground and I had the other. He was always at my wall because he was so quick, so I found myself defending it with my life. We were very competitive growing up, me and David. I think that helped us both.

'Anyway, David had moved on to [Sheffield] Wednesday, which was great, but I was still at Heswall. I was doing well and I remember I got Player of the Year in 1988. Numerous scouts had been watching me, or so I'd been told, but nothing happened. I knew the time was right to go professional, so I wrote to half a dozen league clubs, pretending to be my twin brother recommending me for a trial. Amazingly, Norwich replied and invited me down. The manager of the reserves at the time was Mike Walker, who would go on to manage the first team and Everton, of course. Mike called me up and asked me to play a game for the Norwich reserves. He liked what he saw and invited me back.

'After my second trial game, he said to me, "Don't go on holiday in the summer, because I'll want you in for pre-season training." He said he'd be in touch with the details, but I didn't hear from him again, so I thought, "Bollocks to it, I'm going on holiday to Spain with the lads." I was 20 years old at the time, so why not? While I was in Spain, I phoned home and my mam said, "Norwich City's reserve manager has been on and he wants you down there next week for training!" So, I had to rummage through my suitcase, find my trainers and go running every day while I was still in Spain. It was crazy.'

Despite the madness of tearing along the strip on the Costa Del Sol while his friends soaked up the sunshine and local beer, Reeves made it back to Blighty in time for his make-or-break chance in Norfolk.

'I get back to England, do a two-week training trial at Norwich, play two games for them and get offered a one-year contract,' he says. 'It was great. But while I was mulling that over, Chester City offered me a trial, too. Norwich were in the top tier, though, and Chester, despite being very local to Birkenhead, were in the third tier. I thought I'd give it a go at the higher level, but I didn't realise just how homesick I would be. I was quite a shy boy at the time, especially around people I didn't know, and ended up staying in digs with a family down in Norfolk. As a result, I was coming home most weekends, which didn't help my development as a player.

'By Christmas, I still hadn't made the first team, so I went on loan to Gillingham where the old Tottenham boss, Keith Burkinshaw, was in charge. He'd seen me play for the Norwich reserves and said he liked the look of me. I spent three months in Kent but I still missed home. That issue was still there and it was affecting me.

'When the season ended, Gillingham offered me a two-year contract, Norwich offered me another year and Chester City came back in for me with a two-year deal. That was it for me. I signed for Chester so I could go back home. It was half an hour away from Birkenhead. That's all I wanted. I know what you're thinking: I should've stayed at Norwich. I know that now, but you live and learn, eh?'

While being closer to home was great on a personal level for Reeves, a footballing issue would come to the fore.

'I quickly found out that Chester wanted to play me at right wing-back, which just isn't me,' he says. 'I did OK there, but didn't enjoy playing. During my first season, I played in most games, but over the next season I found myself in and out of the side. Then I had an altercation during a team meeting with the manager Harry McNally. He's passed away now, God rest his soul, but he could be a lunatic. I disagreed with him over something or other and he lost it with me. He basically said, "I'm telling you now, you're getting a free transfer at the end of the season – you'll be at a Conference club next season." I thought that was it. I was facing the scrap heap.'

Reeves would never end up on the scrap heap, however. His Rochdale arrival came at the beginning of Dave Sutton's full managerial reign in the summer of 1991, following the departure of Terry Dolan to Hull the season previous. Goalkeeper Keith Welch had been sold to Bristol City for a six-figure sum and this gave Sutton the ability to perform a desired overhaul of Dolan's squad. While Reeves arrived on a free transfer alongside the likes of then record signing Andy Flounders, he was easily just as valuable to the club.

'Two weeks after Harry had binned me, I got a call from Dave Sutton asking if I wanted to play a reserve game for him,' Reeves recalls. 'He couldn't believe Harry was going to let me go. I played the game and Dave offered me a contract right away. However, the Professional Footballers' Association at the time were doing a thing where they took out-of-contract players over to Hong Kong for trial games. I'd already agreed to go out there and Dave understood that.

'I went over to Hong Kong with 20 other lads. I was the only one that was offered a contract. I can't even remember the name of the club now, but they offered me twice as much money as Rochdale were offering, plus an apartment. I was 24 at the time. If I was eight or nine years older, I would've gone. But I liked Dave Sutton and Mick Docherty [Rochdale assistant manager] when I met them, and I had a sour year at Chester. I wanted to prove I still had it in England. So, I signed for Rochdale and loved it. I was Player of the Year every year I was there. Funnily enough, during the first year, I missed about two months because I got injured against Barnet in a home game, so I won that year's award by just one vote from Tony Brown [Reeves's fellow centre-half], or so Tony claimed any way.

'When I first joined, Steve Whitehall signed about the same time, so I was travelling in with him every day for three years, and later Shaun Reid. Me and Whitey, we were both from Birkenhead. We used to pick Reidy up from the Rocket [junction] on the M62 and then Dave Bayliss joined us later on. We used to have a right laugh.

'Sutty was a great manager but the Doc [Mick Docherty] was the big character. He was a proper player's coach. These days, he'd be classed as being too close to the players, but, in the old days, that's what we had. He was more than just a good laugh, of course. He was a great coach. When I first signed for Rochdale, I was totally right-footed. My left foot was just for standing on. The Doc identified that and picked certain days where, if I transferred the ball from my left foot to my right, he'd fine me a pound every time. Within six months of that, I was transformed. It was highlighted during my second pre-season at Rochdale, when we played Chester in a friendly. A lot of the Chester players were ex-team-mates of mine. They were astounded by the difference in my left foot. That's testament to the Doc.

'We had some great characters in the dressing room at Rochdale, like Jon Bowden and John Ryan. We were all mates and we all got on really well. It was a really friendly place.

'I think that our relationship counted for a lot of our success. We had no training ground for a start. We were training on parks, mud baths and artificial surfaces. How my knees weren't fucked by the time I left Rochdale, I don't know. It was bags for goalposts at times, which wasn't great. The 3G and 4G pitches players have now are carpets compared to what we trained on back then. But, hey, look how well we competed. We almost made the play-offs in my first season.'

Reeves believes players were a lot tougher back in his day, through necessity as much as anything else.

'I remember training on a Friday morning, before travelling to London for a game against Barnet on the Saturday, and I broke my nose. The club doctor, I can't remember his name, was a big old fella who worked in the Rochdale Infirmary. I went down there to see him. My nose was pointing east to west instead of north to south. He got his knuckle and pushed my nose right back in. It was like something cracked in my brain. Then he said, "That's you sorted." Nowadays, if a player breaks his nose, he can't play for weeks and has to wear a mask and so on. I played against Barnet the next day and broke my nose again. There was no health and safety back then, but they were great days.'

After Tony Brown retired, Reeves formed a formidable defensive partnership with Paul Butler.

'Butts started as an understudy, but was a very early developer,' Reeves says. 'He was built like a brick shithouse, even at the age of 18. I tell you what though; he could shift for a fellah his size. I doubt there was a better centre-half partnership than me and him at that level at that time. He went on to have a career as good, if not better, than mine.'

Reeves's performances had not gone unnoticed higher up the food chain, but his level-headedness kept him focused.

'The entire time I was at Rochdale it was always in the paper that "X, Y or Z scout was watching Alan Reeves of Rochdale". I didn't have an agent but other players' agents would say I was being watched. I never heard anything directly, though. I just wanted to keep my head down and keep playing. I had the attitude of what will be, will be, you know?'

And then, in September 1994, it finally happened for him.

'One Saturday, we were playing Hereford at Spotland. Sutty pulled me to one side before the game and said, "Wimbledon manager Joe Kinnear's here to watch you. Unless you have an absolute disaster, you'll be signing for Wimbledon next week." I played the match and did well, despite the result [Rochdale lost 3-1]. After the game, Joe and Sam Hammam [Wimbledon's then-owner] came and spoke to me. They told me to be ready to travel south on Monday. I got a phone call on the Monday which told me to travel to Coventry. I met Joe and Sam in a hotel just off the M6 and it was done within half an hour. As quickly as that, I was a Premier League player. I went home, packed my bag, trained with the Wimbledon first team on Thursday and Friday and played for them on the Saturday. I went from playing against Hereford in the fourth tier one Saturday to playing against Leicester in the Premier League at Selhurst Park the next. It was surreal.'

And Reeves revealed his career got its timely boost with a little help from a football legend.

'Joe Kinnear would later tell me that he became aware of me because he'd sold John Scales to Liverpool for £3.5m and wanted a replacement centre-half that the club could progress. So, he phoned up Sir Alex Ferguson at Manchester United looking for a recommendation from the north-west of England. Apparently, Fergie told him, "There's a lad at Rochdale that, if he was a few years younger, I'd have him myself." He gave Joe my name.'

Reeves was initially in awe of his new Premier League surroundings.

'What I found so surprising, was how big and quick everyone was in the Premier League,' he says. 'I was quick and big enough at Rochdale's level, but I walked into that dressing room at Wimbledon and thought, "Christ." I couldn't believe how big Vinnie Jones was, how big Mick Harford was. Honestly, they were huge. I went out and trained with them and they were so quick and strong, I was gobsmacked. You see them play on TV and don't appreciate the size and speed of them, but when you stand next to them in the tunnel, it's overwhelming. It was quite daunting, to be honest.

'Once I got on the pitch though, I blocked that out. I was just playing against other men. That's how I had to look at it. I blocked out the crowds, too. I had to. If you step back from it all and look at 40,000 people, and all these elite footballers around you, you panic. I just focused on what was in front of me and got on with my job.'

And what a job he did.

'My first year at Wimbledon was the best of my career,' Reeves beams. 'I played against the best players in England week in and week out and I didn't look out of place. I was getting praise from the manager and the press. It was a great place to be and it was the right place for me at that time. A lot is said about the comradeship among the "Crazy Gang" players of that era, and it's all true. It was sensational. I still meet up with most of the lads for a Christmas night out 25 years later in London. Vinnie Jones doesn't join us, mind you. He's gone on to pastures new. Hah.

'We finished eighth in my first season at Wimbledon. Better than we had any right to. I went straight into the first team. I played pretty much every game. I remember when I truly knew the manager rated me. Yellow cards got you disciplinary points back then and, if you reached 21, you got a three-game ban. I reached that threshold just before Christmas that season. I knew I was going to miss three games and was worried about losing my place. I was playing at Maine Road against Man City. I was wound up by Paul Walsh during the game and I punched him off the ball. The linesman saw it, so I got a six-game ban. I got some stick for that, I'll tell you. I was just thinking about my place in the team. When I became available again, Joe Kinnear stuck me straight back in against Everton. He dropped Andy Thorn. That was the vote of confidence I needed.

'But it didn't get that good again. The second year, I probably only played 70 per cent of the games, the third I hardly played at all and the fourth year you can write off. I think Joe had decided he was looking elsewhere by then. We had younger players like Chris Perry and Dean Blackwell establishing themselves. It was obvious I would be moving on.'

After Wimbledon, Reeves moved to Swindon Town where he played over 200 times before calling time on his playing career in 2006. The move would see him make a daily 200-mile round trip from Epsom to Swindon – for eight years.

'I think I was 30 when I left Wimbledon,' Reeves says. 'I didn't think it was the end of my career by any means. I signed a three-year contract with Swindon, who were in the second tier at the time, and

Steve McMahon was the manager. I was living near Epsom race course. My then-partner had gotten pregnant with my first daughter, so I didn't want to uproot her. I thought I'd make the commute for the three years. "Three years," I thought. "I can handle that." After those three years, I ended up signing five one-year contracts. I made that commute for eight bloody years. It turned out that I played most of my career games at Swindon – almost 250. I enjoyed my time there. I played under numerous managers, I was captain, then, while I was still playing, I was reserve team manager and then assistant manager. Politics in football being what they are, I ended up getting the sack from there eventually. It was a sad end considering how long I'd been there.'

This led Reeves to team up with an old pal.

'My fellow Wimbledon centre-half Scott Fitzgerald was youth team manager at Brentford,' Reeves recalls. 'Leroy Rosenior, who was manager at that time, got the sack and they offered Fitz the job on a caretaker basis. He asked me to help him out. We did OK for a few games and we got offered the post full time. However, Brentford were relegated at the end of that season and we lost our jobs. That's the way football goes.'

Reeves then landed a role managing AFC Wimbledon's under-21 side as well as coaching the academy players.

'I got to work with a lot of good young lads on a daily basis. We got a few into the first team, too. My former Wimbledon team-mate Neal Ardley was the first team manager there. He was a former academy manager at Cardiff, so was really open to getting youth into the first team. He's not one of these managers that looks to buy people all the time. He believes that if the youth players are good enough, they're old enough and he chucks them right into the mix. I got an 18-year-old centre-half into the first team for seven games. That said, he then got sent off, so I obviously taught him well. Hah!

'If you work in football you need to be flexible. Back when I went to Wimbledon, there was nothing like the money flying about that there is in the Premier League now. I actually earned more money at Swindon than I did at Wimbledon. Players like Alan

Shearer, Eric Cantona and Dennis Bergkamp will have been on decent money, but I was on peanuts in comparison. Nowadays, if you sign for a decent Championship club, you can retire after playing. It wasn't like that for us back then.'

As we conclude our chat, Reeves reflects on the importance of his time at Spotland.

'Rochdale were a major factor in my career,' he says. 'I didn't have an agent and Chester were going to put me on the scrap heap. If Dave Sutton hadn't made that call, who knows where I would've ended up? As good as Hong Kong might have been for me at that point in time, it would have taken me away from the UK and away from people's thoughts. Rochdale kept me there, gave me the chance to show what I could do in my true position and they looked after me.

'I tell the young lads now, though, that it's always down to the player. You can give them as much help, coaching and direction as you can, but, at the end of the day, they're judged as a footballer. All a footballer needs from someone else is a chance to show what they're good at. That's what Rochdale gave to me and I'll never forget it.

'Even now, as a coach, I'm a very enthusiastic person and a very competitive one. I want to win everything I do. While I was at Wimbledon, I saw a picture of me in a magazine. Under it was a quote from Sir Alex Ferguson. It said, "He's a determined so-and-so." I think that's me in a nutshell. I was bloody-minded. It didn't matter who I was playing against – a striker for Mansfield or Hereford, or Bergkamp or Cantona. Whoever it was, I was determined they weren't getting past me. Obviously, you've got to look after yourself and keep fit, but it was my desire that made me as a player. I think being a defender is a natural instinct that cannot be taught. You can hone your little skills and traits, yes, but I believe only certain people are born to be a defender. Those who will do anything to keep the ball out of their net. I think I had that as a player and, with my desire, I think it got me to the top.'

Matt Gilks

1995–2007

WITH INJURIES blighting the latter stages of regular goalkeeper Neil Edwards' time at Rochdale, the responsibility of custodian would fall permanently on understudy Matt Gilks.

Stood between the sticks, Gilks was everything the Welshman wasn't. He was tall and thin, as opposed to short and stout, and could only draw experience from a clutch of cameos, whereas Edwards had played over 400 career games.

As it transpired, none of this actually mattered. While Edwards will rightly be remembered as one of Dale's best goalkeepers, Gilks proved equally adept during his 12-year spell at the club – as both deputy and sheriff – and his performances elsewhere would eventually take him to the Premier League and international football.

While not an agile, gifted shot-stopper myself, this writer remembers identifying with Gilks more than any other Rochdale player at the time of his emergence due to us being of a similar age.

There is an added pride in meeting Gilks, though. He is a Rochdale-born lad who represented his hometown club and flourished. Even so, Gilks does his best to dampen this feeling of kinship by revealing it was, in fact, near neighbours Oldham Athletic who held his football affections as a youngster.

'Although I was born in Rochdale, I lived in Chadderton and then Royton, so I grew up an Oldham Athletic supporter,' he says. 'They were in the Premier League at the time. I was always aware of Rochdale AFC, of course, but I was a season ticket holder at Oldham for years.'

Gilks then adds with a laugh, 'I came to love Rochdale eventually.'

A thoroughly likeable and level-headed fellow, I speak to Gilks while he is studying for his coaching badges; the staple of every player nowadays, it seems, who is entering the twilight of their career.

But it is at the very beginning of his, where I'm interested in Gilks picking up, and he does so by explaining the origins of his goalkeeping obsession.

'I always wanted to be a goalie, but I didn't get the chance when I was a kid,' he says. 'When I was playing at primary school I was always a centre-half or a striker – every outfield position, really. When I was about 12 years old, I finally got the chance. I got shoved in goal for a game and I loved it. It stuck from there on in. I was a good outfield player, sure, but that was it for me. I wanted to stay in goals.

'We used to have a kickabout on the street up near my mam and dad's house and I used to dive about on the concrete to save all the shots. People said I was mental, but you need to be to be a goalie.

'I then played for local side Heyside Juniors, with my brother, in the year above my age group. It was there I got spotted. Dave Bywater was Rochdale's scout for the local area at the time. He came to watch me and then Rochdale made a move. My mam and dad said "no" to them, though. They wanted me to keep playing with my friends and win trophies. They wanted me to keep on enjoying football. I would have been 13 at the time, I think. A year later, Rochdale came back for me and I joined their youth team on a Youth Training Scheme [YTS], which was what scholarships were called back then.

'I was straight out of school and did a three-year apprenticeship with Rochdale. The club didn't have its own goalkeeper coach back then, so they had former Walsall keeper Fred Barber come in on a Tuesday and me and Neil Edwards used to train with him. I realised at that point just how hard it was to be a professional goalie. I used to get battered. I kept going, though, and worked hard.

'When you're a YTS, you're new to the inside of football and most of your time between training and games is spent doing all the crappy jobs that need doing. I remember one of my jobs was scrubbing the grout between the tiles in the dressing room showers, getting the white bits white again. It sounds awful, I know, but I really enjoyed it. You're not doing it alone, you're doing it with a good bunch of lads and you're all in the same boat. It teaches you respect and the importance of graft. The scholars don't do anything like that anymore, which is a shame.'

Gilks remembers when he was initially flung into first-team action while still a raw trainee in 2001.

'I remember my Rochdale first-team debut like it was yesterday. It was Chesterfield away at Saltergate and we drew 1-1. Paul Connor scored for us and they scored right at the end of the match. I got told I was playing and remember being really nervous before the game. Chesterfield were doing really well in the league – in fact I think they were top – but I think they were struggling financially at the time, too, because people were throwing brown envelopes about outside and inside the ground.

'Anyway, the match kicked off and I got to a through ball before the attacker. It gave me the early touch of the ball I needed to settle me down. To be honest, I realise now how much the back four that day protected me. It was during Steve Parkin's first spell as manager and he had the defence well drilled. Funnily enough, Keith Hill was playing in the defence that day, too.

'For me, Parkin was the best manager I had at Rochdale, with Tony Ford as his assistant. I played under Alan Buckley, John Hollins, Paul Simpson, and Keith Hill, too, but Parkin was the best. He was a tough manager but he was fair at the same time. If you worked hard for him, you were treated fairly. If you let standards drop, he was on your case. I needed that. It showed me how hard you had to work to be a successful footballer.

'Parkin aside, the biggest influence on me at Rochdale was Neil Edwards. I absolutely loved the guy. Being in his shadow was the best thing to happen to me. He is the best keeper I've trained with on a daily basis. He was so quick and agile. He had such a spring for a small guy. I was a young lad at this point, remember, and I'm looking at this fully grown man throwing himself about. I thought, "Will I still be able to do that at his age?" We called him "The Machine" because he never, ever stopped. His quality in training gave me the best teaching I could have asked for.

'When Taffy [Edwards] left, I took over as number one. I believe it was my worst season as a Rochdale player, simply because he wasn't there. Obviously, we both wanted to be playing every week, and I got that wish, but to not have him there with me on a daily basis really affected my game. I didn't enjoy that year at all. I missed watching him and I missed having him there to talk to. I still felt I needed another couple of years with Taffy.'

With Keith Hill preparing for his first full season in charge of Rochdale in the summer of 2007, Gilks decided his future lay elsewhere and he signed a two-year contract with Championship club Norwich City.

'As it happened, I got through my initial concerns about Taffy not being around and had a good career at Rochdale. I had played almost 200 games by the time I reached 24. I felt it was the right time to move on and develop elsewhere. I felt I'd reached my level at Rochdale. I needed a full-time goalie coach with me every day. Rochdale still hadn't addressed that and I was having to go to Bolton Wanderers on a Wednesday to train with Fred Barber. I wanted something that was all inclusive.

'Norwich were offering me all of that and I couldn't turn it down. Even though I didn't make a first-team appearance for them, I found the move fantastic. The place blew my mind. I was still living with my parents, so had to buy my own house down there.

'I was travelling into a training ground that was state-of-the art. They had more than one physio, more than one first-team coach and they even had a goalie coach. I was in the dressing room and I had Dion Dublin on my left, Luke Chadwick on my right. Darren Huckerby was in the corner next to big David Marshall the goalie, and Lee Croft. I was sat thinking, "Christ, I've just rocked up here from little old Rochdale."

'So, despite not playing a first-team game, that year at Norwich was my best in terms of development as a goalkeeper. That is purely because I had a full-time goalie coach who was brilliant with me on a brilliant training ground. I just loved pulling the gloves on and stepping out there and training. I pushed David Marshall all the way. We're still good mates now and still talk about Norwich. He said I made him a better keeper because I was training so hard and doing so well. Marshall is one of the best keepers out there, so for me to push him all the way gave me confidence.'

In 2008, Norwich signed former Livingston starlet Wes Hoolahan from Blackpool. Part of the deal required Gilks to move in the opposite direction.

'Glenn Roeder came in at Norwich and didn't fancy me at all,' Gilks remembers. 'I found myself at Blackpool as part of the Wes Hoolahan deal. Simon Grayson was their manager and they already had Paul Rachubka there. He'd been at Man United and was set in stone as the number one goalkeeper. As a result, my first year was very frustrating. I ended up going on loan to Shrewsbury for a bit. I did OK there and came back hoping to get my chance.

'I remember getting that chance in a game against Crystal Palace, which we won 1-0. I'd just sat down on the bench with a cup of tea when Chubs [Rachubka] got sent off. On I went for my introduction into Championship football. I did well. I was coming for crosses and getting them. I was playing with lads I'd only trained with for half a season up to that point, but we clicked.'

With new-found confidence, Gilks still found opportunities between the sticks hard to come by in the Championship, but he was to be aided by the entrance of enigmatic manager Ian Holloway, who, within nine months of arriving, took the Seasiders to the Premier League.

'Ollie is the best manager I've had at any club. It didn't start so well between us, though. He came in at the end of the season, so I didn't meet him until the summer. I remember waiting for him to finish a meeting, as I was on my way to speak to another club about a transfer. I said, "Nice to meet you, Ollie, but I need to go." He just looked at me and said, "I haven't seen you play. You're not going anywhere. Get your kit on and get out there." I was fuming at that point, thinking, "Here we go again." I went out there and trained as hard as I've ever trained. Eventually, Ollie said, "I can't ignore you any longer. I'm going to put you in." That was it. I became Blackpool's number one.

'He comes across as a joker, but Ollie was such a driven man. I remember us being given the bonus sheet by the club at the start of the next season. It had two options on it. We could choose £1m pro rata to stay in the league or £5m pro rata to get promoted. All the players were going to choose the million. Ollie said, "No, you're not getting rewarded for failure, so take the five." We all looked at him blankly at the time, but then we went on to get promoted to the Premier League.

'I had a lot of self-doubt early on at Blackpool – working hard in training for no reward. Ollie sorted that. I think he liked me as a person. We were similar. We liked a laugh and a joke, but both believed in hard work. He gave me the platform I needed to go and do my job. We were successful together the whole time he was at Blackpool.'

Gilks had achieved a lifelong dream in reaching the Premier League, but the standard was to surprise even him.

'Any player wants to play at as high a level as he can. You do set yourself goals. To play in the Premier League was mine. It's every boy's dream. Playing at Wembley, in the play-off final [the 3-2 win over Cardiff City in 2010], was fantastic, sure, but the Premier League is a special league – all the media, the hype, the talk, the TV. It was magic for a hard-working goalkeeper from Rochdale to reach those heights.

'The first thing I noticed about the standard, from a goalkeeping point of view, was how hard Premier League players hit the ball. Trust me, it's hard. The other funny thing I noticed was how little you can go out to catch crosses. The quality of the crosses tends to be so good, that there is no point. It's going on to the forward's head and that's all there is to it. They know the exact pace and angle to put on the crosses, too. You're best setting yourself to save the resultant header or volley, rather than trying to claim the cross.

'The quality in that final third is so good in that league that, if a team breaks, they're probably going to score. You train for so long to be a goalie that you do need to rely on your instincts a lot more at that level. In the lower divisions, you invariably know where a striker is going to put the ball when he shoots. You can just tell. In the Premier League, a striker can hit the ball while he's still running, without even setting himself up for the shot. You can find yourself out of position quite quickly when that happens.'

Sadly, as Gilks was still acclimatising, his Premier League adventure was to be cut short.

'I broke my kneecap in the November of that season,' he said. 'I ended up playing only the final five games after that. I was in turmoil the whole time in between. I had to have an operation and it felt a little bit like I was starting all over again. You train to play, not sit on your arse. Then, when you're finally able to train again, it takes time to get fit and sharp – and, in the Premier League, you're having to get fit and sharp to an even higher standard. It's a horrible process. Luckily for me, I found a guy called Mick Clegg, who had been Man United's strength and conditioning coach for 12 years. He'd set up on his own. He helped me get back into better shape than I was in before the injury.'

Unfortunately for Gilks, Blackpool were relegated at the end of the season, mainly due to a continued poor run after the festive period. Holloway led the team to the play-offs once again the following season, but there was to be no repeat promotion. When Holloway left for Crystal Palace early the subsequent season, Gilks said the entire club felt his departure.

'I stayed at Blackpool for another three years after relegation from the Premier League,' he says. 'We had such a good bunch of lads and players, but, when Ollie left, that was it. The lads wanted Ollie. That was the bond. When that bond is broken, other clubs come in and dismantle your squad player by player. On and on it went. I was the last one remaining from the promotion season when I left. Other people coming in didn't understand how hard we'd worked to achieve what we did the season we got promoted. I think they thought we could do it again, no problem. It was too much for me, so, when my contract was up, I went to Burnley.'

As mentioned earlier in this chapter, Gilks has international experience. However, it isn't the Three Lions of England on his chest, as one might expect of a Rochdale lad, but the Lion Rampant of Scotland.

In August 2010, the Scotland manager at the time, Craig Levein, was looking for cover for Allan McGregor and was tipped off about Gilks's familial links to Caledonia.

He told STV, '[Gilks] is one we became aware of a while ago and have kept track of his progress. Obviously, he was a key figure in Blackpool's promotion to the Barclays Premier League and while I will not name my squad until tomorrow, he is one I think we need to take a closer look at. He comes highly recommended, is playing regularly for his club and the next logical step is for our goalkeeping coach to work closely with him.'

The goalkeeper himself explains his Scottish heritage.

'When you get to the Premier League, you appear on more people's radars. My grandmother was Scottish. She was born in Perth. So, through that link, Craig Levein knew I qualified for Scotland. I think they wanted another Premier League goalie in the Scotland squad.

'I got the usual stick off the English lads when I declared for Scotland. You know, like, "Did you have a tartan blanket when you were a kid?" or "How you doing, Scottish?" The Scottish lads, strangely, didn't bother about me being from England.

'I went along to training, not knowing what to expect, but it was a proper eye-opener. All of a sudden, Blackpool seemed like a walk in the park. The standard was so high. I remember my first training exercise was with Darren Fletcher and Kenny Miller – seasoned pros at massive clubs – and they trained like it meant everything to them. They didn't take their foot off the gas until the gaffer called time. It made me think, "Jeez, if that's where I've got to be to get on in this game, I'd better pull my socks up." I thought I was doing well at Blackpool, but clearly there was an extra level to aspire to.

'My Scotland debut was in a friendly against Australia at Easter Road in 2012. I was on the bench with David Marshall. Allan McGregor started, but got injured quite early, so I went on. We won the game 3-1 and had already conceded before I came on, so to keep a clean sheet was very pleasing.

'What weighs on your mind when you make your international debut is that it isn't a club you're playing for, but an entire country. It's quite daunting. At the same time, it's a very special feeling. It meant so much to my mam, whose own mother was my Scottish grandmother, who had sadly passed away and didn't get to see me play for Scotland.'

In the summer of 2016, Gilks was still at Burnley, but received an unexpected opportunity to join one of Scotland's biggest clubs.

'I was at a wedding in Cyprus when my phone went. It was Jim Stewart, the Scotland coach. He asked me to go up to Rangers for a chat. I'd actually been speaking to Hearts at this point and I'm not sure if he knew this or not, but, obviously, if Rangers ask you to speak to them, you do. Mark Warburton was manager at the time, but it was his assistant, Davie Weir, who I knew through my involvement with the Scotland squad. I went up, had a look around and, once the contract was drawn up, you can't really say no to Rangers. I'm glad I didn't too, as it was a brilliant place to be. I loved the six months I was there.'

Gilks's role at Rangers was that of a supporting member of the cast. He played primarily in the club's League Cup campaign that season, including the semi-final against Celtic.

'Wes Foderingham was number one at that time,' Gilks says. 'He'd been with the club a while and helped them get back to the top flight after Rangers had been demoted. I was brought in to compete with him. I worked really hard to get in the team, but opportunities were limited to just a few cup games unfortunately.'

Gilks also says the standard of the Scottish top flight is not to be underestimated.

'People can be a bit disrespectful to the top league in Scotland. As well as Celtic, you had Hearts and Aberdeen, who were both good teams challenging at the time. It's unfair to say it's a two-team league. Around Glasgow, though, it very much was a two-team feeling. The passion for Rangers and Celtic in that city is like nothing I've ever experienced.'

Despite enjoying the city and the club itself, Gilks soon felt it was time to move.

'With the lack of opportunity, I was getting a bit frustrated,' he says. 'I'd not played much at Burnley either, prior to signing for Rangers, so I was getting restless. I felt that, if I didn't start playing regularly again, my career was going to be shorter than I would have liked it to have been. I got the chance to go to Wigan in the January of that season and it was a good move on a lot of levels. It was more or less a move back to my own doorstep. My partner and my newly born child were travelling up and down to Glasgow when I was at Rangers and I was doing the reverse back to the north-west. It wasn't ideal. The move to Wigan meant we could all be together again, so, not only was it a good football decision, it was a good family decision too.'

Gilks got more games under his belt once back in Lancashire.

'I was in and out of the team at the start with Jakob Haugaard,' he recalls. 'His contract dictated he had to play a certain amount of games, but I eventually got in anyway, regardless, and played the remainder of the season. Unfortunately, we still got relegated from the Championship right at the end of the campaign. I had an offer from Wigan to stay, but Scunthorpe came in with a better deal, believe it or not, so I decided to up sticks again. I commuted to Scunthorpe, though, rather than move there, so it wasn't too bad. I had a great first year and we just missed out in the play-offs. I did my cruciate in the first play-off game, though, and then, for the next year of my contract, the first six months was rehab.'

The club wasn't the same when Gilks returned from injury and he was soon packing his bags again – almost for the place where it all began for him.

'In the January, Stuart McCall was the manager and he was arguing with the chairman about me staying or going. I ended up talking to Rochdale but, unfortunately, they couldn't get it done. Lincoln then came in for me and, instead of going closer to home, I ended up further away.

'I played about 14 games with Lincoln and got promoted. My next stop was Fleetwood with Joey Barton as manager. I stayed for a year. I knew Joey from my time at Burnley and Rangers. He's a good guy and I think all the off-field stuff gets more air than it should just because it is him, if you know what I mean? He was great with me and still is.

'At the end of that year, Ian Evatt had approached me to join him at Barrow as a player-coach. He then phoned me to tell me he was leaving Barrow for Bolton. Jokingly, I said, "Congratulations, I hope you're taking me with you?" He says, "Yeah, that's why I'm ringing."

'I ended up playing a lot of games and helped Bolton get out of League Two. Now, I'm predominantly coaching at the club, even though I'm still registered as a player. It's great because I get to do coaching and still train at the same time. I'm 40 years old now, though, and I've done my time. I've had a good career and I'm grateful for it.'

As we round off our chat, Gilks underlines the key qualities he believes are required to make an elite goalkeeper and also the role Rochdale played in helping him become one.

'Hard work makes an elite goalkeeper. You cannot get away from not working hard. Any coach that believes this isn't the case is wrong. You also need to have desire and you need to love the job. You can't be half-hearted in that regard. You need self-belief and a thick skin, too. You are the one that is closest to the crowd taking abuse all game. I've seen a lot of sports psychologists over the years to help me deal with that.

'Rochdale gave me the opportunity to learn what it is to be a professional goalkeeper. They put me in the first team when I was needed and took me back out so I wasn't overwhelmed. They built me up.

'Players like Gareth Griffiths, Wayne Evans and Neil Edwards were top, seasoned pros who did everything they could to help me out. It's funny, because now I'm the one advising the youngsters, saying, "Enjoy it, it's a short career, you've got to do more than he's doing or he'll take your place, etc." I got that from the advice I received at Rochdale.

'The fact I did an old-fashioned YTS there was character building, too. It was a harsher world than the one footballers enter into now, but I'd never have wanted it any other way.'

Rickie Lambert

2005–2006

RICKIE LAMBERT is probably sick of hearing the word 'beetroot'. It's not because he's dismissive of his time working in a factory that packed the vegetable, but more because there doesn't seem to be an article in the press concerning his rise to fame that fails to mention it. The beetroot, however, is as much a part of the Rickie Lambert story as his time at Rochdale AFC, where yet another visionary move from then-manager Steve Parkin transformed the life of a footballer forever. He saw in Lambert an intelligent player and natural goalscorer, something everybody else up to that point had inexplicably missed.

Earlier in this book, Parkin says, 'Rickie Lambert was even more pleasing [than Grant Holt]. I'd only ever seen him play in midfield. I never thought he had the legs to play there, to be perfectly truthful. He did have a terrific shot, however. I started thinking, if he's a bit further up the pitch, he could create the kind of space in the box that he does in midfield. I sold this idea to him, I said, "I want you up front with Holty." He snapped my hand off because it meant less running for him.'

Lambert, in this new role, teamed up with Holt to form one of the best strike partnerships ever seen at Spotland. But, like Holt, Lambert had been around the block before his football career finally clicked under Parkin at the age of 23.

In a relaxed manner, and with a softly spoken Liverpudlian accent, he recounts the formative years that took him to that point.

'It was the early 1990s,' he says. 'I was ten years old, playing for a local youth team, and I was spotted by a Liverpool scout. I was invited in for a trial and ended up getting a contract. My dad was so proud. That contract stayed in a frame until I was in my early 20s.

'I joined the tens and 11s age group and stayed at Liverpool until I was 15. I was mostly playing on the right of midfield, which, as you know, isn't really my position. Steve Heighway was the director of the youth team at the time and he called me in with my dad and said, bluntly, "I don't think you're good enough. It's not going to work out." I was devastated. It was like my world had ended.'

Despite being discarded by the club he loved, spells at Blackpool, Macclesfield Town and Stockport County would follow, punctuated by that oft-reported stint in a beetroot factory. Lambert describes these years as frustrating.

'I didn't know what to do with myself after Liverpool got rid of me. Then I heard from Danny Coid, who I had grown up with. He had been let go by Liverpool, too, and was now trying out at Blackpool. He invited me to go down there with another mate and all three of us went on to get a Youth Training Scheme deal at 16 years old.

'It went OK for a while. When Nigel Worthington was manager, I was doing well and it looked promising that I might break into the first team, but then he resigned just before I was about to turn pro. Steve McMahon took over and gave me a month-to-month pro contract when I turned 18. Again, though, it wasn't long before I got that call to the office to be told it wasn't working out. Steve wasn't even playing me in reserve games, which I wasn't happy with.

'It was the middle of the season when Blackpool let me go and I found myself training at Macclesfield, who were in the old Third Division. They wanted to sign me but couldn't afford to. When it came to the summer, I had no money coming in, so I took a job on a farm near Kirby, where I grew up. I had lots of things to do there, including working at the beetroot-packing factory. It reminded me what was waiting for me if the football didn't work out. It made me more determined.

'As it happened, Macclesfield signed me the next season and I did really well there. That led to Stockport coming in to buy me for £300,000 when I was 21. I thought things were going to progress from then on, but my first season there, under Carlton Palmer, didn't go very well at all. He wanted me to play as a deep-lying midfielder and I found it hard, to be honest. I very rarely played and, when I did play, I was subbed. It was a very frustrating time.

'Then Sammy McIlroy took over and he played me as a central midfielder. I liked Sammy and things picked up. I was the leading goalscorer and Player of the Season. But, again, things went backwards. My third season at Stockport was one of the worst I've had personally.

'We were bottom, or near the bottom, of the league most of the time. I don't know why we were so poor, but it cost Sammy his job. The crowd was on our backs because we weren't performing. It was really hard mentally. Chris Turner came in, but things didn't improve and the minute Rochdale enquired about me, I was allowed to speak to them.'

The lure of regular football was enough to persuade Lambert to drop down a division in 2005 and the Liverpudlian committed to Rochdale just a day after his 23rd birthday.

'When I met him, Steve Parkin said to me, "Rickie, I need goals," but we had an agreement that I would play the remainder of that season, which was about three months, as a central midfielder. He needed somebody there. Sometimes he would push me up as an attacking midfielder or as a number ten, if the game needed it. The following summer, during pre-season, he pulled me to one side and offered me the chance to play as a forward. He's right in what he told you, I did bite his hand off.

'Things really changed for me at this point. I came to Rochdale off the back of Stockport, where I'd really not enjoyed myself. I had no confidence. In making me a forward, Steve Parkin brought my confidence back and he got me scoring goals. I loved playing with Holty, too, even though he wouldn't pass to me! We were in competition with each other as to who could score the most goals, but he tried to grab all the penalties, so I had no chance. Seriously though, I loved the guy.'

Lambert quickly established himself as dead-ball specialist at Rochdale. Free kicks won around the edge of the opposition penalty area were greeted by rapturous cheers from the Spotland faithful. They knew what was coming from his malevolent boot.

'I've always been good at set pieces, even when I was kid. I've never been as prolific at them as I was at Rochdale, though. The secret is practice. When I was kid, I would get rows of balls and just practice that technique over and over. I was always good at striking a ball, but the free kick technique is different. It has to be practised and it comes with time. At Rochdale, I hit a purple patch where every single one I took seemed to end up in the back of the net. It got to a stage where the opposition were terrified to concede a free kick anywhere near their own area. To see the ball bend over the wall right into the top corner; it's a perfect thing.'

Lambert recalls his favourite game for Rochdale, which saw him score two goals past a goalkeeper who would himself rise to the elite level of the game.

'It was the 4-3 win against Shrewsbury in November 2005,' Lambert says. 'In fact, it's one the best games of football I've been involved in full stop. We came back from 3-1 down. Holty scored two and I scored two, including the winner, against Joe Hart.'

The freight train Rochdale had become with its unstoppable strike force wasn't quite derailed when Holt was sold to Nottingham Forest in the January of 2006, but it certainly lost more than a few wheels. Lambert without Holt was like an Empire biscuit without a jelly tot.

'I was gutted when Holty was sold,' Lambert says. 'We were in contention for the play-offs and the two of us were on fire. I think everyone felt it when he left. Our league position deteriorated. Listen, though, I know that that's football. It's money to the club and it was a good move for Holty. Personally, I was disappointed, as I really enjoyed playing football with him and he was a great lad around the club.'

It was perhaps inevitable that Lambert would follow his strike partner through the door eventually, although his destination, Bristol Rovers, surprised many, as they were in League Two along with Rochdale at the time. The reported £200,000 fee was considered somewhat meagre too, but the added clauses of that deal have gone on to make Rochdale a lot of money in the years since.

'I was offered a new contract by Rochdale,' Lambert says. 'I wasn't saying no, but I was holding off. I wanted to progress up the leagues and I wasn't too sure Rochdale were going to do it. I didn't want to tie my future down at that time. It was the August transfer deadline day in 2006 and Steve Parkin took me into his office to tell me Bristol Rovers had come in for me. I had three or four hours to decide the next three or four years of my career. It was very stressful.

'There were a few things in my private life that were stopping me being as professional as I needed to be. They were holding me back. It was nothing to do with Rochdale. I loved Rochdale. It was my own issue. I thought if I took the Bristol move, it would force me to leave Liverpool, where I still lived, and the comfort of home. That's what I felt I needed to do. It turned out to be one of the best things I ever did. I wasn't quite isolated in Bristol, but I was by myself a lot and everything became solely about my football career for the first time.'

Lambert's immediate and then continued success with Bristol Rovers led Southampton – in League One at the time – to pay £1m for his services. The fee raised a lot of eyebrows but it was more than justified. Lambert fired Southampton to back-to-back promotions and quickly established himself as a very able Premier League striker.

'I progressed into a better player at Bristol Rovers,' he recalls. 'We got promoted out of League Two through the play-offs and did OK in League One. I had scored 29 goals in my third season. In my head, I was ready to progress and play Championship football. In many ways, it was like Rochdale all over again. I didn't think Bristol Rovers were going to make that step up to the Championship.

'I loved it there, though. I would never have put in a transfer request or anything like that. For me to leave, someone would have to come in for me. I remember that summer came and went and nobody came in for me. I felt disappointed. Not because I was still at Bristol Rovers, but because it felt like nobody believed in me. The season started and then Southampton came in for me after the first game. Straight away, I knew I had to go there. They had just been relegated to League One, but when I met the chairman and spoke to the manager, Alan Pardew, and heard their plans for promotion and beyond, I said, "This has to happen." There were a few scary moments when Bristol Rovers were, quite rightly, trying to get as much money for me as they could, but I was doing my best to get the move pushed through.

'Again, the move to Southampton forced me on further as a professional. I remember Pardew called me into his office a few months after the move and he gave me a right dressing down. He said, "You're not fit enough. You're not looking after yourself. You should be ashamed." I was banging in the goals at the time, so I was in shock. It was a proper eye-opener. From that moment on, I thrived on working hard and doing extra training and being in the gym. Suddenly, I was as fit as everyone else. I was going into games and everything started to feel really easy. That's when I would say I became a proper professional footballer.

'We just missed out on the play-offs in the first season in League One, but we won the LDV [Football League] Trophy. Then we started the next season badly and Alan Pardew got the sack. Nigel Adkins came in and it took us all six months to get to grips with the league. Then we went on an unbelievable run and finished second behind Brighton. Full credit to Nigel for that. He got us into a style of playing, and instilled a belief in us that other teams couldn't cope with. Behind the scenes, the club was being run like a Premier League side. We had the best medical advice, all the stats you could imagine, the best transport. So, when we got into the Championship, we were more than ready for it. We absolutely destroyed the league that season. It was superb. We were promoted to the Premier League in style.

'Once there, it took us a while to get used to the Premier League. We carried on playing like we did in the Championship. We would open up, pass, and wait for teams to get tired, break them down and score. In the Premier League, people don't get tired. People don't make mistakes. People don't open up. They wait until they get the ball, or until you make a mistake, and, straight away, they're through on goal and they score. In the Championship, you would lose it two or three times for them to score one. In the Premier League, you lose it once and they score. I was like, "Wow." So, we changed our style to suit and we stabilised in the league.

'Then Mauricio Pochettino came in when Nigel left and took us up another level. He was a proper eye-opener. He's easily the best manager I've played under. I remember he started running us on a Monday in training. We all went to see him afterwards and said, "You shouldn't be doing this. We've just played 90 minutes on a Saturday. You shouldn't be running us on a Monday." He was all relaxed and said, "OK, yeah, that's fine." The next Monday, he doubled the running. We just looked at each other and decided to keep our mouths shut from then on.'

Lambert's rise to the top wasn't finished yet. At the age of 31, he finally fulfilled an ambition harboured by almost every child in England – he wore the Three Lions. The fact that it was a game against Scotland, the Auld Enemy, made it all the more special. By this stage, Lambert had scored 103 goals in just 196 appearances across three divisions for Southampton. His call-up by Roy Hodgson was surprising only to those who still didn't fully appreciate what he was capable of. Needless to say, he scored on his international debut – with his first touch. It proved to be the decisive goal as England saw off Scotland 3-2 at Wembley in the first meeting between the two nations for 14 years.

'My call up was surreal,' he says. 'I'd been in hospital all that night with my wife, who was giving birth to my baby girl. I went home and went straight to bed in the morning. I woke up at midday to 50 missed calls and 120 messages. I thought, "That's a hell of a lot of well-wishers for the birth of my daughter." One of the first messages said, "Please call the Gaffer". I was like, "Shit, what's this?" So, I called him and was told I was in the England squad. I didn't even know the squad was being named that day. I thought I was being wound up.

'I've had a lot of great moments playing for my league clubs, but that probably is the best moment of my career. It felt like everything had been building up to it. I remember sitting on the bench at the game itself, being absolutely desperate to get on. I was like a tiger in a cage. I knew if I didn't get on and do something, I might never have the chance to represent England again. It felt a bit like I got a call-up because of my league form, but I didn't feel established, if you know what I mean? I felt it would just take another player to start scoring goals again and my place would be gone. Still, I didn't envisage my impact being as extreme as scoring the winning goal with my first touch. That was something else. It was indescribable.'

It was about to get better for Lambert. Following selection for the England squad for the 2014 World Cup in Brazil, Liverpool, the club that released him as a teenager, wanted him back.

'I had just been called up to the World Cup squad, which was amazing enough, and then my agent phoned to tell me Liverpool had come in for me,' he says. 'It was turning into an incredible year for me. The club I supported as a boy, and still do, wanted to pay money for me. I was very emotional, though. I saw myself retiring at Southampton, but the pull of Liverpool was too strong and I was never going to say no to them. Obviously, the training facilities were all new compared to when I was there as a kid, but the ground, Anfield, was exactly the same and inspired the same emotions in me.'

As it transpired, England bombed out of the World Cup in the group stages that summer without registering a single win. Lambert himself was given a mere three minutes of game time against Uruguay in England's second match. It was disappointing that Hodgson then failed to play him in the final game against Costa Rica, which was nothing more than a dead rubber.

After the dissatisfaction of Brazil, Lambert was keen to get back to domestic action,

'Because I was so excited to join Liverpool, I joined up with them two weeks earlier than I should have done after the World Cup. I wanted to make sure I started well for them, but it backfired. I needed more rest, if I'm being honest. I didn't feel as sharp as I did the season before. It took me a while to get a run of games. To be honest, it's a period I don't want to go into too much.'

While Lambert feels disappointed about how his return to Liverpool panned out, he was given the chance to continue his Premier League career at West Bromwich Albion, where he stayed until 2016, before spending a single season in the Championship with Cardiff City.

It was then, at the age of 35, Lambert announced his retirement from playing.

'Long term, who knows?' he says, when asked what the future holds. 'I'd like to think I could be a manager one day, though. That said, if I did it, I would need the same hunger as I had as a player. I would want to learn properly how to do it rather than jumping straight into it.'

As we round off our chat, Lambert is quick to enthuse about the bearing Rochdale had on his vocation.

'Rochdale had a massive impact on me because I wasn't enjoying football and my career was going nowhere,' he says. 'Rochdale brought enjoyment back to football for me. Most importantly, I started scoring goals there. When I was a kid, before I first went to Liverpool, I was striker. I used to score hundreds of goals a season. All those instincts came back to me at Rochdale. That feeling of hitting the back of the net can't be compared to anything else in the game. That's why I started playing football.'

Glenn Murray

2006–2008

ROCHDALE AFC had lost one powerhouse in 2006, but fans were about to celebrate the arrival of another.

With Grant Holt gone (and his strike partner Rickie Lambert too), manager Steve Parkin was once more forced to pan the murky waters of football's wilderness. Against the odds, he found gold among the silt yet again when he signed the unfulfilled potential of Glenn Murray.

Like fellow Cumbrian Holt, it took Murray a little while to hit his stride in Dale colours and, as Parkin laments earlier in this book, Murray only began to properly fire for Rochdale once the manager had left the club.

Of course, Murray's comparisons with Holt go beyond them merely sharing a county of origin. Their early careers followed a very similar path too, with stints at non-league sides Barrow and Workington sandwiching a spell overseas.

'I was on Carlisle's books as a kid and the dream was always to be a professional footballer,' Murray begins, with that Cumbrian lilt the uninitiated usually mistake for a Geordie accent.

'It didn't work out at Carlisle, though, and, by the time I was 17 or 18 years old, I was playing non-league football for Workington and was working as a plasterer's labourer. I had given up on being a professional. I thought my chance had gone.'

There was a glimmer of rekindled hope for Murray, however, when he was invited to play in the USA in the summer of 2004. His destination was North Carolina, where he would represent USL Pro Soccer League side Wilmington Hammerheads.

'I did all right there, but was unsure where it would lead,' he says. 'It was really hot and so you had to play a lot differently than in the UK. You had to keep the ball a lot more. By chance, Sunderland had come out to North Carolina on a pre-season tour. Mick McCarthy was in charge at the time. I played in a couple of games against Sunderland out there and Mick invited me to train with them back in the UK. I jumped at that and spent three or four weeks with them.

'In the end, Mick decided not to offer me anything, but said he would put a word in with anybody I wanted. I asked him to contact Carlisle because it was my local club. [Former Rochdale boss] Paul Simpson was the manager at the time and Mick said he knew him. He said he'd give him a call to recommend me.

'I left Sunderland with my tail between my legs to some degree and I had to go back to work as a labourer. The weeks went by and I heard nothing from Carlisle. I was quite disillusioned and began to think Mick might not have made the call. Six weeks on and I hadn't kicked a football.

'Then, just like that, I got a call out of the blue asking if I could play in a reserve game for Carlisle the next day. I said, "Of course I can." I went through there determined, played the game – I can't remember who it was against – and managed to get myself on the scoresheet. That goal got me a trial period.

'At the time, though, Carlisle weren't in great shape as a club. I used to watch them, as they were my local team, and I'd seen them relegated to the Conference the previous season. Still, just to be asked to go on trial with them was great. I was there a good few weeks and Paul Simpson said to me, "I've not made my mind up about you, but I've had Barrow FC on the phone, would you like to play for them, but train with us during the week?" The idea was that Barrow would pay me enough money to get by. So that was the arrangement; I trained with a Conference National club during the week and played for a Conference North team at the weekend. I scored ten in ten for Barrow and Paul decided to offer me a deal at Carlisle until the end of the season.'

From there, Carlisle were promoted from the Conference via the play-offs, back into the Football League.

'I got my contract extended and, the next season, we got promoted again,' Murray remembers. 'We won promotion from League Two at Rochdale, funnily enough. Despite the success of the club, I was very much a substitute player. I was the impact sub who came on for the last 20 minutes to freshen a game up. I was eager and had the legs, and felt I very much played my part.

'Then we were in League One, Paul Simpson left to manage Preston North End in the Championship, and the club just moved too fast for me. Coming from non-league, with back-to-back promotions, I was struggling with the standard. Neil McDonald took over as Carlisle manager and he saw that. To help me, I was sent on loan back to League Two with Stockport. That step back helped me, to be honest.

'While I was at Stockport, Rochdale manager Steve Parkin sent Keith Hill to watch me. Hilly was youth team manager at that time, but would obviously go on to take over the first-team. He recommended me to Steve. Rochdale came in for me, but then Accrington Stanley did as well, and both were offering very similar deals. The idea was that I would join one of them on loan and sign permanently when the transfer window reopened in January. I told Neil McDonald I wanted to sign for Accrington because it was a bit nearer to where I lived. Neil, to his credit, told me that I had to change my way of thinking if I was going to carve out a career in the game. He felt that Rochdale was a much better club for me and pointed out that it had launched the careers of players like Grant Holt and Rickie Lambert. With his guidance, I signed for Rochdale.'

Unfortunately for Murray, he joined Rochdale at a time when the side was struggling in League Two and it has to be noted that he made his first start in a 7-1 hammering by Lincoln City.

'Steve Parkin was brilliant with me as soon as I got there,' he says. 'He told me I would be starting against Lincoln at the weekend.

Then we got battered 7-1. I, personally, didn't do very well over the next few games, nor did the rest of the team, and Parkin ended up getting the sack.'

Far from fading back into a substitute role, Murray began to establish himself as not only a goal threat but a great outlet for his team-mates, too. He could play the target man as if he had been daubed with a Pritt Stick – a focal point from which his fellow attackers could feed. It wasn't realised quickly enough to save Parkin's job, true, but Murray's talent was fully utilised by the man who replaced him, youth team boss Keith Hill.

'We were all low at the time Steve Parkin left, but then Keith Hill stepped in, brought David Flitcroft in as his assistant, and the transformation was incredible,' Murray recalls. 'Steve signed me, though, and gave me my chance, so I'll be forever grateful for that. However, Hilly and Flitcroft brought a new level of enthusiasm with them. From the way they spoke, to the drills we did in training – everything was new. It swept you along. It was a special time for the club.

'I think the way they showed me attention, and focused on my strengths, brought the best out of me. I'd stay behind after training and Dave Flitcroft would bring out all these new finishing drills. As I say, it was new, exciting and a fun time to be at the club. It brought everyone together, too. We all got on with each other brilliantly. The camaraderie was strong.'

Murray believes the mix of youth and experience was just right, too. Whereas traditionally older professionals may not buy into a young, new manager's philosophy, this didn't appear to be the case at Rochdale.

'Adam Le Fondre came in, and we already had Chris Dagnall,' Murray says. 'We all played well up front together. It wasn't just about the young lads either. The older lads, like John Doolan, Gary Jones, Dave Perkins and Lee Crooks, were brilliant for us, too. They fed off the energy from Hilly and Flitcroft. Crooks had played for Man City, for example, but he didn't think he was better than anyone else. He was as enthusiastic about Hilly's vision as anyone.'

Including his loan spell, Murray made 33 appearances for Rochdale that season, scoring 16 goals. He was an integral part of a side that transformed from one which looked nailed on for relegation into one which narrowly missed the play-offs.

The following was Hill's first full season as Rochdale boss and Murray was a player in fine form. He had found the net ten times when the January transfer window of the 2007/08 season had opened and, when he looked through it, the Seagulls were circling. They finally deemed it fit to swoop on the 25th of the month and Murray departed for Brighton & Hove Albion leaving Rochdale in the region of £300,000 better off.

'I was scoring for Rochdale and the rumours were out there,' Murray says. 'Even over the summer people had been saying clubs were interested in me, but nothing happened. I just got on with my football. Then, one day in January 2008, I got called into the office and was told the club had accepted a bid for me from Brighton. It felt a bit strange. Brighton was a club I'd never paid much attention to, being a northern boy. I think Hilly really wanted me to stay, but Brighton were offering me really good money to step up a division and that's what I knew I had to work towards. I felt I wasn't good enough for League One when I was last there with Carlisle, but I felt ready for it at that point. Rochdale had made me ready for it. My skills had been honed and I was used to playing more than just a bit part with a team.'

Murray spent three and a half seasons in League One with Brighton, each season becoming more prolific. In 2011, after helping himself to 22 goals in 50 outings, it was enough for Championship side Crystal Palace to take a punt on him.

'My time at Brighton was a bit up and down,' Murray says. 'My first year was good, my second year saw me in and out of the side due to injuries, and my last year was special. I knuckled down after I got over the injuries, did really well, and it coincided with the club's promotion.'

With Brighton and Crystal Palace being arch rivals, it's perhaps understandable that Murray was reluctant to discuss his switch in any great detail. One can only assume that, with Murray under freedom of contract, he felt Palace showed a greater interest in acquiring him than Brighton did in keeping him.

Regardless, Murray described the move as an 'opportunity to take on a new challenge'.

And it took him just two seasons to reach the Premier League with Palace – smashing an incredible 31 goals in 45 appearances during the promotion season of 2012/13. He also scored a memorable extra-time winner at Old Trafford against Manchester United in the League Cup quarter-finals the previous year.

'My first season at Palace was not good at all, though,' Murray says. 'I was playing in a very defensive-minded team under Dougie Freedman. I only managed seven goals. I felt comfortable in the division, but didn't feel like I had completely gotten to grips with it. That said, we did go to Man United in the cup and win. I've played against them since and only matched that result once. We were buzzing. They had players like Paul Pogba and Dimitar Berbatov playing. It was a great night for us. I scored the winner and Darren Ambrose scored that wonder goal of an equaliser. We were so close to the final that year, too, eventually getting beat by Cardiff on penalties.

'The next season saw us really kick on. Dougie tweaked the way we played to give me more support up front. I had Wilfried Zaha and Yannick Bolasie on either wing firing balls in. For a striker like myself, it was perfect. Two wingers who wanted to carry the ball to the byline and cross it. While Dougie left us to manage Bolton in the October, Ian Holloway came in, maintained that playing style and guided us to the play-offs.'

Sadly, Murray's season was cut short a game early by a serious knee injury and he wasn't able to take part in the play-off final. In fact, the injury would delay his experience of the Premier League until the following February.

'I snapped my anterior cruciate ligament in the first leg of the play-off semi-final against Brighton. I remember going for the ball in the penalty box and twisting in agony. I missed the next leg and then the final, which was obviously gutting, but the lads took us over the line. I'm at peace with it now. If we had lost, and I felt that my playing would have made a difference, that would have been much harder to take.

'It hindered me for a while did that injury, but I guess the only positive was the period I sustained it – right at the end of the season. It was a nine- or ten-month injury, but I knew I had three months before every other player would kick another competitive ball. I would be well into my rehab by then and that was the positive spin I put on it to get me back. The fact I was now a Premier League player was an added incentive.'

When Murray did return, he found the step up in class a formidable one.

'The obvious thing about the step up is there are a lot less mistakes at Premier League level and the players are much more athletic,' he says. 'Instead of stepping out and engaging strikers, the defenders tend to stay in their line and, if one does decide to engage, then their team-mates cover round. All the teams are well drilled and become hard to break down.'

The change of managers at Palace was also a difficult transition for Murray to handle. He feels Neil Warnock, who had replaced Tony Pulis, who in turn had replaced Ian Holloway, didn't see him as a Premier League striker.

'He had six strikers and, in his opinion, I was the sixth,' Murray says. 'When a manager says that to me, at 30 years old, I'm going to look elsewhere to get games. I wanted to show people that I was fit again and was capable of playing game after game after game. It wasn't even about scoring goals at that point; it was about proving I could play games consistently. I told him I wanted to leave and he said OK.'

Murray moved to Championship club Reading on loan in September 2014, scoring twice on his debut. He went on to score six more times for the Royals before returning to Palace in January 2015.

'Reading was good for me because I played week in, week out and scored goals. It removed all doubt as far as I was concerned.'

Murray returned to Palace under yet another new manager, Alan Pardew, and scored seven times in 15 league appearances. His value as a Premier League force was reignited. After several bids, newcomers Bournemouth lured him to the south coast on a three-year deal, the fee to Palace a not-insignificant £4m. Murray quickly scored a late headed goal for his new club to clinch a famous win against Chelsea at Stamford Bridge.

'Palace felt the bid from Bournemouth was a good one and let me go,' Murray says. 'I didn't play as much as I'd have liked at Bournemouth, but to be part of a squad that everyone thought would be relegated, and wasn't, was a great feeling.'

Murray would go on to return to Brighton, scoring consistently, before his career wound down with spells at Watford and Nottingham Forest.

As we round off our chat, Murray once again reiterates the fondness with which he recalls his time at Rochdale.

'Rochdale was a massive point in my career,' he says. 'The perfect club at the perfect time. Like those strikers before me, Holt and Lambert, the club made my career. It sounds daft, but I wouldn't have been a Premier League striker if it wasn't for Rochdale, Keith Hill and Dave Flitcroft.'

Will Buckley

2006–2010

WILL BUCKLEY emerged from the Rochdale youth team during a period that would become the most successful in the club's history.

The winger made a gradual impact rather than an explosive one, as he matured and learned his craft under the tutelage of manager Keith Hill and his assistant David Flitcroft. He would go on to cement his place as an integral part of a Rochdale side that would seal promotion in 2010 (although he left just before this was achieved), before going on to prove himself at the highest level. For the Dale, he became equally devastating out wide as he did through the middle, and was an integral component of a hugely successful attacking force.

Born and raised next door in Oldham, Buckley joined Rochdale as a youth scholar in 2006 before progressing to the reserves. He explains how he came to that point.

'I joined Oldham Athletic's School of Excellence when I was about nine,' he says. 'I was there until the under-14s age group. I'd stopped enjoying it by then, though, and said to my mum and dad that I didn't want to play anymore.

'I felt there was too much pressure on me. With the way it was run, being a professional environment, football simply stopped being fun. My main position was a striker back then. As I hadn't grown as much as some of my team-mates and opponents, I felt my football suffered for it. I was still confident in my ability but, in most games, I was just not having the impact I would have wanted.

The only thing you want to do at that age is play the game that you love. Unfortunately, at this time, I'd lost the enjoyment factor and therefore the best thing for me to do was leave Oldham in order to find the enjoyment again.

'We approached Oldham to explain, but they didn't want me to leave because I'd signed a four-year contract with them. They did eventually agree to let me leave, but said I couldn't sign for another professional club. I ended up playing Sunday league football for a couple of years. It was the best thing I could have done at that point because football started to be fun again. It was back to what it should have been for a lad my age – a kickabout with my mates.

'I realised then, though, that I did want to have a career in football after all and so I eventually went back to Oldham, as I couldn't go anywhere else. I was 15 years old and they put me on a six-week trial. After that, they decided they didn't want to offer me a Youth Training Scheme deal and they let me go.

'I weighed up my options and decided to go to Hopwood Hall College, in Middleton [just outside Rochdale]. I was accepted into the football academy there. The course mirrored what youth scholars would be doing at local professional clubs – training and studying. Ironically, it's where both Oldham and Rochdale sent their youth scholars after training each day. I think the qualification was equivalent to a BTEC National. You studied sports nutrition, sports psychology, stuff like that – anything that enhanced your knowledge of sport beyond just playing. It was really enjoyable.'

Buckley cites what happened next as the slice of luck that made his career.

'Hopwood Hall's academy was at quite a good level,' he says. 'Every year, they played the Rochdale youth team. I played in that year's game [2006] and we beat them 3-1. It just so happened that Keith Hill was there. It was not long before he was promoted to first-team manager at Rochdale. He spoke to me after the game and invited me and another lad, Ryan Morris, for a trial. I did the trial and was offered non-contract terms. It suited me because I didn't want to tie myself to a two-year youth contract, as I would've been 19 when it expired, which would have made me too old, in my opinion.

'As Keith Hill had been the youth team manager previously, there was a bit of upheaval when I arrived. Chris Beech eventually became my youth team coach. I think he'd just arrived from Bury at that point. I got on really well with him and he helped me quite a lot. It was all very different to Oldham and I enjoyed my time in the Rochdale youth team. Part of that was down to the fact that they would use us in reserve games, which meant we could play with first-team squad players. It gave you a chance to show what you could do against full-time professionals. You got thrown in at the deep end. Keith Hill and Dave Flitcroft would come to these games and watch everybody.'

Buckley's introduction to the first team in 2008 was measured and he believes this is because his manager didn't want to overexpose him to the rigours of league football.

'I was still quite small and weak at that point, to be honest,' he says. 'I knew I had the ability to make it, but I didn't know whether I would get the physicality. In some games I would get pushed off the ball too easily. Keith and David seemed to have faith in me, though, and they eventually selected me for a few first-team squads. I made my debut in the February of that year but only made eight more appearances that season. I was training with the first team every day by then, though. I think the management were looking out for me because, looking back, I wasn't ready for too many games at that point.'

While Buckley would only make a handful of substitute appearances that season, one of them was in the play-off final against Stockport County at Wembley, which Dale lost 3-2.

'I'd like to say Wembley was a defining experience for me, but, to be honest, when I think back to it, it's a blur,' he says. 'I came on for the last 20 minutes but can't remember it. I have to look at the DVD to remind me. I do remember being devastated at losing the game, of course, and I remember thinking it was ridiculous I was playing at Wembley aged 18. It did make me confident that I could kick on.'

After the Wembley disappointment, Rochdale once again made a tilt for promotion the following season and Buckley found himself with more game time, scoring his first professional goal in a 2-2 draw away at the nomadic Rotherham United and then again in the two subsequent games.

'I had a really good pre-season and became a lot more regular in the first team when the season started,' he says. 'I got my first professional goal and I remember how good that felt. I remember the confidence it gave me. We were away against Rotherham, who were playing at Sheffield's Don Valley stadium at the time. It was a shocking pitch and the game wasn't the best, but I remember scoring and sprinting across the running track, which surrounded the pitch, to the Rochdale fans. It felt like they were half a mile away but I wanted to celebrate with them. At the end of the day, you can score 20 goals in the reserves, but that first professional goal beats them all. That is the one feeling you never forget.

'It did feel special at Rochdale during that time. There was a buzz that was created by Keith and Dave and it was felt by everybody – not just the players, but other people at the club and the fans, too. After Wembley, everybody felt we had a chance to go one better. It was my first professional club in terms of being in a first team, so I guess I was spoilt looking back. I thought this is the way it was everywhere. Training was so enjoyable and both Keith and Dave maintained a closeness with the players that made them approachable. You knew both of them were your boss, but you never felt you couldn't go to them. If something ever needed to be said, you could say it to them. It just created a kind of harmony – a feeling that everyone was on the same side.

'Since then, I've obviously learned some managers can be a lot more distant. That was never the case with Keith. It was a relaxed environment, but nobody was ever in doubt of the job that needed to be done. Gary Jones, the captain, personified this. The way he trained and played was an inspiration to us all. It was great to be involved with him. We definitely had the right players at Rochdale, but Keith, Dave and Gary brought a steadiness and calmness that was needed to ensure everybody performed to their best.'

While Rochdale would again miss out on promotion via the play-offs, Buckley had established himself as a rising star. Rumours of his departure were rife. By the January of the following season, the one that would see Rochdale achieve promotion for the first time since 1969, Buckley was sold to Championship side Watford for a reported £250,000, with Dale sitting at the top of the League Two table.

'My contract was coming to an end that season,' he says. 'It was January and I had six months left. My agent mentioned that Watford were interested and it was worth considering because it was an opportunity to play in the Championship. I didn't expect it. I knew I was playing well, but I didn't expect to leap up two divisions. Dave Flitcroft took me to one side and had a word. He wanted me to stay and experience a promotion with Rochdale. He promised I could leave at the end of the season if I still wanted to. I didn't want to let the opportunity slip away, though. I think there was an element of Rochdale realising that, if I left at the end of the season, they wouldn't get any money for me. I think it turned out well for both parties in the end. Rochdale still got promoted, so I was delighted.

'This was my first experience of a transfer, so I was trusting my agent a fair bit. I didn't really hear about Watford's interest until a few days before it all happened. I was actually injured at the time. A few weeks earlier, we were away at Cheltenham and I felt my quad go in the warm-up. I told Keith Hill about it and I think he thought I'd been told by my agent to throw one in. To this day, I still reckon he thinks I was at it! My dad sees Keith now and again and Keith always winds him up about it. Agents do ask players to chuck one in ahead of moves, I'm sure, but I genuinely was injured. I got to Watford and couldn't play for a while because of it.'

Buckley, nursing his quadriceps injury, had to wait until March to make his Watford debut.

'I arrived at Watford and was really impressed with the training facilities and the sessions,' he says. 'The pace of everything was that little bit quicker. No disrespect to League Two, which is a difficult league to play in, but everything here had to be done at extra pace – even thinking. It took me a while to get used to that. It took me five or six weeks to adapt to the step up. It was harder than I ever expected it to be. I had to set myself the goal of achieving the standard, or I knew I wouldn't get a game.

'The manager, Malky Mackay, helped me with this. He was patient and knew what I could offer. He was heavily involved in the team on a daily basis. Maybe he didn't have the banter that Keith and Dave had, he was a different kind of manager, but I enjoyed working with him no less.'

With Watford struggling in the Championship by the end of the following season, Brighton & Hove Albion looked to boost their own promotion chances when entering the division and signed Buckley for a then-club-record fee of £1m. Thanks to a sell-on clause insisted on by Rochdale, some of that money made its way to the Spotland coffers.

'I went on to do well at Watford and played a lot of games for them during the next full season,' Buckley says. 'Personally, when the season ended, despite the club's league position, I thought I had done all right. Brighton had just won promotion from League One and, unknown by me, they had been watching my games. I went on holiday with one of my best mates in the summer and got a phone call from my agent while I was away, telling me I'd been sold to Brighton and that I had to sort out terms with them. They'd put in a few bids for me that had been rejected and I thought that was the end of it. Then they put in a record bid and it had gone through.

'I never thought that would be the last time I'd be at Watford. I never got to say goodbye to half of the lads. The last I said to them was, "I'll see you in six weeks for pre-season training." It was a strange one and one of the harsh realities of football. You rarely get a leaving party.

'The size of the fee Brighton paid for me surprised me, too. It was a record fee for them, well, until they signed Craig Mackail-Smith a week later. It made me feel wanted, though. For them to go back two or three times for me showed how much they wanted me.

'Brighton were a new club to the Championship, true, but they had the big new stadium and big ambitions. Gus Poyet was the manager and obviously he was a great player in his day. I learned so much from him. My first season there, along with my Rochdale days, rank as my favourite in football.'

Brighton finished tenth in the league and reached the fifth round of the FA Cup, beating Newcastle United, and the third round of the League Cup, beating Sunderland.

'The Amex Stadium was packed and created a buzz around the town,' Buckley recalls. 'It was a dream come true for Brighton, what with the league performance and the cups, turning Premier League teams over.'

The next season was even better for Buckley and Brighton, as the club finished fourth, where they then lost out to Crystal Palace in the play-offs. Two days later, manager Gus Poyet and his assistants were suspended. The Uruguayan was famously sacked live on air the following month while working as a pundit for the BBC.

'We got into the play-offs and then it all ended quite badly between Gus and the owner,' Buckley says. 'I think he felt the owner wasn't giving him the money to move the team forward. Gus wanted automatic promotion and had identified a few players. I don't know what happened in any detail after that, but all the lads were gutted that he went, because the influence he had on the club was massive in the three or four years he was there.'

Buckley would stay on the south coast until 2014. During the August transfer window of that year, he finally got his Premier League move when Sunderland paid a fee for him reported to be £2.5m.

'I had another full season with Brighton, managed by Oscar Garcia now, and Sunderland, where Gus was now manager, put a last-minute bid in for me in the January. Brighton rejected it because they couldn't get a replacement winger for me. I understood that. I finished the season at Brighton and we got into the play-offs again, losing to Derby this time. Sunderland came back in for me and I was allowed to leave at the end of that summer.

'From when I was a boy I wanted to play in the Premier League and then I was there. I never once thought, "I can't handle this." The standard increased, obviously, but I felt ready for it this time. My debut was in an away game. I came on at West Brom for 20 minutes. I'd only signed a couple of days before and Gus put me straight in.

'Did I feel pressure? Yes, but not in the way people might think. The TV cameras and the crowd don't matter so much as the pressure you feel from the money. The money players are paid, the money clubs pay for you, and the money TV companies pay the clubs. There is a pressure to perform constantly as a result of that. I felt it. I was sat on the bench with the worst butterflies I've ever had.

'The way the game is played in the Premier League is totally different to any division below it. There is a gulf in class within the league itself for a start, but I was surprised by how much things slow down. People talk about the pace of the Premier League, but you have a lot of time in your own half. Then you're in the final third and it's like, "Woah, what happened there?" All of a sudden, you need to make something happen fast and you're up against the fittest, strongest, quickest left-back around. Bang. It took some getting used to. You watch players every week on the TV and they make it look easy. Trust me, making something happen consistently in the final third, at that level, is so difficult. I've so much respect for the players that can do that time and time again.'

On 16 March 2015, Poyet was sacked by Sunderland after a run of just one victory in 12 Premier League games. Former Rangers manager Dick Advocaat replaced him and, as a result, Buckley found his opportunities limited. He has since spent time on loan at Leeds United, Birmingham City, Sheffield Wednesday and Bolton Wanders before finishing his playing career at the age of 31.

'I was sent out on loan, but I looked back and thought, "I could be doing something else right now." I played one game against Rochdale for a college side and the opposition manager happened to be there. What if he wasn't? Would I have got the same chance somewhere else? Maybe not. Obviously, you've got to have the ability, but you need that luck. You also need a thick skin. Some managers rate you, some don't. You can't take things personally. That's what happened to me during my loan spell at Leeds. The manager preferred someone else in the end. That's fine. You just prove yourself to a different manager.

'I mention Dave Flitcroft frequently to this day because he spent a lot of time with me on the training pitch while I was developing at Rochdale. I needed that time and it's time that a lot of players don't get. The club gave Keith Hill the freedom to do things the way he wanted to, which gave players like me a chance to shine. A lot of teams don't rate youth, or are too scared to put young players in. Rochdale did the opposite. They would take the young lads getting released from Man City, Man United and so on, and they would get played against other reserve sides. If they were good enough, they'd get signed. It didn't matter where they'd been before or where they'd been rejected from – if they were good enough they were good enough. If it wasn't for Rochdale, I wouldn't have been a Premier League footballer and for that I'll always be grateful.'

Adam Le Fondre

2007–2009

WHEN KEITH Hill took charge of Rochdale on a caretaker basis late in 2006, he was lauded for immediately accomplishing spectacular results with the very same group of players left behind by his predecessor, Steve Parkin.

Once given the job permanently less than a month later, Hill's first course of action was to augment this squad of now-motivated players with those of his own choosing.

Stockport County striker Adam Le Fondre was one such. Initially arriving on loan before signing permanently in the summer, Alf (a nickname styled after his initials) quickly became a favourite at Spotland. Celebrated for his hard-working displays and very obvious eye for goal, so successful was Le Fondre's stay at Rochdale that it was surprising the Hatters let him leave at all.

Speaking to him online at his now home in Sydney, Australia, and before we get down to matters of football, I first establish the origins of his exotic-sounding name.

'Funnily enough, Glenville is my first name, but I use Adam,' he laughs. 'My dad's name is Glenville Lyndon Darrell Le Fondre. He named me Glenville and named my brother Lyndon because of that. The name Le Fondre itself is from the Channel Islands. It's a Jersey name. My dad's family is from Jersey, but my mum is actually half French – God knows how they ended up in Stockport of all places! As a kid, Stockport was always my home and my mum and dad are still in the house I grew up in to this day.'

Indeed, born and raised in Stockport, the town's Edgeley Park became Le Fondre's footballing home not long after he first learned he was quite good at kicking one.

'I was brought up in Offerton, which is small part of Stockport,' he says. 'My mum and dad were fantastic with me. I had a good upbringing. We weren't overly wealthy or anything, but I never wanted or needed for anything. We were a football-mad family. My dad used to follow Manchester United all around Europe. As soon as I got to walking, I had a football at my feet. In fact, I can't remember a time when I didn't have a football at my feet. I was involved in team games from five years old. My dad ran the local junior side, both for my age group and my brother's, who is five years older than me. I picked up the habit of scoring goals really early. I actually scored in my first game when I was five, playing against seven-year-olds.

'When I was seven and eight, I was playing with the under-nines at Man United. Stockport County didn't have a Centre of Excellence at the time. They did run community football camps in the school holidays though, so I attended one of these. At the end of the week, I was told I had won every award on offer – Best Player of the Week, Coach's Player of the Week and Penalty King – but I was only allowed to have one, so I chose Best Player. One of the boys I went to the camp with was from my junior team at the time. His grandfather was chairman of Stockport County. I later found out that, after seeing me at the football camp, he told Stockport they needed to start a Centre of Excellence and make me its first recruit. I don't know how true that is, but it's what I was told.

Anyway, they *did* set up an under-nines team and I *was* invited down for a trial and they did sign me. Crewe had also approached me at that time, and their youth setup had an exceptional reputation, but Stockport was on my doorstep and Crewe was an hour away. With both my mum and dad working, it meant less travelling for them, so it was a no-brainer in that regard. I developed with Stockport but then broke my leg when I was 11. Back then, they didn't keep you on the books if you were injured, but, as soon as my leg was mended,

I was invited straight back down for another trial and was signed right back up again.'

Le Fondre progressed through County's Centre of Excellence youth system before making his first-team debut in 2004. With further senior appearances few and far between over the next three years, it was inevitable that he would seek opportunities elsewhere.

'At the beginning of the 2006/07 season, I started really well,' he recalls. 'I scored six or seven goals in the first ten or 11 games. Funnily enough, I then got injured playing against Rochdale, when we beat them 3-0 at Spotland. Stanno [Nathan Stanton] did me and I got stretchered off with ankle ligament damage. I should have been out for six to eight weeks, but I tried to rush myself back within two, which was stupid really. I was a young, naive kid. I had been scoring goals and people were talking about me, so I wanted to capitalise on that. I was miles off it. I was still injured and couldn't really kick the ball. That set me back a further four to six weeks.

'By the time I did come back, the squad was doing really well in League Two. They had experienced strikers who were scoring goals, such as Tes Bramble, Anthony Elding and Adam Proudlock. For me, I was like, "Oh, I've wasted all the good work I'd done." I knew I wasn't going to play at that point. The manager, Jim Gannon, came to me and said, "I think it would be good for you to go out on loan to get some experience and I've had Rochdale on." I turned it down at that point. Steve Parkin was still the manager of Rochdale and the team were right down in relegation trouble. I didn't think Rochdale were going to play the sort of football I wanted to play. However, a month down the line, I still wasn't featuring for Stockport. I was on the bench but not starting games. It was then I decided I would go out on loan, just to be starting games. As it happened, Keith Hill had just replaced Parkin as Rochdale manager and he wanted me, so I went there for a short loan period.'

Le Fondre found the change of scene instantly liberating.

'From the minute I walked into the club I was struck by how different it was to Stockport,' he says. 'You had Glenn Murray there, who was obviously the number one striker, and I was treated as his equal from the off. At Stockport, I was the young kid coming through, but, at Rochdale, I was treated like the main man. This is something I had always craved and, at Rochdale, it was given to me. All I'd ever wanted to do was play first-team football and score goals. Hilly and Flicker [Dave Flitcroft] were loving me at this time – really bigging me up – even though I was just on a short loan. I can't speak highly enough of them.'

Le Fondre's first Rochdale appearance was a memorable debut for a host of reasons. Keith Hill's side destroyed a high-flying MK Dons 5-0, with Le Fondre himself grabbing a brace. It served notice that a side which had been relegation fodder just a few games earlier was rejuvenated and ready to take on all comers.

'It was great to score two on my debut, but it was the game after that, against Walsall, that really sticks with me. We conceded an equaliser in the last minute but I had been brought off with five minutes left. Hilly came up to me and he apologised. He said, "If you'd have stayed on, we'd have won that game." I was only 19 at the time, remember. I was thinking, "Gaffers don't normally do that." So, I was buzzing. I went on to score four in seven and we were playing really good football. I was really enjoying myself.'

However, just when Le Fondre was hitting his stride, he received an unwanted phone call in March.

'I can't remember which game it was, but I'd done an interview for the matchday programme, basically saying how much I was enjoying my time at Rochdale. The Stockport manager sees this and phones me up. He says, "You're not a Rochdale player, you're a Stockport player. You are coming back to us." I told him I wanted to stay at Rochdale until the end of the season. Stockport had gone eight or nine games without conceding a goal at this point. They were on a great run. Then they lost a game and the manager was on to me, saying I had to come back to the club. He said I was going to play. Hilly and Flicker were gutted I had been recalled and, to be honest, so was I. I had already formed a bond with the players. I felt a togetherness at the club after only two months of being there.

'Anyway, I go back to Stockport and play the next game. It was against Hartlepool. We were 3-0 up. I scored and set one up, but was brought off after 45 minutes. Stockport went on to draw 3-3. I then started against Bristol Rovers in the next game and we lost 2-1. After that game, the manager said I could go out on loan again. Wrexham had been in touch, apparently. They were bottom of League Two at the time. The manager says, half laughing, "You can do for them what you did for Rochdale and get them up the league a bit." I told him if I was to go anywhere, I wanted to go back to Rochdale. The manager kind of shrugged and said, "Why not?" I was straight on the phone to Hilly and Flicker. They were on loudspeaker, absolutely buzzing. It was loan deadline day on the Thursday and they said they would sort it all out.

'I went and cleared out my locker, flung my gear in the boot of the car, started driving and got a call after 15 minutes on the road. "The loan's off, come back." I turned around, went back to Stockport and asked the gaffer what was going on. He told me I was now needed as cover as one of the strikers was injured. I went and found the strikers and asked them who was injured. None of them were. It was at that point I suspected I'd done something to annoy somebody at the club. Worse, I was made fifth-choice striker and had to sit on the bench for the rest of the season, including when Rochdale came to Edgeley Park and beat Stockport 7-2.'

His lamentation was not to last. Rochdale's miraculous turnaround under Hill was enough to persuade Le Fondre to sign a three-year deal with the club in the summer of 2007.

'Hilly and Flicker were in touch with me at least once a week, saying they were going to sign me in the summer,' Le Fondre recalls. 'At the end of the season, they sent me the Rochdale shirts I had worn while I had been on loan, with a typed note saying "From mummy and daddy [Hilly and Flicker], can't wait till you wear these for us again". I'd had a rough period of two months without playing. I was like a rubber duck. Yet here were these two guys bigging me up, boosting my ego, and it was such a lift. I went to the gaffer and told him I wanted to leave the club for Rochdale. "Sell me," I said. And he did!'

For the first time since 2002, people at Rochdale were using the 'P' word without any sense of irony. The fact that the coming season also marked the club's centenary seemed to make the revolution all the more poignant.

'The team I joined at Rochdale for my first full season there was incredible,' Le Fondre says. 'It had a great blend of youth and experience. So many players, me included, went on to play at a higher level. That's testament to Hilly and Flicker in both finding the players with potential and then tapping into that potential to help the players fulfil it.'

Le Fondre played every league game that season and finished the club's top scorer as Rochdale made Wembley for the first time in their history, representing the town in the League Two play-off final. Sadly, Dale would lose to Stockport County, the very side Le Fondre left just the summer before.

'It was bittersweet for me, of course,' he says. 'To lose to the team I'd just left, and see them go up, it was hard. It was kind of a grudge match for me, I guess, against my hometown club. Personally, I'd had a good season, scoring 18 or 19 goals and felt that was vital in getting us to Wembley, but we just didn't have enough on the day to see it through. I was happy though, I was playing games and scoring goals. Since then, I've been quite lucky in that I've been available for most games at every club I've been at.'

The disappointment clearly didn't dampen Le Fondre's enthusiasm. He strode through the following season in even better form, once again finishing as the club's top scorer, this time with 21 goals. Again, though, it wasn't enough to secure Rochdale that elusive automatic promotion spot and the side crashed in the play-offs, this time at the semi-final stage to Gillingham.

'After that first season, it opened our eyes as to what we were capable of,' Le Fondre says. 'We had a core of technical players who weren't playing typical League Two football. We blossomed thanks to the guidance of Hilly and Flicker. Yes, we didn't make promotion again, although we were close, but it was an amazing time for me. It was my first experience of brotherhood at a football club. The players had such a great bond. It sounds ridiculous but, if we went on a night out, it would literally be 15 of us out of 20. If we did something, we near enough did it all together. A lot of the time, Hilly and Flicker weren't too far behind us either. This is what really helped us on the pitch, I believe.'

Sadly, Le Fondre wouldn't get a third tilt at firing Rochdale to promotion. Even to this day he is remembered readily as 'the player who was sold to pay a tax bill' (not that he wouldn't have outgrown the club at some stage, such was his talent). In the first month of the 2009/2010 season, Rotherham United, at the time occupying League Two along with Rochdale, paid a sum believed to be around £250,000 for the striker. The transfer, understandably, was met with disquiet from the Dale support, with mutterings of it being essential to keep HMRC at bay.

'It was a hard one for me,' Le Fondre says. 'The two seasons prior, me and Chris Dagnall were always fighting for that number one striker spot. We both scored roughly about the same amount of goals too, so there was nothing between us. Going into that third season at Rochdale, I'm thinking, "I need to be the main man here and I need to score more than 21 goals if I want to play at a higher level."

'It was August, right after the Port Vale game, and I had been on the bench. We drew the game. On the coach on the way home, I got a message from Flicker. It said, "We're going to have to accept a bid from Rotherham for you." I looked down the aisle of the coach to where he was sat. He was looking at me. He looked heartbroken. When I got home, I started crying. I knew I was leaving my brothers behind. However, when I reflected on it, I knew, in a way, it was a move I had to make if I wanted to be the main man. When I spoke to the Rotherham manager, Mark Robins, he made it absolutely clear that's what I would be. As he was previously a striker at Manchester United, I felt he was best placed to help me reach the next level in terms of playing style and, obviously, goals. So, reluctantly, I left Rochdale, but I knew that, without them, I wouldn't have had the opportunity I was now getting.'

He's all white: Alan Reeves, the perfect lower-league centre-half. ©*Rochdale AFC/ Mark Wilbraham*

Mick Docherty takes a training session circa 1993. ©*Rochdale AFC/Mark Wilbraham*

The club's fourth-highest goalscorer, Steve Whitehall. ©*Rochdale AFC/Mark Wilbraham*

Sibling rivalry: Shaun Reid takes on his brother Peter during a Bury v Rochdale derby in 1994. 'I kicked lumps out him,' said Shaun. ©*Harry McGuire/iScoop_Photos*

Shaun Reid and Steve Whitehall in a foot race with Preston North End defender David Moyes in 1994. ©*Harry McGuire/ iScoop_Photos*

Rochdale captain Andy Thackeray with Liverpool captain John Barnes ahead of the 1996 FA Cup third round clash. 'It was an opportunity for the players to show what they had against the best there was at the time,' said manager Mick Docherty. ©*Rochdale AFC/ Mark Wilbraham*

'Are they quick or are they quick?' Rochdale defender Paul Butler summarises the Liverpool attack. ©*Rochdale AFC/Mark Wilbraham*

Steve Parkin stamps his authority on a promotion-chasing Rochdale side. ©*Rochdale AFC/Mark Wilbraham*

Paddy McCourt shows his silky footwork. ©*Rochdale AFC/Mark Wilbraham*

Kevin Townson takes the attack to Rushden & Diamonds FC during Rochdale's first play-off appearance, in 2002. ©*Rochdale AFC/ Mark Wilbraham*

Get in: Paul Simpson nets against Rushden & Diamonds. Rochdale would sadly lose the two-legged play-off semi-final 4-3. ©*Rochdale AFC/ Mark Wilbraham*

Dave Flitcroft in Rochdale's 2003 FA Cup fifth round tie is watched closely by Paul Butler, by now in a Wolves shirt. *©Rochdale AFC/Mark Wilbraham*

Rochdale captain Gareth Griffiths battles gamely as Rochdale lose 3-1 to Wolves. *©Rochdale AFC/Mark Wilbraham*

Matt Gilks takes control of his area against Torquay. *©Rochdale AFC/ Dan Youngs*

Rickie Lambert discovers he is a natural forward thanks to Steve Parkin. ©*Rochdale AFC/Dan Youngs*

'You what?' Keith Hill begins his crusade to take Rochdale AFC out of the 'Rochdale Division'. ©*Rochdale AFC/Dan Youngs*

Ben Muirhead hits home the winning penalty against Darlington in 2008 to send Rochdale to Wembley for the first time. ©*Rochdale AFC/Dan Youngs*

Keith Hill takes in the fact he is the first manager to lead out Rochdale at the national stadium. ©*Rochdale AFC/Dan Youngs*

Rochdale captain Gary Jones gets to grips with the Stockport County midfield in the play-off final. ©*Rochdale AFC/Dan Youngs*

A young Will Buckley is thrown into the mix at Wembley. ©*Rochdale AFC/Dan Youngs*

Adam Le Fondre celebrates one of his many goals for Rochdale. ©*Rochdale AFC/ Dan Youngs*

He's one of our own: Craig Dawson becomes the new Alan Reeves for Rochdale. ©*Rochdale AFC/Dan Youngs*

Chris O'Grady just prior to hitting the goal against Northampton Town that will promote Rochdale to the third tier for only their second promotion. ©*Rochdale AFC/Dan Youngs*

Neither Steve Eyre nor John Coleman could recapture the magic of Keith Hill as Dale slid back into the 'Rochdale Division' in 2012. ©*Rochdale AFC/Dan Youngs*

Ian Henderson cushions a side-footed volley beyond Paddy Kenny as Rochdale knock Leeds United out of the FA Cup in 2014. ©*Rochdale AFC/Dan Youngs*

Calvin Andrew rushes to greet jubilant fans after keeping Rochdale's League One play-off hopes alive in 2015. ©*Rochdale AFC/Dan Youngs*

It was ironic, then, that, despite selling their primary goal-getter, Rochdale went on to be promoted that season while Rotherham did not, regardless of Le Fondre scoring an incredible 30 goals for the Millers.

'Funnily enough, it was like the Stockport situation at Wembley,' he chuckles. 'I seem to move to a club and my previous club goes up. Of course, I was buzzing for all the people at Rochdale, but was disappointed I couldn't get Rotherham promoted. We'd been in the top three most of that season and then fell away in the last month. We put so much effort into it and looked like one of the best teams in the league, but lost in the play-off final. We threw it away, really.'

Le Fondre did eventually escape League Two when he signed for Championship side Reading for £350,000 in August 2011. It was here the initials A.L.F. would gain wider recognition.

'I think I missed just two games for Rotherham and scored close to 60 goals for them,' he says. 'I knew people were watching me. Rotherham offered me a new contract but I said no. I'd done four years of League Two and scored nearly 100 goals at this point. I knew now was the time to move higher. I didn't give them an ultimatum, but they knew if they didn't sell me at that point, they would lose me for nothing at the end of the season.

'They rejected a few bids from Sheffield Wednesday, who had come in for me. It was then getting close to deadline day and I'd scored four goals in the first five games of the new season. I was playing more as a number ten than a number nine, kind of like a split striker, and I was enjoying it, but then my agent said, "Something is going to happen here really fast and it will be between two big clubs." Before I knew it, he was back on saying Reading had had a £350,000 bid accepted and I was to go and discuss personal terms. To be honest, I wasn't bothered about personal terms, I just wanted to play in the Championship and prove myself there. I got in my car and set off for Reading. I went the wrong bloody way in the pissing rain, too!'

Once he did find his way to Berkshire, Le Fondre had no trouble settling in.

'It was a bit like Rochdale in a way,' he says. 'It was a family club, and had a very welcoming dressing room. Obviously being a player from League Two, you have to adjust and prove yourself. The levels of ability and commitment required are massive and I knew I had to achieve them quickly. The tenacity and intensity of players in this league is immense. The demands on me as a player were huge. It took a lot of work on my part.

'We had a great run, though. From Christmas onwards, I think we only lost two games. To get promoted to the Premier League just 12 months after moving there was beyond anything I could have dreamed of. We had a great formula. We played 4-4-2 with Noel Hunt and Jason Roberts up front. Roberts at that time was the best striker I'd ever seen in terms of being capable of bullying the opposition. There wasn't a centre-half in the Championship who was physically capable of stopping him. He could pretty much take on a whole back four on his own. This was perfect for me. When I came on, the defenders were too worried about getting in a wrestling match with him, so I could just dance around and do my thing.'

Le Fondre scored 12 goals as Reading won promotion to the Premier League and, from there, he enjoyed massive success and acclaim. Not only did he score on his Premier League debut against Stoke, he netted against his favourite club, Manchester United, and followed that up with goals against Arsenal and Chelsea, culminating in him eventually winning January's Player of the Month Award in 2013.

'Adapting from League Two to the Championship was much harder than Championship to Premier League for me,' he says. 'I didn't find the step up as hard as that and that's the truth. The hardest bit was it sinking in. I had to pinch myself. I'd gone from League Two to the Premier League in 12 months. I was now on *Match of the Day* on a Saturday night. It was surreal. You get recognised a lot more and you get more things for free! People are looking to sponsor you all over the place when you're in the Premier League. For me, though, it didn't change my life that much. My lifestyle was still very much family first.'

His goal against Manchester United caps Le Fondre's highlight reel, however.

'To bag a goal against Manchester United the day after my birthday must have been written in the stars,' he says. 'It was an amazing game. I think that game still holds the record in the Premier League for the most goals scored inside 30 minutes. I think it was 4-3 after 35 minutes. Crazy. Yes indeed, I have a lot of fond memories from my time in the Premier League.'

Despite Le Fondre's efforts, Reading were relegated after one season back in the top tier and he became something of a Championship nomad, having spells at Cardiff, Bolton and Wolves without ever capturing his earlier form.

'I stayed with Reading for another season and we thought we would bounce back right away,' he says. 'However, we missed out on the play-offs by one goal. Then financial trouble hit and the threat of a points deduction. It pushed me out of the door. My boyhood hero, Ole Gunnar Solskjaer, phoned me and said he wanted me at Cardiff. Sadly, I didn't get the goal return there I would have liked, but sometimes the football didn't suit the way I played and these things are out of your control as a player. That's life.

'I then began to bounce around clubs. I enjoyed Bolton first time around, but made a bad decision joining Wolves. Rangers in Scotland were interested at one point, but I ended up at Wigan, before going back to Bolton. This time, I was back to being on the bench a lot though, and it did get to the point where I was questioning if this was the life for me. I'd always just wanted to play football and score goals, not rot in a stand. It was mentally draining because I was doing more than enough in training to warrant a start. Something had to give. As it happened, the club had to sell Gary Madine in January, so I got a bit more game time and helped the club stay in the Championship that season with a few goals. I thought that would stand me in good stead for the next season. I had a great pre-season, scored a few goals and then ended up not playing in the first two games of the season. I thought, "Nah, I'm not having this. I'm tapping out."'

Since 2018, Le Fondre has become a household name in Australia, playing for Sydney FC. Life in the A-League seems to have also helped him rediscover that lethal touch in front of goal.

'Sydney came in for me and Bolton boss Phil Parkinson said I could go. He said I had to wait until we'd played Leeds midweek in the cup, but I'd already sorted my flight. I said, "Thanks but no thanks." It was very emotional that day. Me and my partner knew moving to Australia would be a huge change for both of us, but we said, "Yeah, let's go for it." It's been absolutely brilliant out here. I've not looked back. I'm scoring goals and winning trophies. It's what makes me happiest and it's all I've ever wanted to do.'

Inevitably, Le Fondre will have to consider his long-term future, however. A huge player of football management computer games, could this be his future path for real?

'It's hard to be a manager these days as they don't have a long shelf life,' he says. 'I don't fancy spending long spells unemployed, so I don't think it's the job for me. I like the idea of being an under-23 or under-18 manager, though. I like the idea of developing players, managing their growth into the first team. I think I have a lot of good experiences I can pass on. For me, that's something I would've loved as a kid myself. Someone who had played X amount of games and scored X amount of goals telling me they could get me to the next level quicker than I currently was doing. I do this with my second cousin who is currently at Burnley. I advise him on the pitfalls that you can fall into and how to avoid them.'

We round off our chat with Le Fondre identifying the traits that made him an elite footballer; the difference between him and the thousands of other hopefuls.

'If you speak to a lot of the coaches I worked with, they would say I was ruthless,' he says. 'I wasn't born ruthless, it was something I developed. Hilly and Flicker played a huge part in my desire to achieve – to work relentlessly on my finishing. There were countless times I had to be dragged off the training pitch because I would spend 45 minutes on finishing drills. It was my bread and butter and I was determined to make the most of it. Would I hold the ball up? Now and again, yes, but, at the end of the day, my job is to put chances away and I made sure I worked so hard at that, that, if a chance fell to me, it would more often than not result in a goal. That's what got me to the Premier League and it was a path started by the management at Rochdale.'

Craig Dawson

2009–2011

FOOTBALL FANS take great delight in chanting 'he's one of our own' when a homegrown player performs admirably on the field of play.

It's no different within the stands at Rochdale AFC, where there have been few local players to attract the native pride Craig Dawson has.

It's easy to understand how a great many who have played for nearby Manchester United or Liverpool have grown up supporting these clubs and claim to have fulfilled a boyhood dream when stepping out in their colours.

It's not so easy to recall many Rochdale players who have made the equivalent claim.

But when Dawson delivers just that assertion, there's no doubting him. Here is an affable, genuine fellow whose love of the club, and football in general, is palpable. He entered the professional game the less fashionable way and his career trajectory since has all the substance of a *Roy of the Rovers* comic strip.

It's a cliche, granted, but there is no denying the involuntary double take one performs when considering Dawson went from playing non-league football to the Premier League in just two years, before going on to win England under-21 caps, representing Great Britain at the Olympic Games and playing in a Europa League semi-final.

Not that the man himself is in any way thunderstruck. There is no arrogance or showy cockiness here, just a quiet self-confidence in his ability and an unwavering dedication to the biggest factor of all in achieving success – hard work.

Born in Rochdale in 1990, Dawson was raised in the Spotland area of the town, just half a mile along the road from the stadium of the same name. He attended Meanwood Primary School and Oulder Hill High School during his seminal years.

'When I was at Meanwood, Rochdale's football in the community coach, Keith Hicks, used to come in a couple of times a week to run a soccer school,' Dawson recalls. 'I got involved and, as part of that, we'd get invited to Rochdale games. A lot of my school friends were big Rochdale fans anyway, so there was a good few of us used to go when we were young. I remember Kevin Townson was playing up front around that time and Steve Parkin was manager. Rochdale were doing quite well and it was good to watch. I collected quite a few replica shirts growing up.

'It was definitely always my dream to be a professional footballer, but I had never signed for a club's centre of excellence or academy. I just didn't get that opportunity. Nothing came of the Rochdale soccer schools or anything that I tried anywhere else. It didn't look like it was ever going to happen. As I went through high school, I kept myself fit by running a lot and I played other sports, too. I was a batter for Rochdale Cricket Club in the summer months, but it was always football that interested me the most.'

A teenage Dawson kept himself in pocket as a glass collector at the Dog and Partridge pub on Bury Road, and kept himself fit by turning out for Rochdale St Clements, a local amateur side.

'I suppose I got my first proper taste of "men's football" when I was playing for St Clements' first team,' he says. 'My brother Andy is four years older than me and he had been playing for them for a while. He was in the first team and I had started out in the fourth team. I got a lucky break when the first team was a player short one day and I found myself drafted in just because I was there. I did well and got a run of games after that. I know I'm a defender now, but I was playing right wing, up front, everywhere, back then. It was my first experience of adult football, and it was a steep learning curve, but I loved it. I stayed in the first team for the rest of that season and we won the league and cup double.

'That was my life at that point. I was working in the Dog on a Thursday and Friday night, glass collecting, as I wasn't old enough to serve beer, and playing for St Clements on a Saturday, before going back to the Dog to do another shift at night.

'By this time, I was at Hopwood Hall College, too, studying for my A-levels. I was studying PE, IT and sociology, of all things. I suppose I eventually saw myself going to university to study sports science or coaching.'

In 2007, with Dawson aged 17, a well-known representative from Northern Premier League side Radcliffe Borough saw potential in the teenager and, before long, he was an integral part of their starting XI. It was here he established his reputation as a goalscoring centre-half, notching 15 times in 95 appearances.

'Bernard Manning Junior was the chairman of Radcliffe at the time,' says Dawson. 'I went to high school with his son, Ben. He knew of me because both me and Ben played football for Oulder Hill and he would watch the games. He'd seen me play for St Clements a few times, too. He was in the Dog one Friday night and he said, "Are you coming down to Radcliffe for training?" I laughed it off. I thought he was joking. He kept on at me, though, and then I knew he was serious. I agreed and he took me down there.

'Initially it was just for pre-season training. I did OK and they put me in the team for a friendly against Salford. The manager at the time, Kevin Glendon, was worried about me because I was only 17 and I was playing in an adult league. I ended up making a tackle on the halfway line and took this guy right out. I remember seeing Bernard and Kevin on the sideline laughing and nodding in approval. Radcliffe signed me on the basis of that match.

'The standard in the Northern Premier was way higher than I'd experienced at St Clements up to that point, but I really liked the challenge of playing centre-half. There were a lot of ex-pros there – such as Mike Flynn who had been at Stockport. They all looked after me and taught me quite a lot.

'When I was at St Clements, I had played higher up the pitch and scored a few goals. My brother was a centre-half and always used to score from corners, so I tried to copy him. It became a habit. Everybody wants to score a goal in a game, but it's harder for defenders, obviously. I guess I got the knack from having played in different positions while I was developing as a player at St Clements.'

By now, Rochdale manager Keith Hill, in his first spell in charge of the club, was developing a reputation for bringing on promising young players. Word of Dawson's Radcliffe performances reached Spotland. However, it took Hill a while to decide that the teenager would be more than capable of making the step up from non-league to League Two.

'I'd played a good six months at Radcliffe and was doing well,' Dawson remembers. 'I was on £50 a week and was made up that someone was paying me to play football. I really enjoyed the laugh I had with my team-mates and the experience on the pitch. I'd gone from playing on fields and parks to a tidy little ground. It was still a far cry from the professional environments I've played at since, but I wasn't really thinking about anything else too far into the future. Then I got told Accrington Stanley were interested in me and then Rochdale and Crewe Alexandra shortly after.

'Rochdale invited me down to train with them and I couldn't believe it – my hometown club. I went there for a month and trained with the first team, but it was a massive step up. Massive. After the month was up, I was told they weren't interested. I was gutted. Then Crewe put a decent bid in, which was accepted by Radcliffe. I went down to speak to them but I turned Crewe down. I felt it wasn't the right move for me. It was a huge decision to do that, being a part-time footballer, but it didn't feel right. A week later, [Rochdale assistant manager] Dave Flitcroft phoned me up and said, "We want to sign you, if you still want to be part of what we're doing here?" He told me they were willing to take a chance on me. I was over the moon. Radcliffe accepted their bid and I went straight over there and signed. It was funny, because all my mates were still watching

Rochdale every week. I didn't tell them I'd been training with the club. When I told them I'd actually signed for Dale they were all well chuffed. They couldn't believe it.'

Dawson signed a two-year contract with Rochdale in February 2009, but was allowed to see out the season with Radcliffe as part of the deal. He left the club in style, too, being named their Player of the Year.

'Hilly decided I could still play for Radcliffe at the weekends and train with the Rochdale first team during the week, getting to know the lads and so on. I wasn't going to walk straight into the first team, so he wanted me playing competitive games. During the week, Hilly and Dave Flitcroft put a lot of work into me. I think they saw me as their little project. They wanted to make me a success. They were doing one-on-one drills with me – a lot of extra work. I took that into my games for Radcliffe and felt I improved massively. The difference training every day made to me was immense.

'I had a good year at Radcliffe and was sad to leave. It was a good club and I made a lot of friends. It was great to be honoured the way I was, being named Player of the Year, and everybody there wished me well, now I'd achieved what I'd wanted to do since I was a boy. I was a full-time footballer.

'I remember walking into the office at Rochdale with Colin Garlick [the club's chief executive] to sign my contract and Kevin Glendon was with me. He said, "Everything you want is right here. This is just the start. You need to crack on and work hard. This is your opportunity." I knew he was right. I thought, "I'm finally on the ladder."

'Rochdale gave me a programme to work on over the summer to get me ready for a full-time pre-season. I was the fittest I'd ever been after that. I met up with everyone for pre-season and we went away to Spain for a week of intense training. I was welcomed fully into the fold and very much felt part of the squad.

'Nathan Stanton and Rory McArdle had formed a great partnership the previous season in the centre of Rochdale's defence. I accepted that it would be a very difficult partnership to break.

Part of the deal that saw me move to Rochdale was that Radcliffe got a friendly out of it. I started that game alongside Rory, but then he dislocated his shoulder. We were only a couple of weeks away from the first league game. I was given my chance a lot earlier than expected because of Rory's injury and I found myself starting against Port Vale away to start the season. I remember Joey Thompson scored for us in a 1-1 draw and the away end going mad. It was incredible. I would have been stood in there myself a few years ago. I remember going back to Rochdale Cricket Club after the game, because my brother had been playing for them that day, and the attention I got was amazing. Everybody wanted to speak to me about the game and how it felt to play.'

Dawson's first season at Spotland was a rousing success. His goals from centre-half and his ability to play the ball out from the back contributed to Rochdale's first promotion since 1969. Quite rightly, he was named in the League Two PFA Team of the Year.

'To establish myself and get that much success in my first full season as a professional footballer was unbelievable. I owe so much to Keith Hill and Dave Flitcroft for that. I joined a very well-organised, talented side that was already well on the way to being successful. I felt like I slotted straight in and, even to this day, I'm still in touch with a lot of lads from that time.

'The morale was superb. Rory McArdle was a big character in the dressing room and Tom Kennedy was the biggest joker when I was there. I got on best with Jason Kennedy, I would say, though. We were both quite quiet in the dressing room, so we seemed to gravitate towards each other. Joey Thompson was a Rochdale lad as well, so we shared car journeys. We were both the focus of extra training, too, so we spent a lot of time together.'

However, just as his performances for Radcliffe had attracted Rochdale, his performances at Rochdale enticed the Premier League. As the summer transfer window was about to close, West Bromwich Albion snapped up Dawson for an undisclosed fee on a three-year contract. The Dale faithful were not to be deprived of seeing the star defender continue to light up League One, however, as the Baggies loaned Dawson back to the club for the remainder of the 2010/11 season.

'I was aware of the interest from West Brom and was conscious that Rochdale had turned down a few bids,' says Dawson. 'In the end, the club decided to let me go and it was a chance for me to go to the Premier League, which nobody would ever turn down. From a football point of view, I was excited but, emotionally, I was very sad to leave Rochdale. I knew I'd be coming back on loan for the rest of the season as part of the deal, so that made it easier. The best place for me to keep developing at that time was at Rochdale, as I wouldn't have gone straight into West Brom's first team.

'Having finished the season strongly with Rochdale, I arrived at West Brom in the summer of 2011. I did a full pre-season with the club. I felt ready, but the step up was incredible. Roberto Di Matteo and Dan Ashworth had been the ones to sign me, but, by the time I arrived at West Brom, they'd gone and Roy Hodgson was in charge. He was a great coach, but, in hindsight, I maybe should have had a spell in the Championship first, as I can't overstate the increase in standard enough. That said, I learned so much by training with Premier League players. It's an experience you can't beat. Yes, I had two frustrating years at West Brom where I didn't play enough games, but I never stopped learning. Learning was all well and good, but not playing games did hinder my development. Looking back on it, I should definitely have gone out on loan sooner.

'You see, you get away with so much more in League One and Two. Here, in the Premier League, every tiny mistake costs you – and the pace the game is played at doesn't give you any time. It was difficult to get in the team.

'I was given my debut against Bournemouth in the League Cup in August. They weren't a Premier League team back then and we won 4-1. I remember I was then given an opportunity in the Premier League at Swansea a few weeks later. We were 2-0 down after 25 minutes and lost the game 3-0. After that, Roy Hodgson decided to go with Gareth McAuley and Jonas Olsson and they formed a great partnership.'

One positive that did follow Dawson's Baggies debut was him being called up into the England under-21 squad by Stuart Pearce.

'It was out of the blue,' Dawson recalls. 'I remember the car picked me up at the house to take me to training. It was an England-branded car and everyone on the street was out looking at me. I didn't even think I would make the bench for the qualifying game against Azerbaijan, never mind start. I scored with my first touch down at Watford wearing an England shirt. It was very special.

'We won almost every game in that qualifying campaign and then went to Israel for the European Championship finals in 2013, but we simply didn't perform out there and finished bottom of the group. It was great for me to experience an international tournament, though. I had so many texts of support after each appearance for the under-21s. It was great.'

Clearly impressing while with the national under-21 side, Dawson was also selected by Pearce for the Great Britain 2012 Olympic football team, where he went on to score a penalty in the quarter-final shoot-out defeat to South Korea.

'I was doing some running ahead of pre-season, and had my phone buried in my bag somewhere, when the Olympic squad was announced,' Dawson says. 'I didn't have a clue I was part of it. I dug my phone out later and had so many missed calls and text messages from friends and colleagues. Loads of media people were trying to get hold of me, too. I thought, "Wow, I'd better go home!"

'To be a part of Team GB in London was a huge honour. I played alongside Ryan Giggs and Craig Bellamy, who were absolute perfectionists. Stuart Pearce is a very passionate man, too, but he's really calm in the dressing room, which is probably not what people would expect to hear. He puts a lot of work into developing his players. He was brilliant during the Olympics. Never in my wildest dreams did I think I would be part of something like that. The opening ceremony alone was breathtaking.'

On the domestic front, Dawson had committed his next three years to West Brom but further management changes hampered his first-team progress. Blackburn Rovers, Leicester City, Leeds United,

Nottingham Forest and Bolton Wanderers all vied to exploit the situation, with the latter managing to get Dawson in on loan. While it meant dropping down a level to the Championship for a while, Dawson was simply happy to play regular football again, scoring four goals in his first six appearances.

'I just needed to play games and it was only the England under-21s that had kept me going in that regard. Bolton provided an opportunity to play on a more regular basis. They needed a centre-half and I was it. My time there gave me the confidence I needed to reaffirm I was more than capable at a higher level.'

He certainly is. A spell at Watford would follow and then a move to a rejuvenated West Ham United, under David Moyes, where a Europa League semi-final would beckon in 2022.

'I want to play at as high a level as I can for as long as I can,' Dawson says. 'I'll just keep working as hard as I can every day with the ultimate aim of making the senior England squad. Look at the career Rickie Lambert had after leaving Rochdale. That's what I aim to do. If I look after myself, hopefully I'll keep improving.

'You know, when I look back, Keith Hill and David Flitcroft made Rochdale an unbelievable experience for me. They made the place like one big a family. If it wasn't for the work they put into me during and after training, I wouldn't be where I am today.'

The Others

BEFORE WE can finish this section, there still remain other players to occupy the timespan covered by this book who turned out for Rochdale and went on to play at an elite level. For differing reasons, I was unable to speak to them directly. Still, it would be remiss of me not to reflect on their time at Rochdale and the impact, if any, the club has had on their subsequent careers.

Paul Butler
1991–1996

Unfairly maligned for several seasons as being carried by Alan Reeves, Butler triumphantly proved his doubters wrong when his centre-half partner left for the bright lights of London and the Premier League.

While Reeves was the elegant ball player of the two, Butler was the tough-tackling but pacey foil as the pair formed, under manager Dave Sutton and then Mick Docherty, a partnership that helped Dale make repeated pushes for the play-offs in the early 1990s.

Once Reeves signed for Wimbledon in 1994, Butler, far from being lost, stepped into the role of leading man with aplomb and his performances would eventually pave the way to him earning a big-money move of his own.

It was something Butler had never imagined when he was younger, growing up in the Manchester district of Moston, the antithesis of a leafy suburb (said confidently as this writer's grandparents were born, raised and still live there). His tough surroundings clearly helped form his no-nonsense approach to football.

Physically imposing and possessing a face that said 'don't mess with me' even when relaxed, Butler typified a fourth-tier centre-half. Unlike Reeves, however, he took a while to find the kind of form that made him stand out. One early appearance saw him come on as a substitute, give away a penalty and then get carried off injured.

After several seasons of competitiveness in the top half of the basement division, many Rochdale fans felt the 1994/95 season could be the one to remember. However, losing Reeves in the September was a blow to compound a string of inconsistent results and, by November, everybody, including Sutton himself, had had enough. Mick Docherty, son of Manchester United legend Tommy, eventually stepped up to take charge of the first team. Results improved enough initially that relegation never seemed a real issue, and there was an area final appearance in the Auto Windscreens Shield, but the early swagger of the Sutton era had gone. An end-of-season slump left many fans despondent. The following season followed a similar pattern. Shining through it all, however, Butler was one of very few positives.

His fine form in a mostly poorly performing Rochdale side attracted interest and his expected departure came in the summer of 1996 – a few miles down the road to arch rivals Bury. His destination proved somewhat disappointing to the supporters, even though the reported £100,000 fee paid by the Shakers was a welcome boon.

As it turned out, Butler's move to Bury proved an inspired one, and his presence helped push the Shakers up to the old First Division (what is now the Championship). However, as he did at Rochdale, Butler outgrew Gigg Lane and an amazing £1m offer saw him move to Sunderland, where he went on to achieve promotion to the Premier League and an international cap for the Republic of Ireland. However, his first attempt at football in the top flight was not a fruitful one and, after only a handful of appearances, he was left in the dark at the Stadium of Light.

He next found himself at second-tier side Wolverhampton Wanderers, where he had spent some time on loan the previous season, and would again go on to compete in the Premier League with the Black Country club. After Wolves' relegation, Butler began a third assault on achieving Premier League status, this time with Leeds United. However, despite initially coming close by reaching the play-off final in 2006, manager Kevin Blackwell lost his job the following season, paving the way for Dennis Wise. By his own admission, Butler failed to see eye-to-eye with the self-styled hardman and so began his downward trajectory.

He returned to League Two with MK Dons and then Chester City. When playing against Rochdale for the latter, he scored an own goal that led to him offering the Dale faithful a less than complimentary salute.

Butler has now retired as a player.

Grant Holt
2004–2006 and 2016

Despite the number of clubs on his CV, it is more than fair to suggest that, if it wasn't for Rochdale AFC, Grant Holt's career could have petered out into something unremarkable.

As it transpired, the prolific, powerful forward, for a time at least, became the most sought-after English striker in the Premier League.

It was in 2004 that the then-Rochdale manager Steve Parkin first saw something in Holt, something that all before him seemed to have missed. At the time, Holt was what Parkin described as a raw striker, mostly treading water in Sheffield Wednesday's reserves – but the potential was there.

Running a club like Rochdale, where lavish transfer fees and ego-massaging wages are about as likely as caviar in a pound shop, Parkin's strategy hinged on finding players such as Holt – low-cost risks that could yield both short-term success for his team and long-term profit for the club.

The risk paid off. Holt made 83 appearances for Parkin's Rochdale side, scored 42 goals and created countless others before he was sold to Nottingham Forest for around £300,000.

Holt wasn't a novice to the senior game before he first found success at Rochdale. The Cumbrian had already dealt with plenty of the knocks life dishes out to sports people all too regularly.

Holt began his career as a youth player at his hometown club Carlisle United, but was released when he was 18. He has said publicly that he found this to be a sobering experience, one that forced him to find a 'proper job' as a tyre fitter, while he endeavoured to keep himself sharp on the football field by turning out for part-time outfit Workington Reds.

He did eventually manage to win a contract at Halifax Town who, at the time, were in the old Third Division, but, when that didn't work out, he tried his luck in a different hemisphere at Western Australian club Sorrento. A return to part-time football in England beckoned with Barrow and then a summer in Singapore with Sengkang Marine.

It has been documented that Holt went there on the understanding that he would be signed by Carlisle on his return. However, the Cumbrian club entered administration and the deal was cancelled, so he had to go back to Barrow and make ends meet with a part-time job in a factory.

Holt was resigned to spending a further two seasons at Barrow, at the time in the Northern Premier League. His resolve hadn't dampened any, however, and he continued to put himself out there, travelling all over the country for trials with full-time professional clubs.

It was Sheffield Wednesday who eventually signed him in March 2003. By January 2004, aged 22, Holt had made 30 appearances for the Owls, half of them as a substitute, but only managed four goals. Regardless, he had done enough to persuade the eagle-eyed Parkin to bring him to Rochdale for the meagre sum of £10,000.

In the previous section of this book, Parkin described Holt as thus, 'I'd seen Grant Holt a little bit before I signed him. He was very raw but effective. I knew I could bring him on. He had the right attributes to be a fantastic striker and just needed a little work. He proved a very worthwhile investment of our time.'

The rawness referred to by Parkin was evident as Holt made a slow start to his Rochdale career. Holt himself has since publicly joked about the fact his new team-mates questioned the manager's sanity after a few of his early displays.

However, it didn't take long for Parkin's faith (and management) to be repaid. The remainder of the 2003/04 season brought three goals in 14 appearances for Holt, but it was during the next – 24 goals in 45 games – where the striker would show what he was capable of. The emergence of Rickie Lambert only helped his game further, each bringing out the best in the other, and together they formed the best strike partnership this writer has witnessed at Spotland.

A powerful forward, with technical ability and a sound reading of the game to boot, Holt very quickly became the nemesis of lower-league centre-halves the country over. As well as unsettling defences, he also held up the ball brilliantly, which brought others into the fray.

The 2005/06 season brought optimism for Rochdale fans as both Holt and Rickie Lambert hit top form. By January, Holt had bagged 15 goals in 24 games and a first promotion since 1969 did not look such a far-fetched notion.

It was then the harsh truth of what it is like to be a Rochdale supporter came to bear. Like a shy child with the best toy in the nursery, our prize asset was coveted by more illustrious rivals. Holt was sold to Nottingham Forest for a fee reported to be around £300,000.

A bitter pill for the fans to swallow perhaps, but were it not for the initial chance Parkin was willing to take, and the time he was willing to invest, Rochdale would never have benefited from Holt's buried brilliance in the first place.

As it transpired, his transfer to Forest wasn't quite the expected springboard to greatness many of the Dale faithful thought it might be. Despite landing a Player of the Year award from the fans of the previous European Cup winners, Holt's time on the Trent was marred by an uneasy relationship with manager Colin Calderwood, who would often play the striker out of position.

A brief loan to Championship club Blackpool seemed an ideal move for Holt at the time, but, surprisingly, his next permanent move would be back down to League Two, where Shrewsbury Town, managed by former Dale boss Paul Simpson, broke their club transfer record by signing him for £170,000. His time with the Shrews was a tremendous success. While there, he inevitably scored against Rochdale and, spectacularly, scored five goals in a single game against Wycombe Wanderers.

In 2009, Holt moved to Norwich City where he would become part of Paul Lambert's amazing revolution, which took the Carrow Road club from League One to the Premier League in successive seasons. He scored his first Premier League goal in the third game of the 2011/12 season, against Chelsea, and went on to score a total of 15 league goals in that first campaign at the top table. He was the darling of football pundits across the land and widely tipped to make Roy Hodgson's first England squad for the 2012 European Championship. They even went as far as to ask for his medical notes. Not bad for a player in his 30s.

From there, things turned a little sour. Holt handed in a transfer request not long after being named Norwich's Player of the Year, before eventually signing a new three-year-contract to stay at the club. He wouldn't see it out and, in 2013, Holt's time in East Anglia came to an end, the player eventually frustrated by the system employed by the defensive-minded Chris Hughton, who had replaced Paul Lambert in charge. Norwich sold Holt to Championship side Wigan for about £2m, from where he spent marginal spells on loan at Aston Villa, Huddersfield Town and Wolverhampton Wanderers. He also suffered a serious knee injury during this period.

With Wigan's relegation from the Championship in 2015, Holt was released five months into the following season.

But, just as some people out there were suggesting Holt's career as a first-team regular had entered terminal decline, the powerhouse forward decided to come 'home'. In February 2016, Rochdale manager Keith Hill surprised everyone by announcing

Holt's return to Spotland on a deal until the season's end. While he would only score two goals during this 14-game spell (mostly substitute appearances), he brought a visible lift to the other players on the field.

Regardless, Holt was released by Rochdale at the end of the 2015/16 season and went on to sign for Scottish Championship side Hibs, fresh from their Scottish Cup victory. He has now retired from playing.

Keith Hill spoke to me about Holt's second spell with Rochdale.

'What separated Grant from the rest and made him an elite footballer? Well, first and foremost it was his ability and that has never been in question. On top of that, he matched the attributes he has as a striker with hard work, endeavour and game knowledge. That's what separates the talent from the rest. Grant Holt had that game knowledge in abundance. He was capable of marrying his ability with game management during a match and that equalled performance. He knew exactly what to do and when and where to do it – that intelligence definitely separated him from the rest.

'When he came back here to play for me, everybody at the club already had a respect for him, myself included. He brought a lot of knowledge to the changing room. He's been there, seen it and done it, so the younger pros looked up to him. We also saw the impact he can have on the opposition. He still possessed that game knowledge that made him stand out during his first spell with the club. Putting it into action is a lot more difficult the older you get, but he demonstrated he still has all the attributes needed. I've no doubt he'll make a successful coach. He's got a lot of experience to pass on from every level of the game. He would make a very good coach for any manager because he was very good in the changing room here, not just for the younger players, but the senior members of the playing staff as well.'

Part III
The Cult

Shaun Reid

1982–1988 and 1992–1995

WHILE GARY Jones will rightly be remembered as one of the best Rochdale captains of all time, if not *the* best, there was another to dent the Spotland turf before him who may have fancied laying claim to that title.

Shaun Reid was a hard-working, tough-tackling, in-your-face midfielder who epitomised basement-division aggression and was the embodiment of what it is to be a terrace cult hero.

Perhaps, to a wider audience, he was slightly in the shadow of his more famous and successful footballing brother Peter, but Shaun was a decent footballer in his own right and loved by the Spotland faithful, who would sing with glee, 'Who needs Cantona when we've got Shaunie Reid!'

Interestingly, Shaun would only face Peter once in a competitive game: Bury v Rochdale in 1994, won by Shaun's side and not before he 'kicked the hell out of Peter', who had to be subbed off injured after 20 minutes.

Reid's steadfast contribution to almost perpetually struggling Rochdale sides during his two spells with the club was to his immense credit, as he racked up 289 appearances (which, at the time of publication has him ninth in the club's all-time list) and 19 goals.

Interestingly, Reid's 432 Football League appearances overall – which took in clubs such as Preston North End, York City, Bury and Chester City – were all in the 'Rochdale Division'.

'I could've played at a higher level,' he explains. 'But I had a lot of injuries throughout my career. Jesus Christ, when I look back – ankle reconstruction, two cruciate operations, three broken legs, two achilles tendons operated on – if there was an injury out there, I seemed to get it. It was down to the way I played the game. I was combative. A tackle in those days was a tackle. Not like it is now. I played against some hard people.

'For example, I remember we played Wimbledon in the League Cup [in 1987]. I always remember standing in the tunnel for the first leg at Spotland. They had John Fashanu, Vinnie Jones and all those names from that era. I heard this voice say, "No one fucks with the Wimbledon mafia." I looked round and, it was the funniest thing, because you've got all these hardmen, big six-footers, and it was little Terry Gibson at the front mouthing off. I've never laughed so much in my life. In that game, I was up against Vinnie Jones. It was a tough old battle but, that night, I battered him. I battered him and I outplayed him. He went on to bigger and better things, of course he did, but it proved to me I could compete with that level of player. I'm convinced I could've played at a higher level, I just never got the chance.'

Reid is a hard, up-front man, who makes no secret of his working-class background and political views, all shaped by his upbringing on Merseyside.

Raised in Huyton, a Liverpool border town that is the final resting place of original Beatle bassist Stuart Sutcliffe, Reid said it was football rather than music that mattered there.

'In Liverpool, back in the day, growing up in the mid-70s, it was all about playing football. I joined Huyton Boys and did quite well with them. We got to the quarter-finals of the national trophy. When I was in third year at school, I played in the fifth year's team as well. I was busy. I played most nights. Saturday morning, Saturday afternoon, Sunday morning and Sunday afternoon. That was my life growing up as a kid.

'My memories of Huyton itself are that it was a friendly place. Warm people. Kids playing footie. Everything was based around having a game of footie under a light. Wherever we *could* have a game, we *would* have a game. We'd finish school and we'd be in the playground until four, half four, and then we'd go home for a bite to eat and be back out playing footie. That's all we did.

'The actor Rex Harrison was born in Huyton, but from the football world there was obviously our kid [Peter Reid], Stevie Gerrard, Craig Hignett, Tony Hibbert and Joey Barton, either from the town itself or the surrounding area. For a small area, it's produced some decent footballers.

'It all started in the '60s when our kid [Peter] played for Huyton Boys and won the English schools' trophy. Huyton had only four schools at that time, so it was an astonishing achievement. From then on, it seemed to spark a football culture in the town and it seemed to produce player after player. It was a great place to be brought up.'

Reid says his brother actually had little influence on his own footballing path, however.

'Peter left home when he was 15 years old and I was only five at the time. He went to Bolton as an apprentice, so I hardly saw him. My football upbringing had little to do with him. I remember playing football outside, and, where we lived at the time, there were four houses on one side and three houses on the other, with gateways into each house. I remember playing there with a tennis ball against the older kids. Everyone joined in. It's all we lived for. Playing football with anything you could get your hands on.

'Nowadays, a lot of kids seem content to play football on a games console rather than doing it for real. That's reflective of society as a whole, sadly. It deprives them of learning to be sociable in a real environment. Of course, you fall out with people playing football, but you build a camaraderie. Even school football seems to have fallen by the wayside these days. I understand that teachers have got other things to concentrate on, but I always felt that football brought people together and built societies and communities.

'There's less places for kids to play footie now, too. Back in the day, we could throw a couple of coats down on a side garden and have a game. In the winter, you'd get covered in mud and then go home and get battered by our mam and dad – but we did it and we did it every night. You got the hump because you actually had to stop playing to eat your tea. You don't see it now. There are a million more cars on the road and less green spaces. As I say, society has changed.'

Reid's footballing prowess eventually led to him being invited to train with Bolton Wanderers during the school holidays, but nothing more formal than that materialised. It was while he was training with the Trotters, however, that his long association with Rochdale would come about.

'Roy Greaves went to Rochdale and had a word with the manager Peter Madden. He'd seen me at Bolton. I was invited to train at Rochdale and eventually joined the youth team under, I think, Bob Taylor it was, when I was 16. It grew from there and, all of a sudden, I got offered a YTS. I accepted and moved into digs in Bamford [a suburb of Rochdale] so that I didn't need to get six buses a day. I still remember Mrs Ainsworth. She was brilliant. She really looked after me and made staying away from home a lot less daunting.

'It wasn't like the academy that Rochdale has today, though. No way was it. It was more like Rag-Arse Rovers, to be honest. You didn't have a training kit and you trained wherever you could find a patch of grass that was empty of people and clear of dog shit. There were no facilities for the youth team.

'I remember playing with the son of one of the directors. Neil Butterworth his name was, son of Trevor. There was Jimmy McCluskie, too. He was a good lad. It was great. That's where my love for Rochdale started to grow. Obviously, being a kid, it felt like my first proper club and it was, really.'

Reid showed steady progress while at Rochdale and eventually made his first-team debut on 14 January 1984, in a 1-0 win at Crewe. He was 18 years old.

'Geoff Thomas had made his debut a few games earlier and he scored that night,' Reid remembers. 'He went on to have some career, didn't he? It was a really heavy pitch and we were two kids trying to find our way. We both had decent games, I seem to recall. That's when I learned what footie was about. Crewe had a lad playing for them called Bob Scott [who formerly had played for Rochdale]. He was about six foot four and built like a brick shithouse. I thought I was quite handy as a kid, y'know, strong and hard? Well, I hit Bob and I felt like I'd run into a wall. I always remember thinking, "Wow, I really am playing against the big boys now." These were *men*. I learned bloody quick because you had to. It doesn't happen these days, does it? You get the odd ones who are outstandingly brilliant at 17 and 18 getting into the first team, but it's taking them a lot longer now, especially at the top end.'

Reid's first goal for Rochdale came more than a year later, in a 2-1 defeat against Swindon Town, February 1985.

'I saw that goal on YouTube not too long ago, actually,' he says. 'A lot has happened since then and, honestly, to this day, I can't remember the goal itself. I remember the feeling, but not the goal itself, if that makes sense? Scoring my first league goal was special feeling. I was a kid. I was playing for a club that I loved and I scored my first goal for them. Scoring wasn't important to me, though. I felt I could have gone on to be more of an attacking midfielder, sure, but I was an aggressive player as well, so I was used more as a leader. I suppose they'd call someone like me an enforcer now.

'Football has changed a lot these days, though, to the point there's no tackling anymore. It's a different game to the one I grew up playing. My job was to break up the play and get the ball to the players who could go past people. That became my job and was what I was known for. I sort of fell into that niche but, as a kid, a schoolboy, I scored goals for fun. As a professional, I was seen in a different light and I took that on board.'

And as if to prove that point, three days after his debut goal, Reid was sent off at Scunthorpe while being carried from the field on a stretcher!

Already on a yellow card, Reid had injured himself making the challenge which led to his second booking. There was no sympathy from referee George Tyson, who brandished red as Reid's team-mates and staff sought to tend to his plight.

'It was a feisty game, to say the least,' he says. 'I went in for a 50/50 and I may have gone in a bit high on that occasion, which was usually the case, but I was a winner, do you know what I mean? As it happens, I came off worse. It was a heck of a gash. I think I had to have nine stitches in my shin. The referee deemed that I deserved to be sent off. I may have said something as well, to be fair, because I was a bit gobby. I tell you what though, you got up and got on with it in those days. I probably played the next game I was available.'

Reid was also knocked out by John Bramhall in a clash with Halifax Town in 1987. Nobody appeared to care as Bramhall scored.

'I was on the end of a high challenge in the middle of the park. I was hit from behind. Just a normal challenge in footie in those days. It's funny, because Brammy came and joined us at Dale after that, didn't he? I played in the same team as him.'

Beyond being rendered unconscious or being dismissed, Reid has other fond memories of his time at the club, and also the managers and directors he played for.

'Most of my time at Rochdale was synonymous with actually just scrapping to stay in the Football League,' he says. 'Staying up was like we'd won the FA Cup. The atmosphere was unbelievable. It was simply a case of survival and that seemed to be accepted by all at the club. When I go back to Rochdale now, I see how far the club has come. It's phenomenal. I'd like to think it's down to that period where we battled to keep the club in the league. The facilities and everything have improved no end, but the club is still true to itself. I mean, I remember sitting in the bath at Spotland, looking up, and there were holes in the roof where leaves were dropping in and rain was coming in. I was thinking, "Is this being a professional footballer?" but, do you know what, it was. It was a club on its knees but it kept going. It was a club like the town's people – warm but very strong.

'Look at the clubs that haven't kept their league status over the years – York City, Chester City, Hartlepool, Darlington – they were big clubs in the day. Anything could have happened to Dale if they went down. I remember people carrying me off the pitch on their shoulders when we kept the club up. I was thinking, "Jesus, what's it going to be like if we actually win something here?" Rochdale could have been one of those clubs that just went out of existence, like Bury. For a small-town club to do what it's done since, is incredible. You have to give credit to the board too – Mr Kilpatrick, Mr Morris – these people weren't millionaires but they kept the club going and people shouldn't forget about that.

'The most important thing for a football club is the people, the fans. Those men got that. Anyone can have their name at the top of the paperwork, saying they own it, but they don't. Not really. It's owned by the fans. The custodians of the club, at any time, should be mindful of that.'

So much did Reid enjoy his time at Rochdale, he says it is easily the best club he played for.

'I've enjoyed everywhere I have played, but Rochdale sticks out for me, it really does. I learned to be hungry there – hungry to play games and battle. I also learned respect. When I heard of the sad passing of David Kilpatrick, who is a former chairman of the club, it reminded me of one of the great lessons he taught me. I had a problem off the pitch. I was 18 years old. Vic Halom was the manager and he called me in. He said, "I'm going to fine you three weeks' wages." David Kilpatrick, hearing this, looked over his glasses, and said, "Vic, we don't pay him enough to fine him." I laughed, but then he said, "I'm going to make you come over to my house in the afternoons after training and dig a garden." He was disciplining me but he didn't want to financially hurt me. He was a clever man. Mind you, I only went to dig the garden once and I was a pain in the arse, so he told me not to come back.'

While in the first team, Reid played under managers Jimmy Greenhoff, Vic Halom, Eddie Gray and Danny Bergara. It was an unrequested wake-up call from the latter in 1988 that Reid recalls most readily.

'I was captain at the time and I remember it was two on a Saturday morning,' he says. 'I'm in bed, obviously, as we have a game that day. The phone goes. It was only bloody Danny Bergara, the manager, still in the office at the ground. He'd had a whisky. He was under a bit of pressure at the time as we'd lost a few games. "Captain," he says. "I need to see you." I tell him it's two in the morning, but he demands I go to the stadium to see him. I resist for a bit, still half asleep, but he's adamant I go in. So, I get down there, go into his office, and he's sat there. He doesn't say anything. I'm thinking, "He doesn't even know he's fucking phoned me, him." I got his attention and he says, "Shaun, I wanted to speak to you after training yesterday." I says, "You've left it a bit fucking late." He was totally unaware of the hour. Anyway, it turns out he just wanted my opinion on the team he was choosing for Saturday. Fuck's sake. That's pressure, you see. He loved football, did Danny. He was so determined and that's how it gets people. He wanted to win football matches and I loved him for that. He was a great man but he was mad as a hatter, like.'

Reid left Rochdale for the first time in 1988. It's not a time he remembers fondly.

'The club was always run on a shoestring, wasn't it? It wasn't an affluent club. York City's Alan Little, the assistant manager, remembered me playing against him. He was a hard player and I had given him a right seeing to on the day. It had clearly stuck in his mind because he persuaded John Bird, the manager, to come in for me. They offered about £30,000 plus a goalkeeper called Scott Endersby on loan, I think. I didn't really want to go, I'll be honest, hand on heart. I would've been 22/23 years old then and was happy, but the club needed the money, apparently, so off I went.'

However, after more than 100 games for York, Reid couldn't deny the lure of Rochdale and he came 'home' in 1992.

'Dave Sutton was manager of Rochdale and he phoned me,' Reid recalls. 'He knew I was leaving York and he said, "Do you want to do a bit of pre-season with us?" I had other clubs asking me too – Mansfield, Bury and Blackpool – but I had an affinity with

Rochdale and I liked Sutty, so I came back. It was a completely different squad and it was packed with decent players. They also had a really good coach in Mick Docherty. Mick really took a shine to me and told me I hadn't achieved what I should have in the game. He was a big influence on me. He had a great way about him. I look back now on some of the things he used to tell me and I wish I had taken them on board. If I had, I'd have played at a higher level, I know it. He was a font of knowledge and me, as a young lad, I thought I knew more. It's a common problem with young players. They think they're the finished article but they're nowhere near it.

'Sutty had his way, but Mick was a player's coach. I mean, Sutty used to shout at me and I used to laugh. It was funny when he lost his temper. Mick, though, was different. I knew when he had the hump with me because he just used to look at me a certain way. That was enough for me. I knew I had to give over or pull my finger out. I think Sutty knew, as manager, that his number two, Mick, was vital to that team.'

Perhaps this writer's strongest memory of Reid, one that demonstrated both his leadership qualities and ability, was the second leg of the Auto Windscreens Area Final in 1995. Dale were 4-1 down from the first leg away against Carlisle. A place at Wembley awaited the winner – something that seemed an impossible task for the hosts prior to kick-off.

'They were flying in the league and the weather was horrible in that first leg,' Reid says. 'I remember playing into the wind one half and, when we swapped ends second half, the wind dropped. Bloody awful. The return leg was a night match as well and had a great atmosphere. Carlisle packed out the away end. It was behind the Pearl Street goal in those days, but Dale supporters were just as loud. I was up for that game, I tell you. When I came away from the first leg, it hurt me. I didn't think it was a 4-1 game. In those days, we were on the cusp of being half decent. We had some good players, didn't we? I always felt it was a team that could have gone up, but it never quite seemed to click. When it came to the return leg, though, there was an extra ten per cent in every challenge. We drove forward. We caused them problems. We were unlucky in the end because we missed some chances. We won 2-1, but it wasn't enough.

'Mick was manager by this time and he held me in high esteem. People who watched me play would have seen that boisterous and mouthy aggression, but it was Mick who actually made me believe it. He said to me, "You're a leader, so go lead." I took that on board.'

Reid would depart Rochdale a second and final time in 1995.

'I kind of just knew my time at the club was up,' he says. 'I went to Bury for my sins. I was there for a good few years and then went to Chester. Me and [Bury manager] Stan Ternent fell out. It was a clash of two people who were headstrong. Gary Shelton rung me, said, "Come and play for me at Chester." I had a few other irons in the fire, but he persuaded me. We got to the play-offs and played Swansea. They won. Swansea then went one way from there and Chester went the other. It was a sliding doors moment. Had Chester gone on to get promotion that year, who knows?'

When he finally threw his boots into the back of his airing cupboard for the last time in 2000, Reid kept himself busy by obtaining a UEFA B licence and took on spells coaching at Swindon Town and Plymouth Argyle. In January 2012, he was appointed as manager at Merseyside non-league outfit Prescot Cables before leaving in March of that year to become manager at Warrington Town. His success was marked. In the 2014/15 FA Cup Reid took Warrington to the first round proper for the first time in the club's history, where they defeated League Two's Exeter City 1–0 live on TV.

'I got my badges and spent a year and a half with Andy King at Swindon and then he got the sack,' Reid reminisces. 'I then went down to Plymouth and worked with our kid for a bit. Then I ended up out of the game. My only involvement was watching it. I then got the chance to take over a little club called Prescot Cables, just down the road from me. They had about eight games to save their league status. I went in, kept them in the league and the chairman of Warrington approached me and asked if I would manage them. They were very ambitious. Wanting to do what Salford have done and get into the Football League, you know? I went there and had a great time, won a trophy, got us into the second round of the FA Cup and got us promoted the next year.'

It was then that tragedy struck.

'I had a brain haemorrhage,' Reid says. 'It happened while I was managing a game against Trafford. It just felt like something hit me in the back of the head. The recovery was a difficult period for me. I had to take a bit of time out, obviously, but I'm fully recovered. Now, I just enjoy watching football – anywhere and everywhere. Maybe, at some point, I'd have another go. Without wanting to sound big-headed, it's what I'm good at, it's what I know most. They can change the terminology all they want, you know, all this playing through the lines and this, that and the other, but, at the end of the day, the game doesn't change. If you squeeze, keep the ball better and you're more organised, you win football matches. The most important thing is, you've got to have a desire to win football matches. Any team I've coached certainly has that. They either have that or they don't play for me, simple as that.

'The first thing I say to them is, "Listen, I'm not here to be your friend. I'm not here to love you. I'm here to get the best out of you." That desire to win was evident in a lot of people I shared the pitch with at Rochdale. Alan Reeves and Paul Butler especially. It should be a given for every footballer, but it isn't always. Again, society in general these days has a big say on this. People want everything for nothing and think they should simply just have it. There is no, "I'm gonna go and get that," it's more like, "I should have that." Call me old-school, but if you haven't got a desire to want to go and get something, then you aren't going to get it. You might play at it, but you won't do it.

'If people aren't giving their all on a football field, you're entitled to dig them out. If they don't like it, I say, "Ring your agent and move on." I was a player once and I thought I knew everything. I didn't, clearly. Players need to listen and they need to learn. Hunger and desire are just as important on the field as dropping your shoulder and going past people. You're not playing for a shirt, you're playing for the people. It's their football club. When you go home on a Saturday night, if it doesn't hurt you, you shouldn't be playing for that club. You get well-paid, so it's not about the money. It's about desire and putting a smile on people's faces. Making them come back the following week in hope of a win. You've got to engage and make them feel part of it. It's not for the people who have the shares, it's the people who travel across the country on a wet midweek. It's their club and they deserve respect.

'I watched football matches during the Covid-19 pandemic, without the fans, and I'm telling you, it isn't the same game. Club owners should be mindful of that.'

Steve Whitehall

1991–1997

GOALSCORERS INGRATIATE themselves into football fan affection more quickly than most players. The very nature of their stock-in-trade usually makes this a formality, especially those who can find the net in struggling sides.

Affable Liverpudlian Steve Whitehall played in both promotion-challenging and doldrum-slumming Rochdale teams (sometimes within the same season) but never struggled to provide his primary commodity. His reliability ensured his name constantly rose in chorus from the Spotland stands. In short, he was loved.

Whitehall made 282 appearances for Rochdale across six years, scoring 92 goals, making him fourth in the club's all-time scoring list behind Reg Jenkins, Albert Whitehurst and Ian Henderson.

One would think such a natural predator would have honed his talent since childhood, under the tutelage of top-class coaches and the watchful eye of talent scouts. Surprisingly, neither is true. In fact, Whitehall didn't take up football until he was 17 years old.

'I did a bit of football at primary school, in the Wirral, but won a scholarship for my secondary school, St Anselm's College in Birkenhead, and that was kind of like a private school, I guess,' Whitehall says. 'They did cross-country and rugby in the winter and cricket in the summer, so those were the sports I did through my early to mid-teens. There was no football, not even in the playground. It wasn't until I got to the sixth form there that I started playing football. My next-door neighbour at the time was the secretary of a local Sunday league team, and asked me to go and play for them. He was also associated with one of the West Cheshire League teams, Heswall, so I got games for them too. Tranmere were interested for a while, but nothing happened. I then played against Reggie McGuire, who also played for Southport. He recommended me to Southport's manager, Brian Kettle, who got me in for a look, and then I signed for them.'

Whitehall supplemented his part-time football income with a job in the Civil Service, working with the Land Registry and Charities Commission.

'Southport were in the HFS Loans League [now the Pitching In Northern Premier League] back then,' he says. 'The equivalent of the Conference North now, I guess. They were a part-time team. By now, I'd graduated from university with a biology degree and joined the Civil Service. I started in Land Registry and was promoted up to the Charity Commission, working in Liverpool city centre. It worked for me. I trained at Southport Tuesdays and Thursdays and played matches at the weekend – although we played a lot of games on Tuesday night too, what with the number of cups you were in at that level. I was earning not bad money between the two jobs and they never conflicted.'

Despite this, Whitehall still harboured the dream of playing league football.

'If I'm being honest, I had a job for life with the Civil Service, and all the security that goes with that, but it isn't what I wanted to do. I just wanted to play football all the time. Not many people get the chance to do it and I always said to myself that, if I did get the chance, I would take it.'

That chance did come, in a fashion. Whitehall had been lined up for a trial at Sheffield United but, the day before, Southport had agreed to send some players over to Liverpool to bulk up the numbers for a reserve game. It was a dream come true for the native Whitehall – until he was dealt the bad news.

'Southport wouldn't let me go to Anfield,' he says. 'They didn't want me getting injured for the Sheffield United trial. I was gutted. I almost had the chance to go and play for the team I supported. Well, kind of. Me and another lad at Southport at the time were invited down to Sheffield for a week. Brian Kettle, as well as managing Southport, also worked for Liverpool FC as one of their community guys. Liverpool had a reserve team fixture against Coventry and most of the first team were away in Europe and a lot of the reserve players were away somewhere else, I forget where now, but the bottom line was that they were short of bodies for this fixture. So, Brian Kettle asked us to come down to help out. I could've worn the Liverpool jersey – but the Southport chairman wouldn't let me play because of the Sheffield United trial. I went to Sheffield and played a match against Hull and then a game against Nottingham Forest in which I scored. I got invited back for another trial a week or two later. In the end, they opted against signing me. It all ended up being for nothing.'

Then, in 1991, it did happen for him. Rochdale offered Southport an acceptable sum and Whitehall was offered terms.

'Chester were interested and rumours of a few others – there's always rumours aren't there? – but it was Rochdale who made the firm offer. I didn't have to think too hard about it, to be honest, even though it would be less money than my two combined jobs, because it was a chance to play football for a living. I had vowed to take the chance if it came and here it was.'

But any dreams of big-time glitz and glamour quickly evaporated when Whitehall arrived at Spotland.

'I was dead enthusiastic,' he says. 'I'd signed a two-year deal and was going to play league football – but then I got to the ground and it was horrendous. It was falling apart. There was a leak in the changing room roof and the grass on the pitch was about a foot high. It was an eye-opener, but it also put me at ease, too, that maybe the step up wasn't going to be so big. I was still pretty raw and obviously now training all the time rather than two days a week, but it was brilliant. My experience of football up to now, at the level I had played at, was about just making sure I didn't get my legs cracked. As far as I remember, I didn't find any difficulty with the transition to being a full-time pro.'

Whitehall was signed for Rochdale by manager Dave Sutton.

'He was an eye-opener, to be honest,' says Whitehall. 'I'd only had one manager previously and Brian Kettle was a manager who didn't even swear! Dave Sutton liked to throw a tea cup around the dressing room every now and then, if you get me?'

Knuckling down, Whitehall's primary objective was to establish himself in the first team.

'I was sub pretty much all of pre-season,' he recalls. 'Then we went from a back five to a back four for the first game of the season, which created an extra spot up front and it got me in the team. It was a 1-1 draw as far as I can remember [against York City]. I was subbed off and I don't think I had a very good game. I then scored two goals against Carlisle in the League Cup in my next game – right in the Sandy Lane end. It was brilliant. I got man of the match. The League Cup was sponsored by [electronics retailer] Rumbelows back then and the man of the match used to get a prize from the sponsors. I ended up with a 24-inch TV. Not bad for my second game, eh?

'Don't forget, I was the number two guy that season, too. Sutton had spent a lot of money on Andy Flounders, so he was the main guy. He was on penalties and everything went through him. My focus at that time was just getting in the team. Towards the end of that season, I was back on the bench a lot. I thought I was playing well, so was a bit confused. There were rumours flying around that it was because Rochdale would have to pay Southport more money if I scored a certain amount of goals. I really don't know if that was the case, but I was happy with the 11 goals I'd scored that season.'

Whitehall went on to establish himself as a firm favourite with fans and fellow professionals alike, scoring the goals that kept Rochdale in the play-off hunt over the next two seasons, netting 15 goals each time.

'I felt I was making up for lost time,' he says. 'I'd missed out on playing football between 11 and 17 and I was having to learn how to play the game. Sometimes it was about instincts, which I had, and other times it was about going against them, such as retaining possession late in a game rather than going for goal. I felt I got better and better.'

However, Rochdale could have bizarrely lost their goalscoring talisman in 1994, as Whitehall reveals.

'I came in one day and Dave Sutton says, "We're selling you to Chesterfield. You need to drive there now, sit down with their chairman and see if you can work out a deal." So, I drove to Chesterfield, I met the manager, John Duncan I think it was, and we negotiated a contract and I signed it. I actually signed it. I went back to Rochdale to get my gear and Dave Sutton pulls me aside. He says, "You're not going to Chesterfield now. The chairman won't allow it." I'm thinking only the chairman could have sanctioned the move in the first place. I don't know if Dave had just been in touch with their manager and thought he could use the £100,000 that was being offered to buy more players, but our chairman clearly didn't want to get rid of me and that was that. I stayed. I was happy about that, as I didn't want to leave.'

Not long afterwards, Sutton was dismissed as Rochdale manager and his assistant, Mick Docherty, stepped into his shoes.

'Mick Docherty was great in terms of organisation and coaching,' Whitehall says. 'He did a lot more than Dave in that area, in terms of working on individual things with individual people. I really enjoyed working with him. When he became manager, he was very rigid with his system. I used to feel sorry for Dean Martin, one of our midfielders, actually, because he only got to play in away games because of the way Mick set up the team.'

Under Docherty, Rochdale reached the third round of the FA Cup and Whitehall finally fulfilled his ambition to play at Anfield. Despite losing 7-0 to Liverpool, Whitehall retains fond memories of the occasion.

'The week leading up to the Liverpool game was great,' he remembers. 'I was living in the city at the time, so I got a lot of media attention and did quite a lot with the papers. Then, to play at Anfield as a Liverpool fan, against their first team, was a dream come true. I still talk about it now. Other than the result, it was fantastic. In fact, some people still ask me what my best and worst games were for Rochdale – I tell them it's the same game. The Liverpool one. We were doing great to keep it at 1-0 coming up to half-time and then Stan Collymore gets two out of nowhere. Going in at half-time 3-0 down is completely different. You're right up against it then, aren't you? Chasing a game against a Premier League team, when they're just stroking it around? It isn't fun. Still, I've got good memories of the day, I've still got a Liverpool shirt and photographs, and I can still say I've played at Anfield against Liverpool's first team.'

What had started as a promising season for Rochdale petered out into mediocrity after the Liverpool game. Despite finishing the season with 24 goals, even Whitehall himself wasn't immune, missing two penalties in a defeat to Wigan Athletic, a game also remembered for goalkeeper Lance Key completely missing a back-pass that led to the opening goal.

'Lance Key did me a favour that game as people tend to remember his mistake before they remember my penalty misses,' Whitehall chuckles. 'Seriously though, I hit both of those penalties far too high. That's penalties for you. We didn't get another penalty that season and John Deary took the next one we got. I got back on the horse after that, though. I think we got another penalty two weeks later and I just knew I was taking it. I just remember Loaf [Deary] said, "Are you all right taking this?" and I said, "Yeah, course," and he says, "Well just keep it bloody low."'

That season's poor finish ultimately cost Docherty his job, too.

'None of us were expecting Mick to leave when we finished up for the summer,' Whitehall says. 'We were expecting him to be there when we came back. Instead it was Graham Barrow waiting for us. He brought his own lads in and his philosophy was, "We'll keep it to 1-0." You know, keep the ball, don't concede and maybe we'll get one? That style didn't really suit me. I had one season with him and I did all right. I'm sure I finished that season leading scorer. My contract was up at the end of that season, but I didn't want to go. He came to me and said, "We're not going to give you another contract, we're going to sell you somewhere." In this day and age, I'd have gotten a bit more money, but I had to wait around for someone to come and sign me. I didn't want to go. I was close to getting 100 goals for the club and wanted to see that through. Anyway, Steve Parkin bought me for Mansfield and we beat Rochdale 3-0 the next year. I scored a nice free kick.'

Despite how it ended, Whitehall still has great affection for Rochdale and his time spent at the club.

'I love the place and still get back whenever I can,' he says. 'I played with some great people and the camaraderie was always top notch. I would say Dave Lancaster was my favourite strike partner while I was at Rochdale. We were a big and little fella act [Whitehall is 5ft 9in]. Decoy Dave, I called him. Andy Flounders was a bit greedy, but then strikers are, aren't they? I had a good laugh alongside Jamie Taylor, too. So many good players. We had a really good group travelling in from the Liverpool area. There was me, Shaun Reid, Alan Reeves and Darren Oliver. I was made up for Reevesy when he signed for Wimbledon but it just meant more driving for me.'

When it came time for Whitehall to finish playing, he had already ensured a backup plan was in place.

'The PFA ran some part-time physio courses and I was actually the PFA rep for Rochdale,' he says. 'So, I got all the info and, as I already had a biology degree, it appealed to me. I went to Salford University on a Monday and a Thursday after training, making those very long days, as I still had to get back to Liverpool afterwards. I also did my study on some of the longer away trips, rather than play cards, you know? It paid off because I qualified. That was the thing back then, people think footballers are loaded. Not in the Third Division they're not. You very definitely needed another career after playing football. Once I was finished with playing, I went off and put my qualification to use and I still work for the NHS now.'

Whitehall's Rochdale legacy wasn't done there, however. His son, Danny, joined the club's academy in 2012.

'Our Dan joined Liverpool at the age of eight, and they let him go when he was 16,' Whitehall says. 'I phoned Tony Ellis, who was by now heading up Rochdale's academy, and I asked if he'd have a look at Dan. He played a few games, scored a few goals and then Rochdale took him on. He finished leading scorer in the league for two years on the trot.

'Despite that, Rochdale never took him on as a pro. I've no idea why not. He went to Southport for a bit but then decided to do a soccer scholarship at Hastings College in Nebraska. He was there for four seasons and still, even now, he is Hastings' top goalscorer by 20 goals. He then could've signed for Southend but they changed manager, so he was unlucky again. He had a trial at Kilmarnock and got a year's contract there. He's still trying to stay in the game. He's playing for Eastleigh in the National League. I tell him to keep at it. It might just happen for him like it did for me.'

Gary Jones

1998–2001 and 2003–2012

WHEN GARY Jones left Rochdale AFC in 2012 at the ripe old age of 35, it was a sad day.

Sad not just because he was the club's record holder for the most appearances – an amazing 531 of them – but sad also because he still had so much more to give.

Watching him lead League Two club Bradford City to the League Cup Final at Wembley the following season only served to remind all onlookers of the qualities Jones still possessed, which had seen him become one of Rochdale's most effective captains and single-handedly drag the team over the line on too many occasions to recite.

The Gary Jones who played for Bradford that day was certainly a far cry from the Gary Jones who arrived at Spotland on loan from Swansea in 1998. Back then, the Birkenhead-born midfielder was an unknown, brought in to help bolster a Rochdale side that had already endured 18 months of struggle under the management of Graham Barrow and, as Jones explains, it wasn't where he imagined himself ending up when making the transition from Sunday league to professional football.

'While there seems to be a myth that I was part of Liverpool's academy, I actually never did an apprenticeship with any club,' he says. 'I learned the game playing Sunday league football and turning out for [League of Wales side] Caernarfon on a Saturday.

'Funnily enough Jan Mølby, who was Swansea manager at the time, used to come and watch the Sunday league team I played for. I think he knew a couple of the people involved. After one particular match, he invited me to Swansea for a week's trial. I went down there for a week, stayed in a hotel, and, at the end of it, they offered me a year's contract. That's where it all started for me, from a professional perspective.

'It was OK at Swansea but then Jan got the sack and Micky Adams came in. I was only young and still new to professional football. He never really took to me and so I never got a look-in.

'Graham Barrow was aware of me, I believe, and asked if he could take me on loan to Rochdale. I went there and saw they had some really good players – Robbie Painter, Dave Bayliss, Mark Stuart, Andy Barlow – so I wasn't sure why the team was struggling in the league. But then you realise that good individual players don't necessarily guarantee team success. There has to be something else there. We were always at the wrong end of the table and that era is, sadly, synonymous with a really poor team.

'And, while my move had been made permanent, I was in and out of the side and was very close to being released – then Graham Barrow got sacked. I played in the last away game that season, against Brighton, and I had a really good game. I showed what I was capable of. On the strength of that, [caretaker manager] Dave Hamilton pleaded with the chairman [David Kilpatrick] to give me a new contract – and he did. Sometimes you need a little bit of luck in the game and that was my little bit of luck right there.'

It was under Barrow's successor, Steve Parkin, that Jones really came into his own, coinciding with the formation of a Rochdale side that seriously looked like achieving promotion from English football's fourth tier for the first time since 1969. Under Parkin's leadership between 1999 and 2001, Jones eventually established himself as an essential first-team player, his box-to-box dynamism an integral part of a side that inched closer and closer to the play-offs with each passing season.

'It was funny when Steve first came in,' remembers Jones. 'First day back for pre-season training and he's calling all the players in to see him, one by one, to say hello and give them their squad numbers and whatnot. I didn't get called in and I'm thinking, "What's going on here, like?"

'I mentioned this to Dave Hamilton, who went in to see him and it turned out Steve didn't even know who I was! I think he thought I'd been released. Needless to say, I wasn't in his plans at all and players such as Jason Peake were ahead of me. But then I started to gradually improve in training, got noticed and I got my chance. I think my first start under Steve was at home against Exeter. I did enough to keep my shirt and the rest, as they say, is history.

'I became captain of the club aged 23, which was a massive honour. It was on the way to Chesterfield, I think, and the current captain, Neil Edwards, was injured. Steve came up to me and said, "Gary, you're going to be captain today." When a manager says that to you, and puts his faith in you in such a public way, it's like a massive shot in the arm. It raised my game to a level that I aspired to for the rest of my career.'

Jones believes that act is the perfect summary of Parkin's attributes.

'Steve was a fantastic man-manager,' he says. 'When you talk about good players alone not being enough to create a good team, that's what Steve offered – he knitted everybody together. Yes, he signed a lot of good players, and was given money to do that, but he created an unbreakable team spirit. He had a magnetism that drew people to him, even the lads who weren't playing. He certainly knew how to get the best out of his players.'

Sadly, late in 2001, with Dale competing for the top spot in the division, Steve Parkin left for second-tier Barnsley and took Jones with him.

'The team that season was the pinnacle of what Steve and Tony [Ford, assistant manager] had been building since 1999,' confirms Jones. 'It was good enough to take the title. When they left, it was a massive blow for all of us. Massive. I had no idea at that point that they wanted me to join them at Barnsley. I remember driving in for training a few weeks after they had left, I think it was a Thursday, and being told by Dave Hamilton that Rochdale had accepted a bid for me from Barnsley and I was to go over there right away to sort out terms. It felt strange, of course it did, but football is a short career and this was my chance to play two levels higher. I drove to training in the morning as a Rochdale player and came back Thursday night as a Barnsley player – that's how quickly it happened.'

While John Hollins came in to replace Parkin, and gamely kept Rochdale in the hunt for promotion, the side fell at the first hurdle in the play-offs. It was to be the end of another era for the club and, for the next six years, normal business was resumed, with the team reacquainting itself with the tag of perennial fourth-tier strugglers.

During this period, in 2003 to be precise, Jones returned to Rochdale on loan, after finding his Barnsley appearances limited. The deal was made permanent once again in 2004, with Jones going on to re-establish himself as club captain, a role he didn't relinquish until leaving in 2012.

'I did my metatarsal in training at Barnsley and so hadn't been playing,' explains Jones. 'I wasn't really in the manager's plans and Alan Buckley was manager of Rochdale at the time. He asked if I would be interested in coming back. I told him absolutely, but warned him I wasn't the player I was due to me being out for so long with an injury. I was right. I was miles off, to be fair. I kept breaking down with scar tissue and so on. I just wasn't doing myself justice. However, at Rochdale, I was given the time I needed to get myself fit and I did just that.'

In late 2006, with Steve Parkin, who had replaced Buckley, leaving Rochdale for a second time, youth academy coach Keith Hill stepped into the first-team manager role and led the club into the most successful era of its history, culminating, finally, in that long-awaited promotion from the fourth tier in 2010.

'Hilly came into management at just the right time for the club,' Jones remembers. 'It needed that breath of fresh air and a new approach. Hilly brought sports science with him via John Lucas, and he brought in Dave Flitcroft as his assistant, who was previously part of the dressing room with me under Steve Parkin. It was the perfect combination. Dave acted brilliantly as that go-between with players and manager.

'I still remember Hilly's first day in the job, as caretaker manager at that point. He got me and John Doolan into his office and told us that, as the elder statesmen of the dressing room, it was on us to get the players going and that's what we did.

'Under Hilly's leadership we just hit the ground running from day one. His training techniques were modern, new and interesting with short, sharp ball work – every single player was engaged. Revolution is not too strong a word. We knew something massive was happening. We began beating teams by four or five goals – I'm talking out of sight by half-time. It was a no brainer to give him the job full time.'

Prior to Hill achieving that 2010 automatic promotion, he led Rochdale to a first Wembley appearance courtesy of the play-off final in 2008. While it would end in a 3-2 defeat at the hands of Stockport County, Jones said he was proud to lead the team on such an occasion.

'What an amazing experience that was,' he says. 'To captain a football club in its centenary season at England's national stadium was unbelievable. I go back to the amazing semi-final win against Darlington when I remember this experience, too, because we came back from 1-0 down to win on penalties in front of nearly 10,000 supporters. I can still vividly see Ben Muirhead wheeling away after banging in the winning penalty that got us to Wembley. The result at Wembley wasn't what we hoped for, but we dusted ourselves down and made the play-offs again the next season, albeit we didn't do enough to get to Wembley again.'

In 2009/10, Rochdale's eventual promotion season, the team looked set for the League Two title before a late wobble saw the team finish third – while it was enough to achieve a step up to League One, there was still a lingering sense of what might have been for Jones.

'I think our slump coincided with Notts County getting a boost from signing all these big-name players like Kasper Schmeichel, and us running out of steam. We didn't take our foot off the gas, I think it was a mental thing. We were at the top of the table for a long time and we should have seen that through. It's as if something got to us collectively and after one bad result, we couldn't shake it – I recall getting absolutely smashed 5-0 down at Torquay and then we lost to Darlington at home, too. It was getting a bit daft. We got promotion in the end, though, and achieving that at home against Northampton, and the scenes it created with the supporters, with what it meant to them, will live long in my memory.'

Jones was a rare absentee through injury during the winter of that season, too, and he was forced to look on from the sidelines as Jason Taylor and Jason Kennedy swept all before them in the Rochdale midfield. He would still go on to make the PFA Team of the Year, however.

'I couldn't get back in the team,' Jones recalls. 'It was tough as captain but, if you're winning football games, it doesn't matter who you are, you can't change a winning team. That was the situation I was in. I didn't like it, but I understood it. If you're smashing goals past all comers, then you don't disrupt that. I just kept working hard and waited for my chance to come again.'

Jones would continue to excel during Rochdale's first season in the third tier for 36 years and his performances are perhaps best encapsulated by a single moment of brilliance at Southampton's St Mary's Stadium. His 30-yard thunderbolt secured Rochdale a 2-0 league victory and is widely regarded as one of club's greatest goals.

'I've got to be honest, I found the step up easy,' Jones says. 'We all did. Hilly had been preparing us for this transition before it arrived, so we were ready. Everyone thought we would struggle, but we weren't far off the play-offs by the time the season ended.

'For me to score 19 goals from midfield also made it a fantastic season personally. I've still got the DVD from that season and sometimes put it on to show my son that I wasn't a bad player in my day!

'The goal against Southampton still looks good. Anthony Elding laid the ball off and I just concentrated on hitting it as best

I could. Fortunately for me, it flew right in. But that goal was just part of a terrific team performance. It was boiling hot that day and they had a fantastic team containing Rickie Lambert, Morgan Schneiderlin and Jason Puncheon – and we outplayed them.'

Like Steve Parkin a decade before, Keith Hill's success at Rochdale took him to second-tier Barnsley, only this time Jones stayed behind. With Hill gone, the club slid back into League Two within a single season, under the guidance of Steve Eyre and then John Coleman. It was under the latter's management that Jones ended his association with Rochdale.

'When Hilly left, Bradford wanted to sign me at that point,' Jones reveals. 'Obviously, I was out of contract, so I went to speak to Bradford manager Peter Jackson, but it didn't seem the right move for me at that time. Rochdale had just had a good season and, even though Hilly had gone, I didn't see why we couldn't do it again. I went on holiday and Steve Eyre phoned me up. I'd never heard of him, to be fair, but I liked what he had to say and he got me a new two-year deal at the club. Sadly, managing the youth team at Man City, which Steve did before getting the Rochdale job, is a big difference to managing seasoned professionals and he struggled with that. It didn't work out for him.

'Then John Coleman came in and it started off really well with a good win over Bury. To be fair, and this might surprise you, I loved the way he wanted to play football, I really did. Where I had an issue was in the preparation. With Keith Hill, everything was done meticulously and on time. Everything. I needed that structure and it got the best out of me. With Coleman, that all changed – we were starting at different times and that discipline just wasn't there. That didn't suit me. We didn't fall out or anything, we just didn't see eye to eye. Don't get me wrong, I had total respect for him and what he had done for Accrington, it just wasn't for me.

'We were eventually relegated and the opportunity came around again for me to speak to Bradford after the club accepted an offer. John Coleman OK'd it. By now, Bradford were being managed by Phil Parkinson and Steve Parkin, and it was a much better proposition for me. That was that, my time at Rochdale was over. It was sad, especially on the back of such a poor season, but football works that way and you have to get on with it.'

And when Hill retuned to the club in 2013, leading Rochdale back into League One, was there ever any chance of Jones returning?

'No, there wasn't,' Jones says. 'The opportunity never came around again. Hilly is an amazing manager and I would have loved to work for him again, but the chance just didn't arise. It's not just Hilly, though, it's the club. It will always have a special place within me. It was the club that took a chance on me instead of discarding me, it allowed me to find my leadership qualities and it gave me time to get back to my best after injury. I would not have had the career I did were it not for Rochdale and for that I will be eternally grateful.'

Paddy McCourt
2000–2005

MANCHESTER UNITED fans still enthuse about the late George Best to this day – those who have seen him first-hand and the latter generation who have pored over endless YouTube footage.

The Northern Irishman was the archetypal crowd-pleaser. A dying breed of footballer who, alone, is capable of making an admission fee one worth paying. Players such as this nowadays tend to be deemed a luxury, or lazy.

In my time supporting Rochdale AFC, I have been fortunate enough to enjoy the talent of another Northern Irishman who put me in mind of Best. He, too, came over to England at a young age and, when given the chance, demonstrated the kind of footwork that would tangle the legs of opposition players as if they were string on a parcel.

While debates still rage in Rochdale fandom about the unfulfilled potential of Paddy McCourt, he is undoubtedly a cult hero. There is almost a childish triumphalism in telling the football world, 'We saw him first.'

McCourt takes his place in this book for achieving cult status at Rochdale, but he could easily fall into the elite class, too, having eventually achieved his own boyhood ambition in signing for Celtic and playing international football. The road to Glasgow from Rochdale's youth setup was anything but smooth, nor has the road been since, but the talented boy from Derry has gifted fans of both football clubs with memories they'll cherish forever.

To this day, there is an imperturbable style to McCourt when he speaks, which very much matches the way he played.

'I would class myself as a street footballer,' he shrugs in summary of himself. 'Someone who isn't afraid to try new things or bring some creative flair – whether that be on the street or in the more structured environment of a football team. My game never really changed from when I started playing as a young boy to when I retired as a senior professional.'

This outlook was shaped on a Derry council estate where, as the youngest of six children, McCourt took to his very apparent football ability with unsurprising diffidence.

'I was probably similar to most people,' he says. 'I grew up playing football with friends – school friends and street friends. There wasn't much to do where I lived other than play football, you know? As time goes on, you start getting better and, by the age of ten, 11, 12, you start to realise you're probably better than the lads you're playing with. Then you go to secondary school and get opened up to a broader range of player and realise you're better than the majority of them as well. It's at that point you start to think you might be quite good at it. That gives you more confidence. It was always a dream of mine to play professional football, but I'm not sure when I realised exactly that a career in the game might be a realistic option for me.'

McCourt turned out for youth team Foyle Harps and it was there his first chance to realise his dream came to pass.

'Foyle Harps is a club that has players from all the areas local to me in Derry and it is very close to my heart,' he says. 'My young boy plays for them now, actually. Because it was full of boys I knew, I felt very comfortable in that environment, which gave me great confidence to express myself as a young player. There was a scout at the time called Matt Bradley, who was also a local football coach. He was friendly with Dave Hamilton, who was assistant manager at Rochdale at the time. I was playing in a game that Matt was watching. I was 16 and a half at this point. I knew Matt anyway, and am still very friendly with him to this day, but he was watching this game and he asked afterwards if I would be interested in going over to Rochdale on trial. I said, "Of course." It was as quick as all that. I went over to Rochdale for a trial, did quite well and was offered a YTS scholarship.'

This presented a tough decision for the teenage McCourt.

'It meant leaving Derry,' he says. 'It was very difficult. I was very close to my mum. I am the youngest of six children, so I was used to always being in and around my family. To be suddenly packing my bags and heading to another country, while still a teenager, is a big deal. I knew, though, if I wanted to be a professional footballer and have a career in the game, these were the sacrifices I needed to make. As tough as it was, it was something I felt I had to do at that time.'

However, upon arriving with his suitcases at the fourth-tier English club, it didn't take long for reality to kick in.

'It certainly wasn't glitz and glamour,' McCourt recalls. 'We didn't have a training ground at Rochdale, so we would often train at different venues. We'd meet at the stadium and head off somewhere else each day. As a YTS, you'd then come back to the stadium and clean the dressing room and clean the first-team players' boots for the next day. Whatever jobs needed done around the stadium, we were doing them. It certainly wasn't like it is today where players rock up to state-of-the-art training grounds with jacuzzis and saunas, and canteens where they get their dinner.'

McCourt's progression wasn't hampered by any off-field hardships, however.

'I was doing quite well in the youth team,' he reflects. 'I was scoring goals and making a bit of a name for myself in terms of how I played and got my goals. This led to me being given a spell in the reserves, you know, with seasoned pros, and that, in turn, led to me getting an opportunity in the first team. It was a dream come true for me, that. It's easy for people to say, "It's only Rochdale," but, for me, setting out to be a professional footballer, I'd left Northern Ireland to achieve this. To do it so quickly was brilliant. It gave me that belief that I could go on and have a successful career.'

McCourt was first introduced to the Spotland throng during an LDV Vans Trophy match as an 82nd-minute substitute against Southport in 2001. However, it was only after Steve Parkin had left that McCourt found any real sustained joy in the first team. New manager John Hollins rated the youngster and, despite much rawness in his game, used McCourt regularly. This faith was rewarded with match-turning performances as Rochdale made the play-offs, McCourt firmly establishing his trademark style of slaloming through opposition players as if they were statues.

'Steve Parkin was a very old-school manager,' McCourt says. 'Very tough and very demanding of the players. He gave me my opportunity in football and I'll always be grateful for that, but he wasn't a very warm manager for a young player coming in, you know? He was a tough man in general, never mind the football side of it, and he was very successful, so I'm not for one second saying his management style was wrong, but, for a young player, it was hard to work out what he was thinking or what he thought of you. He would never take time to speak to you, or encourage you, or even find out more about you.

'John Hollins was the complete opposite. He was, for me, a legend in the game for the career he had with Chelsea, but also, as a man and a person, I can't speak highly enough of him. It was almost as if football was secondary, you know? He just wanted to make sure the young players were OK. He asked constantly how I was and how the family was back in Ireland. I assume he thought if my welfare was OK, he would get the best out of me on the football side. I loved the time he was at the club. It's a shame it was all too brief. He was someone I felt I could speak to about my problems. I could go to his office and speak to him without worrying he would think of me as weak or not strong enough to be a footballer.'

Empowered by Hollins's protective shroud, perhaps McCourt's most notable contribution during this period was his last-minute winning goal against Halifax at The Shay. A mazy run capped off with a difficult finish from a return ball kept Dale on target for promotion.

'To be honest, I don't remember much about the particular goals I scored.' McCourt laughs. 'I've played nearly 500 games since, so it's hard to remember that far back. I certainly remember that period was a good one for the football club. It wasn't a club littered with success, so, when it was doing well, you could sense around the town and the club that people were enjoying themselves. To be a part of it was something I was very thankful for. People I would meet about the town were very grateful. That was great for me, being so young.'

McCourt's form also led to him being called up to the Northern Ireland under-21s before he received his full senior international debut that season, against Spain in a friendly at Windsor Park, which Northern Ireland lost 5-0.

'It was a proud moment,' McCourt says. 'I think Lee McEvilly was called up around that time, too. It was unusual back then for a club at Rochdale's level to have full internationals, so it was a very big thing for the football club as well as for me.'

Rochdale would ultimately miss out on promotion, falling at the first hurdle of the play-offs, and Hollins would not renew his contract. The team would go on to struggle the following season under new manager Paul Simpson, but McCourt would continue his role as an impact sub, his performances attracting the attention of Premier League scouts.

'I was fairly new to professional football and it was the first time I experienced an ex-team-mate now being the manager,' McCourt says of Simpson's appointment. 'I remember finding that strange because he was a team-mate sat alongside me in the dressing room and he then obviously had to change to be our boss seven weeks later. I found it difficult, to be honest. I'm sure Paul found that too. I know a lot of the other players found it strange. As a young player, I was used to older, more experienced managers, so this was a real change for me. We ended up having a pretty poor season. I thought Paul was a good man and he has gone on to have a very respectable career in coaching, but that was definitely a strange season.'

And it was a season that could have been very different, as McCourt reveals.

'I remember getting a call from my agent while I was back home for the summer. He said, "Be ready to jump on a flight to come over, as Man City have put a bid in." I was waiting by the phone but it never rang. I was told later that Paul Simpson and the board felt that spending another year at Rochdale would have been better for me, especially if the club got promoted. I'm not sure if that was the case. Whatever happened, I ended staying at Rochdale.'

With yet another managerial change at Spotland, this time Alan Buckley stepping in to replace Simpson, McCourt's opportunities began to wane. More and more he was viewed as nothing more than a substitute and questions were raised over his stamina and ability to last the 90-minute duration of a match – questions that have dogged him his entire career.

'Alan Buckley was very similar to Steve Parkin for me,' McCourt says. 'Not as tough, but very old-school. I remember his style of football was horrendous for a player like me. I thought very early, "This is not going to suit me at all." There was no talk of playing football. It was all about structure. He mentioned many times that he knew how to get teams out of the bottom division. We lost convincingly at home to Yeovil in the first game of the season. He took me off early and then came in at full time and had a right go at me. I knew then how that season was going to pan out. To be fair, it did. I never really felt I belonged at the club while Alan was manager. He preferred the senior, more experienced players. I could never get any kind of rapport going with him at all.'

Buckley's know-how failed to have any impact at Rochdale and he was replaced when Parkin returned as manager in late 2003, but there was to be no reprieve for McCourt.

'By the time Steve Parkin came back, I was so disinterested in football, and so not enjoying doing it for a living, it wouldn't have matted who came in to replace Alan. I would have classed myself at that point as a dead footballer. The love had gone. I spent so much time being in and out of the team, I just couldn't build a relationship with anyone because the managers were changing that quickly. I just found the whole thing monotonous. It was really hard to stay focused. The inevitable thing happened where Steve sensed this right away. He saw that the young enthusiastic lad he had met three years previously, who would have done anything to succeed in the game, was gone. If someone told me at that point my career was finished tomorrow, I wouldn't have blinked an eyelid. In fact, I would have been thankful. I just didn't like it anymore. When Steve pulled me into his office to say there was interest from a club back in [the Republic of] Ireland, meaning I could go home every weekend, I couldn't sign the release papers quick enough.'

While speaking to McCourt, it's hard not to think Rochdale could have done more for him, given his circumstances, but, as he points out, this was very much prior to the days of player liaison and welfare officers.

'I'm not blaming the club for this,' he says. 'The club was where it was at the time. I'm pretty sure it's changed now. When you left training at 1.30pm, the day was your own. Like any young person living in another country, of course I went out – to bars at weekends or playing snooker during the week. I built up a bit of a reputation for being out and about, but Rochdale is a small town. I lived in the town and I didn't drive, so I was seen a lot.

'I think a lot of the stories about me were exaggerated, if I'm being honest. Like many Irish players living in England, away from home, they were all going out on a Saturday night. When you go out on a Saturday night and you're not playing well, then the Saturday nights get the blame. See when you're playing well? Well, everyone thinks it's great that you're out and chatting to fans. It's just the way football is.

'Looking back, it was a learning experience. There was no real stability for me. Leaving home, having dreams of being a professional, and going into a setup like that, was difficult. I coped the only way I knew how. Rochdale gave me great experience and a platform to grow from a young boy into a man. It was something I had to do very quickly. It taught me to deal with being on my own. I was lucky that the people I stayed with were very good to me, and treated me like their own son, but when you're outside of that house, and about a strange town, football is a very unforgiving world if you're not ready. It'll eat you up.'

It would be here that a lot of young footballer's stories would end, but a steely resolve to hone his abundance of natural talent ensured McCourt was well-primed to effectively start his career from scratch. March 2005 arrived and, along with spring, the month heralded the beginning of McCourt's revival. Former Carlisle manager Roddy Collins, at the time manager of League of Ireland side Shamrock Rovers, brought McCourt to Dublin. By May he topped the scoring charts.

'At that stage, my only ambition was to get back to enjoying football,' McCourt says. 'I never thought of going back to England and so I played the best football I had for years. Roddy, like John Hollins, put his arm around me. He always made sure I got home to see my mum. Again, my football just flourished because, managing the person rather than the footballer, always seemed to work best for me. The League of Ireland season starts in February, so I had a great five months and could have gone to QPR, Motherwell or Bristol City after that. I could've earned good money, but, the bad experience I had at the end of my time at Rochdale, meant I just wasn't ready mentally to go back and go through all that again. Money was secondary. I was just so enjoying my football and my life, I just wanted that to continue. That was more important to me than taking another stab in the dark at football over the water.'

Financial difficulties meant Shamrock reluctantly agreed to sell McCourt to his hometown club Derry City at the end of that season. Despite the switch, he still managed to win the Professional Footballers Association of Ireland Young Player of the Year award.

While many assumed McCourt was spending the following three years in football's wilderness, he was, in fact, carving himself a new reputation. With Derry, McCourt won the League of Ireland Cup twice, won the FAI Cup and played in a UEFA Cup run, in which the club eventually lost to Paris Saint-Germain.

'I also met the woman who is now my wife,' McCourt adds. 'Stability was all that mattered to me. I had three really good seasons at Derry and, by now, I was 24. I had grown up a bit, you know? Clubs started to come back in for me and I was very much ready to give things another crack on the full-time football front.'

Come June 2008, McCourt was once again in vogue. Derry received two offers – one from Premier League side West Brom and the other from his boyhood heroes Celtic.

The choice was, as you might expect, a no-brainer.

'It was a bit of whirlwind, to be honest,' McCourt says. 'I was due to sign for West Brom, who had just got promoted to the Premier League. I'd had meetings with the manager, Tony Mowbray, and the agent involved, who was Northern Ireland-based. Derry had accepted their bid, so I flew over to Birmingham, drove down to their training ground and met the chief executive, Dan Ashworth. I was shown around, all normal stuff when you're about to sign for a club. Then Dan said, "Look, the hospital is now closed for your medical, so we've sorted a hotel for you and you can do it at 9am tomorrow." While I was at the hotel, my agent got a call from Derry saying Celtic had matched the bid of West Brom. I got a call from Celtic's chief exec, Peter Lawwell, and, for me, there was nothing to think about. I had supported Celtic since I was a boy. It was a surreal moment. My agent explained to West Brom the situation and we set off up the road to Glasgow that evening.'

McCourt made his competitive debut for Celtic on 25 October 2008, in a 4-2 win over Hibernian, although he was mainly used in the club's successful reserve side that season.

'It was very daunting,' he says. 'Derry was a full-time club, but they are in the League of Ireland – not a league readily recalled in world football. Moving to Celtic, which is a club that is in the world top 20 in terms of size, was very daunting. There was also added pressure being a Celtic supporter and the whole of Derry seemed to be talking about it at the time. That said, I felt really ready to go and experience what it was to be at a top club.'

The following season, McCourt scored his first Celtic goal. It was one that dazzled the travelling Bhoys but one that Rochdale fans would not have been surprised to see. It was during a League Cup match at Falkirk and involved a trademark run whereby he beat five defenders before chipping the keeper.

'My first goal was a long time coming,' he says. 'My first year, I only made five or six sub appearances while I took time to adapt to this new level. I then had a really good pre-season over the summer and was in and among the first team. I then got a start against Falkirk in the League Cup and that's when I got that first goal. It was a dream come true to do it in the manner I did. You dream of it as a boy. Picking the ball up on the halfway line, going past three or four men and then dinking it over the keeper. That's what it's about.'

McCourt continued in this fashion when given a run in the SPL and it saw him rewarded with an improved contract, as much to ward off suitors in England as to keep him happy. He was enjoying life playing under Gordon Strachan.

'Gordon was a bit of a mix as far as management styles go,' recalls McCourt. 'He was very tough on the players, but the players loved him. He was very honest, though, and he would back his players to the hilt. I learned a good thing from Gordon, actually, on how to work with players. At Celtic, the players could lose or draw and he would absolutely batter them in the dressing room. I mean, he would really go after people, but then, in the press, he would stick up for them all. He would make an excuse or take the blame for the result himself, saying he got the team selection wrong. He always backed the players in the press and I think the players really respected him for that. They would run through a brick wall for Gordon, there's no doubt about that.'

Then, seven years after his first international appearance, McCourt won a second cap for Northern Ireland, against San Marino in a qualifying match for the 2010 World Cup. He went on to be named in several international squads during his time at Celtic.

'It tends to be the way with international football,' he reflects. 'At Derry I was flying but didn't get a look-in. As soon as I signed for Celtic, I'm getting picked again. I wasn't a better player a few months after signing for Celtic than I was at Derry but that's the way of it. It depends what league or club you're at.'

Come the 2010/11 season, McCourt was firmly established in the Celtic ranks, despite managerial changes. Highlights included scoring in a 9-0 annihilation of Aberdeen, snatching Celtic's 600th home SPL goal and winning the Scottish Cup, his first silverware in Scotland.

McCourt failed to hit his previous heights during the next two seasons, despite Celtic winning both the 2011/12 and 2012/13 SPL titles, and the 2013 Scottish Cup. That final, a 3-0 victory over Hibernian at Hampden Park, was his final appearance for the club.

'I felt it was the right decision to leave Celtic when I did,' he muses. 'I had the opportunity to stay, but I felt the previous season that I wasn't playing as much and I was now 29. I felt I wasn't having as much of an impact on the team as previously. It was time for a new club and for me to be more influential on a team and play more regularly. I was aware time was passing me by. I didn't want to look back on my career and see myself on the bench more than on the pitch.'

McCourt's next move was back to England, signing for his former Rochdale team-mate David Flitcroft at Championship side Barnsley.

'Dave gave me a licence to go and play,' McCourt says. 'First half of the season, I absolutely loved it and was playing well. But the team wasn't playing well. It wasn't a big shock. Their budget wouldn't have been that of the bigger clubs. We were nowhere near dead and buried though, so it was a big surprise to me when the board decided to move Dave on.'

Spells at Brighton, Notts County and Luton followed, each time seeing McCourt move down the English leagues, before a life-changing event took precedence over his career.

'My wife, she took ill in April 2016,' McCourt says. 'She had a brain tumour that was causing her to take fits. She wasn't able to drive. We decided it was time to go home. I was 32 and had two young children. It was the best decision for all of us. I played part time for a couple of years and then, in 2018, I was offered the role at Derry to become the head of the youth academy. I did that for a year and was offered the role of technical director, which I still hold to this day. I have a much boarder role within the football club. I'm a lot more involved in the first team. I draw on the experiences that I had as a young man, to help me deal with young players who work with me on a daily basis now.'

McCourt says he'd like to return to Rochdale one day – both as a supporter and an academic of the game.

'It's a club that I still hold very close to my heart and I still check for the result every Saturday. It's a club I support, basically. I wouldn't rule out being back there someday. I'd especially love to come back to compare how it is now to when I was there. To see how, or if, the infrastructure has moved on. What do they now see as the best way to develop young players, for example? If I was joining as a 16-year-old now, would these methods make a difference? My opinion would be, if the club ever came into some kind of money, the most important thing it could ever do is to get its own training base. If you had that, I'm sure a lot more names like those in this book would follow on.'

Ian Henderson

2013–2020 and 2022–

DUE TO Rochdale AFC's lack of financial clout when compared to other clubs, manager Keith Hill once referred to his exploits in the transfer market as having to look for 'broken toys'. The analogy referred to him picking up players who had raw talent but who had also lost their way in the game, and so needed to be 'put back together again'. In other words, players that would have otherwise been out of his league.

Ian Henderson is possibly one of the most successful projects to emerge from Hill's toy workshop. A player from East Anglia, Henderson had once upon a time made a handful of Premier League appearances before tumbling down the divisions. He rocked up at Rochdale in 2013, aged 28, with a slight journeyman reputation, before going on to prove all doubters wrong, becoming the club's third-highest scorer by 2020 with 126 goals in all competitions at the time of publication.

During this time, he became a captain who led by example on the field and was a key contributor to the club during the most successful period in its history. But, as a child, the predatory instinct Rochdale supporters would come to love and admire was not initially Henderson's key strength. It was, in fact, his hands!

'I started off playing in goal, funnily enough,' he recalls. 'It wasn't until I asked to play outfield that I realised I could actually play football. My Sunday team put me up front and I scored a hatful of goals in a short space of time.'

Born in Bury St Edmunds, Suffolk, but brought up in the Norfolk town of Thetford, Henderson was aware of Norwich and Ipswich being the two major football clubs in the region. It was the former who eventually came calling.

'Norwich scout Colin Watts saw me play and invited me for a trial. I remember the trial vividly. I was only about seven or eight years old. I played against Colchester United and scored a couple of goals. However, on the debrief, Colin said it was a "no" from Norwich at that present time. So, I went back to my Sunday league team and just kept on playing football and scoring goals.'

Undeterred, a resolute Henderson refused to let his dream slide.

'I think this is where I learned a lot about myself early on in terms of being proactive,' he says. 'I had an older brother, who was already at Norwich, and I remember writing a letter, in pencil, to Colin Watts asking for another trial. Colin still has the letter actually. In the letter, I said I was better than my brother. Maybe that's a bit self-proclaimed and overconfident, but it worked. Colin offered me another trial, but this time it lasted nearly three months! They just couldn't come to a decision about me, for whatever reason.

'It got towards the latter stages of the trial, and I remember them still humming and hawing as we went to play against Watford. I scored a hat-trick. I was thinking, "Surely they've got to offer me some sort of deal now?" Thankfully, they did. I was only eight or nine years old at this point but something magical happened. I made a mature decision to fully commit myself to football. I was dedicated and professional. I made sacrifices. It paid off, as I started to jump years. I started playing in older age groups. I was playing in the under-19s when I was 14 or 15. All of a sudden, a pathway at the football club seemed a lot clearer to me. I then got called up to play for the reserves. Steve Foley was the reserve team manager back then. Obviously, the structure of football clubs has changed now, but, back then, that's how it was. Steve took a liking to me, for whatever reason, and he played me. I was absolutely buzzing because I got half a day off school.'

However, just as Henderson was getting to grips with balancing life in a professional club's youth team with schoolwork, he had to deal with the loss of his brother Tommy, who tragically died in a car accident shortly before Christmas 2000.

'If you lose someone you love there is always a place in your heart and your mind for them,' he says. 'I always have a thought for my brother and my grandad before a game. I use the sad losses in my life as a catalyst to help me keep on going and give me motivation to be the best version of myself.'

And so it proved. Henderson knuckled down and worked towards his ultimate goal.

'From that period of me doing my GCSEs to leaving school, it was a big jump, as I then went into full-time training and started right at the bottom of the food chain. I was a youth team player doing all the odd jobs around the building, as well as training and playing. However, I started to perform consistently for the under-19s and the reserves and I got called up to the first team when I was 16. It was at Coventry City, but I didn't come off the bench. I always look back at that moment with huge honesty. Was I ready, physically and psychologically, at that time? No. No way was I ready for first-team football, but I understood why the manager did it. It was to give me some experience and dangle that carrot.

'After that, I literally wasn't involved with the first team again until one year to the day later. I made my full first-team debut against Coventry at Highfield Road, the team I was on the bench against a year earlier. That moment, that emotion, that feeling – it will stick with me forever. All of the hard work put in since I was eight years old had paid off. It was a reward for all of my sacrificial behaviours prior to that moment. The only thing was, all through the ranks at Norwich, I played up front, either as a lone striker, in a two, or as the middle man in a three. When I made my debut at 17, the manager [Nigel Worthington] put me on the right wing and I'd never played there in my life!'

The positional switch didn't faze Henderson, however.

226

'It all evolved from there very quickly,' he says. 'I started to feature more for the first team and got a bit of a run of about ten or 15 starts in a row which, for a club of Norwich's size, was a good achievement. I still had a lot to learn, though. All of a sudden, we had gone from the Championship to the Premier League. I had a hand in that by scoring a few goals, but I had a lot of work to do to stay in that first team.

'By nature, football is highly competitive and we had some extremely good players at the club at that time with the likes of Dean Ashton and Darren Huckerby, who had a reputation and a goalscoring statistic that far outweighed mine. Nonetheless, it was an amazing learning curve and upbringing. I am eternally grateful to Nigel Worthington for giving me my debut, and mentors such as Aidy Boothroyd, Sammy Morgan and Colin Watts. I still keep in touch with them all to this day. I have made a point in my career to keep in touch with the people who have helped me.'

As Henderson struggled for game time at Norwich, he eventually realised it was time to move on.

'I left Norwich in the summer of 2007 and I was maybe a little bit lost in the sense that I'd been at a football club since I was eight and I was now 22. I didn't know anything else. I had an ingrained football make-up from one system and one culture, which was hard when I went somewhere else. It took me maybe four or five years to adapt to life away from Norwich, if I'm being honest.'

Spells at Northampton and Luton followed, but neither managed to fulfil an ambitious Henderson.

'I didn't really play at Northampton and, looking back, it probably wasn't the right move for me,' he says. 'However, there is always learning to take from a move – even the ones that don't work out. After 18 months and playing only 20 or so games, I had the opportunity to go to Luton for six months. Luton had been deducted 30 points, if I recall rightly, so it was always going to be an uphill battle to retain their league status. In the end, we fell short but the team did win the Football League Trophy at Wembley, which is something they deserved with their great fanbase. However, Luton wasn't the right fit for me in the sense of my own career direction and I left.'

This led to what Henderson refers to as the nomadic period of his career.

'I'd got myself into a situation where no football club wanted me in the UK,' he says. 'I ventured away from England and signed for a team in Turkey called Ankaragücü. I went to Austria for a three-week trial first, as that was where their pre-season training camp was. The coach was really good with me. Hikmet Karaman was his name. He was Turkish-German, I think, and he spoke broken English, but, as we all know, football is a universal language and he put an arm around me and played me.'

Once in the Turkish capital, Henderson had to adapt to a new way of life, right down to managing his own business affairs.

'It was very different in Turkey,' he says. 'They train twice a day – early morning and early evening – to mitigate the climate, but I had a really good time. My contract was for two years but I ended up only being there for six months due to a couple of factors. Firstly, the team merged with Ankaraspor, the other team in the city, and the president from there brought all of his players over to us. Then there was a limit on overseas players in Turkey and, as a result, they decided they didn't need me anymore. One day, the manager called me in and said, "You've got to go." I wasn't going anywhere. They tried all sorts of tactics. It taught me a valuable lesson – to thoroughly read a contract! Essentially, I was going to the notary in Turkey every day to document the prior day's activities, while liaising with a lawyer in the UK, trying to negotiate my way out of the football club. I had to return to the UK without any money, but I fought that case and eventually won it, which was quite pleasing.'

The experience left Henderson with an existential crisis,

'I was now in my mid 20s and it was at this point I asked myself a deep, penetrating question, "What do I want from football?" I had become sick and tired of moving here, there and everywhere. I wanted to be settled and have consistency in my life. I had always lived out of a suitcase. I had never owned a house in which I hung up my clothes. My partner, Nicola, who I'd been with for about five years at that point, said, "Why do you not hang your clothes up?" I didn't know. It was perhaps a fear thing of always having to move on. Luckily enough, she helped me with that, psychologically.'

And then an old mentor saved Henderson from another trip overseas.

'It was by now November, and I'm back in the UK without a club again. I was due to fly out to Germany to sign for a team that was interested, but I didn't have international clearance to play until January, due to the situation in Turkey. My old youth team manager from Norwich, Aidy Boothroyd, had just taken over at Colchester. He asked me to come along and train with them. I did this for about a week or ten days and he offered me a contract. It was a small one to start with – I think 18 months – but I signed it. However, I didn't play much under Aidy. It was his assistant, John Ward, who took a liking to me. When Aidy left, and John took over, I got a lot more game time.

'John Ward says to me, "You're going to play every game, I don't care if you play good or bad, you will play." He played me on the wing, sometimes up front, and it was great. I did well for John and, just when I thought I was getting that consistency in my life, John lost his job. A new manager came along and deemed my services surplus to requirements.'

Dejected, Henderson relocated to Manchester with his partner, where he even considered giving up football and returning to education.

'I was 27, 28 when I left Colchester and I was seriously considering going to university to study dentistry,' Henderson reflects. 'I had braces when I was a kid. I didn't have the most aesthetically pleasing teeth and had braces and I was really intrigued by it. I looked into studying it, but never pursued it in the end.'

Instead, Henderson opted to stick with football, hoping for a slice of luck that would reinvigorate his career. It came in the form of an old team-mate.

'I got a call off a mate I'd played with at Colchester, Michael Rose,' Henderson remembers. 'He had signed for Rochdale and said the manager, Keith Hill, wanted me to come in and train. I felt, every time I'd played against Rochdale previously, I'd scored or done well against them, so I understood why Keith perhaps wanted me to come in. It actually came at a good time for me because I was supposed to have signed for Preston North End but, the day I went to sign for them, the manager, Graham Westley, got the sack, so the deal was off. I was thinking, "Jesus Christ, not all this again." Then, after that, the same thing happened again. I went to Notts County to sign but, the day I got there, Keith Curle got the sack. I just couldn't believe what was happening.

'So, the call from Rosey was very welcome. I thought I'd just go along, train with Rochdale and enjoy it. For whatever reason, and I can't put my finger on it exactly, I just hit it off with everyone at the football club, especially the manager and the players. I don't want this to come across all cheesy, but it felt like home. It felt comfortable. Like I could really be myself. I've always been myself, but here it was even more so. There was a level of freedom given to me, too, and I played with that freedom. It allowed me to play with a smile on my face and that elevated my game. One thing I will always take from Rochdale is the attitude of the people who live there. There is a never-say-die-attitude and an identity of hard work. The team mirrored that. They gave their all for the cause. I really respected that.'

Henderson suitably impressed Keith Hill and was rewarded with a contract until the end of the season. He was immediately thrust into a dogfight with Rochdale sitting at the wrong end of League Two.

'When I joined Rochdale, it was a similar situation to Luton for me, in that Rochdale were struggling in the league,' he says. 'However, Keith had not long come back to the club and was already turning things around. We dug out of it and we finished the season relatively strongly. I could always sense, with the way our team set up, we would always score goals, but we were a bit vulnerable to conceding goals too. It created entertaining games for sure, but it was also to the dismay of the fans at times.'

Henderson was given a two-year contract at the end of the season and, with his manager, could look forward to creating a new era for Rochdale.

'That summer, Keith began his rebuild phase,' he says. 'There was good recruitment with Ollie Lancashire and Peter Vincenti, among others, who added huge value not just on the pitch, but off it too. Keith always recruited the right characters. Added to this, Scott Hogan was brought back to the club and both Jamie Allen and Callum Camps were promoted from the academy. There was the perfect mix of youth, experience and personalities. As a team we just rocketed. There wasn't a great deal of tactics in terms of, "You're gonna do this and you're gonna do that," it was all based on working hard on the field, you know? See how Liverpool play now [2022]? It was like that. I'm not comparing us to Liverpool, I'm comparing our intensity and the way we attacked each game, week in, week out. We'd be relentless in that approach. We would run teams off the pitch with our energy, enthusiasm and our ability to move the ball fast across the deck. We had dynamic players who allowed us to do that. We didn't have a big team, on paper, it was a team built around energy and enthusiasm. That's what Keith wanted.'

Henderson believes the manager allowed him to flourish into the player he always believed he could be.

'Keith Hill, tactically, was exceptional. His understanding of formations and what opposition teams were going to do was phenomenal. He would always set us up to win a game. Always. It was attacking football. For me, however, it was his man management. He gave me the autonomy to run the changing room as captain, and do what was needed. In short, he saw a leadership quality in me that allowed me a certain freedom. He was inclusive of my business ventures outside of football [Henderson had set up a network marketing business upon joining Rochdale]. Keith allowed me to pursue this – in fact he encouraged it. He was a very fair man and very honest. If you did well, you did well. If you didn't, you didn't. There were no grey areas. It was simple, effective leadership.'

That season, Hill led Rochdale to promotion from League Two for a second time, and a remarkable FA Cup third round victory over Championship side Leeds United.

'Maybe there's method in the madness from Keith,' Henderson chuckles. 'Against Leeds, he dropped me back to create a three-man midfield. He must have known that they played with two players who were relatively slow in midfield and our style of play totally disrupted them. Scotty Hogan that day was unbelievable. One of his best performances for Rochdale and it quite rightly won him his big Championship contract with Brentford.'

During the 2-0 victory, Henderson scored a magnificent side-footed, cushioned, looping volley over the stranded Leeds goalkeeper Paddy Kenny.

'I tried that technique earlier on in the game and it didn't come off,' he recalls. 'I can remember the ball coming over vividly. It was as if it was in slow motion. I just caressed the ball into the far corner. People always mention that goal to me, but I practised that technique so much in training and so much over the years, that I wasn't surprised it happened in a game. I don't want that to sound arrogant in any way, but there is a catalogue of those types of finishes over the years in my game. However, on this occasion, it felt like the whole stadium sucked me in when I scored. It was like a beehive exploding. Not quite the Azteca Stadium in Mexico, but definitely that type of feeling. It was a magical moment.'

With promotion to League One, Henderson would undergo a positional revolution.

'You'll probably remember, I started the promotion season as a left-winger,' he says. 'Lots of people forget that and they wonder why I only started scoring prolifically towards the latter end of my career. Well, that's why. I was an up-down-inside-out winger.

'I got my fair share of goals as a winger, of course I did, but it got to a point – the first season we were back in League One actually – when we had a lot of injuries. The manager was scratching his head. We were playing Crewe away and he only had me or Matty Done to choose from to play up front. To be honest, he didn't want to choose either one of us. So, he came up with a formation called split strikers, where me and Doney would act as inside wingers playing up front. It just suited the whole profile of player at the football club. It unleashed the two of us, to be honest. Doney ended up going to Sheffield United on the strength of his performances in that role. We had one of the best league finishes Rochdale has ever achieved, too. I think we surprised a good number of teams with the way and style in which we played that year.'

Rochdale would go on to confound critics and bookmakers over the next two seasons, starting the season as relegation certs before mounting a realistic challenge for the play-offs or even promotion.

However, the side then began to wane, as Henderson explains,

'Those first two years in League One, we really pushed hard at the play-off positions but, as a team, and as a football club, we reached our level, I believe. You see it now with teams who rise from League Two to the Championship. The organisational structure needed to maintain that level of success and status is incredibly difficult. The budget increases are eye watering and the ability to track and keep the type of players needed is also incredibly difficult. For a club like Rochdale, even in League One, this became a challenge. The third season in League One was a case of consolidation. We knew we were going to lose players because of our success and with the younger players evolving and developing.'

As Rochdale began to struggle in League One, Henderson said he did what he could to rally players,

'We should have been relegated in the 2017/18 season. No doubt about it. I could see it and I could feel it early in the season. Myself and, let's call it the leadership squad, we called numerous player meetings to share our views and experiences. For me, it boiled down to simple key fundamentals not being met consistently enough to withstand the pressures of League One.

'However, the moment that will always stay with me from my time at Rochdale actually had nothing to do with me. It was Joey Thompson's winner against Charlton on the last day of that season. The goal that kept us in League One. From a human interest point of view, it had everything. What he had been through, beating cancer, and then to do that? Wow.'

Henderson would spend another two seasons at Rochdale, each time finishing as their top scorer. He was zeroing in on the all-time club record of 129 goals held by Reg Jenkins, who set the figure in October 1972 when he passed Albert Whitehurst's 124 with Rochdale's second goal in a 2-2 home draw with Bolton. Could Henderson have beaten Reg had he not missed a few penalties and avoided suspensions along the way?

'What a wonderful question!' he laughs. 'No, I don't have any regrets about missed penalties or missed games through suspension. I know that I did the best that I could. I know, had I stayed at the club longer, I would have topped the club's all-time goalscorer list in my first spell.'

And that's the rub. Henderson's eventual departure in 2020 left a sour taste for all concerned. It was far from cordial and eventually led to lawyers being involved on both sides. The club had undergone a lot of changes in quick succession around this time, with chairman Chris Dunphy stepping down to be replaced by the less-visible Andrew Kilpatrick, and Keith Hill being replaced as manager by his understudy, Brian Barry-Murphy.

'I had multiple offers every single year to leave the football club,' he says. 'I always declined because, and I've always been open about this, money is not my driver. For me, I am driven by being part of something and achieving something as part of a group. Not everyone has that view, and I totally understand and respect that, but it's not me. I didn't ever come close to accepting any offer to leave. I had conversations with Keith frequently, but he knew I had no interest in leaving the football club. None whatsoever. I wanted to finish my football career at Rochdale AFC, simple as that.

'Things had changed at the club. Keith left, yes, but I was still offered a new contract. A lot of speculation has emanated from this, but the nuts and bolts of it are very simple. I didn't ask for any more money, the only stumbling block in the negotiations was that there was a stipulation that stated, in order to get my third year, which would have taken me up to my tenth year at the football club, I had to play 50 per cent of the games. After nine years of service, I didn't feel I needed to prove myself to anyone to get that extra year and a testimonial match. There is a trail that shows I also said I would give 50 per cent of the net profit from my testimonial match back to the academy to reinvest in players.

'I'm aware things have been painted in a way that perhaps shows me as money-grabbing, but, I'll say again, I didn't ask for any more money, I was offered the same money that I was already on and I was OK with that. I just wasn't happy with the 50 per cent game clause. I let the club know this and then there was a complete breakdown in communication across the board. Then someone said something had happened, which didn't happen, which in turn then led to an internal investigation at the club. This investigation proved what I said was correct. As I'm sure you can understand, I can't say too much more about these events, and it, very sadly, resulted in me leaving the club. I was upset. I publicly came out and made a statement and we can all use excuses about the pandemic, which I am not saying lightly, as it affected a lot of people in a lot of ways, but it was multi-faceted, let's just say that.'

A two-season spell at League Two Salford City followed Henderson's Rochdale exit.

'Salford came in for me as soon as they found out Rochdale were going to retract the contract they had offered me,' he recalls. 'It was a very good offer, but it came with a stipulation that I perform a mentoring role. I declined it. Deep down, I guess, I hoped Rochdale were going to come back for me. When it became clear that wasn't going to happen, I knew I had to move on. Salford came back with a new offer, as did several other clubs, but everything about Salford, from the outside looking in, seemed like an exciting project – big ambitions and big goals. I also knew some of the players who were already there, so it wouldn't be a case of completely starting from scratch. I opted to sign for them, but didn't want the responsibility within the contract of mentoring or coaching. I was very much still focused on playing.

'The season got off to a really good start and I think I got four or five goals in the first three or four games. However, there then came a lot of change in management in a short space of time. For whatever reason, they decided to release the manager, Graham Alexander, and his coaching staff. I got on really well with Graham. I liked his approach of getting the fundamentals right and doing the basics over and over. He brought a lot of professionalism to Salford. When he and his team left, it felt like we were in the middle of nowhere, to be honest. I've never had that in my career where a management team is replaced while the club is doing well.

'We then had Paul Scholes coming in with Warren Joyce, and then Chris Casper was getting involved on matchdays. No one knew if they were coming or going. Richie Wellens arrived for a bit – but didn't last too long, before Gary Bowyer was given the job. Now, Gary at least managed to get us going again and brought the belief back into the playing squad. We pushed on under him, but, again, the club decided it was going to go in a different direction and he was relieved of his duties.'

Henderson, too, became a victim of the reshuffle.

'I kind of had an inclination that Salford wouldn't offer me another contract because I saw the way they were setting up for the new season and the type of players they were targeting,' he says. 'I don't have an issue with this and, as you have seen by now, it has happened to me enough for me to understand this is how football works.

'If I had to sum up my time at Salford, how would I do it? Well, my objective at Salford was to score goals. Did I do that? Yes. I think my average was just under one every two games. Did I assist? Yes. Did I help the team achieve the strategic objective of promotion? No. Were there a lot of variables within that, such as having four managers in two years? Yes.

'Let's use Rochdale as an example. In the history of the football club, it has only ever achieved a certain level. On the flipside, a team like Salford, that has had a heck of a lot of investment put into it, hasn't even achieved the levels Rochdale has, but, the pressure to do so – and then more – is always there. They have been used to promotion after promotion through the non-leagues and the expectation to do so again is ever present. However, they have reached a level now where the infrastructure needs to catch up with their ambitions. That wasn't the case while I was there, but I'm sure it will be before long. Rochdale, on the flipside, maybe doesn't have all of that investment, but it has all of the people behind the scenes in place to make the club operate the way it does, to make it a community football club.'

Rather than fizzling out at the age of 37, Henderson was brought back to Rochdale by a new regime – a new board and a new manager in Robbie Stockdale – offering him one last chance to crack the record that was cruelly denied him previously. There was certainly a Pavlovian reflex of optimism from this writer upon seeing him wearing blue and black again for his 'unveiling'.

'When Salford finally told me I wouldn't be staying, I went away with my family on holiday to reflect,' Henderson says. 'We had a good time and I came back refreshed. I said to my family, "I'm going to get myself fit and into a good state." I didn't expect the requests to come flooding in from football clubs, nor did I see myself as an instant first pick, but I wanted to be the best and fittest I could be to at least give clubs that option. Once I reached this level, I said to my agent, "OK, I'm ready," and then the phone started ringing. I was a little surprised, to be honest. I thought I would have to wait much longer. One of those calls was from Rochdale. My agent said the new manager, Robbie Stockdale, wanted to meet me. I was excited by the prospect of coming back. As I said before, I wanted to finish my career at this club. I wanted to create modern history at this club and help it get where it wants to be. I met Robbie for a coffee and he outlined his plans, his philosophy, his preferred team set-up and so on. He's actually not that much older than me. We clicked. It was just a case of going back and forth over the contract, to make sure both parties were suited, and then it was a case of a rigorous fitness examination and medical.'

And on the prospect of surpassing Reg Jenkins as Rochdale's all-time top scorer?

'I will just keep hitting the goals,' Henderson says casually. 'I will always go into a game believing I am going to score during it. Always. That is my football DNA. I'd like to score the goals that break the record and then enough thereafter to hold the record for a long time. It won't be the scoring of the actual goals that I cling to, it will be the feeling attached to scoring the goals, if that makes sense? It will have been done over such a long period of time.

'Sorry if I appear a bit deep here, but I am really big on longevity and sticking at something. A person doesn't become a neuroscientist overnight. No, it takes years of dedication and refinement. That's my mantra with everything in life – family, relationships, business – it's always built on solid foundations but then it takes work and dedication to stay the course. In football, that is very rare these days. Players can be seen as transient when it comes to football clubs. I have taken a 45 per cent wage cut to come back to Rochdale. I don't say that flippantly, I say that from the point of view that my exit from the club last time was totally misconstrued. I am here for personal achievement, collective achievement – but not money. I want to create a legacy so that when my children grow up they see what their dad has achieved and think to themselves, "That's why we stick at things."

'By the time people are reading this, I hope that record has been broken.'

Henderson was given an initial one-year contract, but his already evidenced longevity may well see that extended.

'Growing up, football has always been my life and I never want to let go of that dream of playing it professionally,' he says. 'You are a long time retired but, if you surround yourself with younger people and you're in and around a squad, and they're pushing you day in, day out, and you still have that desire to match them, you'll have longevity regardless. There are fundamentals, obviously, in looking after yourself and working incredibly hard, but the desire and enjoyment have to be there. If they are, there will be longevity.

'That said, my first spell at Rochdale is the most I've ever enjoyed football in my career. I played week in, week out, the manager got me, understood me, and, as a team, we did well on limited resources. The underdog attitude we developed carried us a long way. That period is the greatest in the club's history and I'm glad I was part of it. I hope I can make many more happy memories for the club.'

Calvin Andrew

2014–2020

HAD THINGS panned out differently, the name Calvin Andrew could have been up in lights in London's West End rather than featuring on a Rochdale team sheet.

It's hard to imagine now, but, as a youth, the multi-talented 6ft 2in forward showed a penchant for the dramatic, to the extent he had agents urging him to tread the boards professionally.

'I was always big into my drama,' Andrew says. 'At school I was doing stage shows, you know, *Oliver!* and things like that? It was like a hobby for me, I enjoyed it, but I had talent. I realised this as I was constantly being asked by people to take it further. People from London were coming up and trying to get me to try out for West End stage shows. It really did appeal to me and, if football hadn't worked out, I definitely would have gone that way. Hey, I still might.'

A striker who isn't known for scoring goals usually has to work doubly hard to endear themselves to supporters and managers alike. It's fair to say Andrew's record will never be held up to the likes of Reg Jenkins, Albert Whitehurst, Steve Whitehall or Ian Henderson when anyone is perusing the pantheon of great Rochdale forwards, but that still wouldn't prevent supporters looking back on his time at the club fondly.

A mobile target man hailing from Luton, Andrew came to Rochdale with a decent pedigree. He had played in the second tier for both Luton Town and Crystal Palace, and had gone on to ply his trade at enough third- and fourth-tier clubs to warrant the 'experienced player' tag. While not a goal-every-two-games man, his knack for scoring vital ones led to the birth of the affectionate chant, 'Calvin Andrew, he scores when he wants.'

Andrew made 231 appearances for Rochdale, scoring 28 goals, yet 118 of those appearances were as a substitute – a club record.

Regarded fondly around the club for his demeanour and community work, Andrew – apart from one freak, out-of-character moment that we will come to – epitomised everything Rochdale AFC sought to be: a part of the community that people felt they could reach out and touch.

'I seem to get a lot of accolades from people about my community work, but I don't see it as me doing anything special,' he says. 'I always remember, as a kid, having a presentation at my Sunday league team from Marvin Johnson [who made more than 400 appearances for Luton Town between 1986 and 2003], who came to speak to us and present some awards. He was a Luton legend at the time. You were just in awe of this guy. You listened and would hang off every word that he said. These guys probably don't realise how much of an effect they have on kids. They're stars, at the end of the day.

'When I got my opportunity to be a professional footballer, I realised this and knew I had a platform to inspire and mentor people. Whenever Rochdale ever asked me to do something in the community, I jumped at it. Yes, there is personal gratification in knowing you can help or inspire someone else, but it's also something every footballer should be doing. It is part of the job, as far as I'm concerned. A lot of the lads were probably not too keen on me at times, as I'd bully them into coming along. They'd be giving it, "I can't, I've got something else on," and I'd be like, "Yeah, you're cancelling that and coming with me."'

This caring demeanour was shaped by having two supportive parents as he was growing up who, according to Andrew, never once pushed him into any one career path.

'They took me to everything and they were fantastic, but they never forced me to do anything,' he says. 'I was super lucky to have two parents who supported me in everything I did, the whole way through my career. I think that really benefited me. I saw a lot of kids, at ten and 11 years of age, being forced by the parents to go on trial with Arsenal, Watford and teams like that. They would get knocked back and their parents would march them somewhere else. Before you know it, the kid's fed up with football and not enjoying it anymore. For a very long time, I was playing football for the love of it. It wasn't something I was looking to do professionally. I had a broad spectrum of things I could have done. I was playing Sunday league football for a very long time before I was part of any professional youth setup. For me, I never had any of the pressure the other lads had, to make the grade at a pro club.'

And, as well as an acting career, Andrew could well have had his pick of numerous sporting professions too.

'I was fortunate growing up in that I was athletically gifted. I don't want that to sound like I'm blowing my own trumpet or anything, but I just seemed to be good at any sport I tried. I did athletics, rugby, cricket, you name it. I wasn't focused on just football at all. Every day, after school, I would be playing one sport or another at a very good level. There were always people coming in and trying to get me to sign for clubs, be that cricket, rugby or football.'

But it *was* football that Andrew enjoyed best.

'From a very young age, I was playing football out in the street with the other kids,' he says. 'My brother is six years older than me, so I was playing with him, too. We started to play against kids from other streets and it built up from there. A lot of the kids were six or seven years older than me, because of my brother, so I got a lot of football education because of that. I had to grow up very fast and be more physical, and cleverer with the way I played the game, or I wasn't getting a touch.'

Finally, Andrew did have a decision to make about his future – and football won the day,

'I was 16 and I was at college, studying sports science. I had been asked to go in and train with the Luton youth team now and then, but it wasn't formal.

'I had been approached by Peterborough United prior to that. I had gone in to train with them for a few weeks when I was 15 and they wanted me to sign a YTS [Youth Training Scheme] with them. I played a game against Luton Town, the week before I was due to sign, and did really well. It drew Luton's attention to me. They said, "You're a Luton boy, why are you not in with us?" Because football still wasn't something I'd set my heart on at that point, it made more sense to go to Luton. Instead of my dad having to ferry me over to Peterborough to train with them, which was an hour and 15 minutes' drive one way, Luton was on my doorstep. A lot of the kids I knew from Luton were there and, even though I was an Arsenal fan, I grew up going to Luton games, so it all fitted for me.

'When I did sign for Luton, I was signed on a YTS for just three months before I was offered a professional contract. It took off from there really. Luton were in the third tier at the time, with Mike Newell the manager. In the first three reserve games of the season, I scored nine goals. Then we played Portsmouth, and Sol Campbell and Linvoy Primus were in that game, coming back from injury. I think we beat them 3-2, but I definitely had a stormer against those two guys. I then went on to make 11 or 12 appearances for the first team and we won the league, gaining promotion to the Championship. I would be playing up front with Steve Howard some games, and then cleaning his boots afterwards. That was how young players were introduced to the professional game back then, which is very humbling and teaches you a lot.'

Luton's promotion, however, saw Andrew's chances consequently limited.

'The next season we were in the Championship and I went right down the pecking order,' he remembers. 'I was just turning 17 and more experienced pros were arriving. I was sent on loan to Grimsby first, in League Two, and it was an eye-opener. I'd never been away from home, so this was the complete experience of what it is to be a professional footballer and to be an adult. Russell Slade was the manager at the time. We played Newcastle in the FA Cup at home and I was marking Alan Shearer on corners. I held my own, too. It certainly stands you in good stead an experience like that, not feeling a million miles apart from the top players. I scored my first senior league goal while I was at Grimsby.

'From there I went back to Luton for a bit and was then sent on loan to Bristol City. That was a bigger club and I had an apartment to myself. Again, it was a learning curve – all of these experiences building me up.'

Then something happened that changed Andrew's career forever.

'My time at Luton was hampered by some bad injuries,' he says. 'I had a cruciate ligament injury when I was 18, which kept me out for most the season. It hindered my development and completely changed my body. People see me now and say, "Yeah, you're a big, strapping centre-forward," but I wasn't prior to that injury. I was always a tricky winger with pace to burn. That injury changed the whole way I approached football. It changed my body and my position.'

Luton were relegated from the Championship in 2007 and would go on to fall into administration and suffer heavy points deductions.

'I was supposed to leave to go to Stoke but there was a transfer embargo on the club, so I couldn't go,' Andrew says. 'You can imagine my disappointment. When the embargo was finally lifted, I signed for Crystal Palace. I think they paid about £80,000 for me.'

However, Palace's enigmatic manager Neil Warnock led to some interesting conversations in the Andrew family home.

'I discussed the move with my parents and my mum was a bit against it, due to what she had seen of Warnock on the telly. He was a bit of a terrier and certainly played the media. She said, "I'm not sure you'll get on with him." But I did. He was a fantastic person. I went down there with my dad to have a medical. It took about four and five hours because of all the injuries I'd had at Luton. While I was doing that, Neil Warnock took my dad to the cricket. Kent were playing next door. He then took him for food. My dad was well impressed. Warnock was a great manager and a fantastic person, too.

'I started that season for Palace and was doing really well but, towards the end of that season, I ended up doing my other cruciate and was out for a whole year again. This one was a bad one and they said I might not play football again. I just refused to accept that. I had up days and down days but I grafted and worked hard. I got back to playing and went on loan to a few other clubs. Eventually, Dougie Freedman became manager. I struggled with injuries again, though, so didn't play a lot of games and we ended up parting ways.

'I didn't play football for about six months after that. I just needed to get my body right. Most of my career has been me focusing on overcoming bad injuries and career-threatening stuff. I wouldn't say I was lost at that point, but I knew I needed to take time to get my head and body right.'

By his own admission, Andrew failed to get the timing of his return correct, however.

'I went to Port Vale but it was a terrible season for me. I was not myself. I'd come back too soon, I was just trying to get my foot back in the door. I shouldn't have.

'I was at Mansfield next. I enjoyed it there as it was the first time I felt like me again after I'd left Crystal Palace. My body and mind felt capable again. Sadly, I didn't play as much as I should have done towards the end and I ended up moving on again.'

In March 2014, Andrew signed for another League Two club, York City, on a contract for the remainder of the season.

'It was while playing for York that I encountered Rochdale for the first time in my career. It's weird because I remember thinking what a good team they were. Something about the game, which I can't explain, stayed with me. I remember thinking afterwards, "I really like that team." Anyway, York got to the play-offs but were beaten by Fleetwood. I ended up without a club again.

'I was sat at home, contemplating my future, when I got a call from [Rochdale coach] Brian Barry-Murphy. He said Keith Hill was interested in signing me, but he wanted me to do a trial first. I'd never done a trial for a club in my life. I was going to say no, but then I remembered the impression Rochdale had left on me after I played against them and I thought, "You know what, this could be good for me." So, I got down off my high horse and gave it a go. I stayed at the Norton Grange Hotel for two weeks, trained with the squad, played in a few pre-season games, got on with everyone and then Keith Hill offered me a contract. That was the beginning of my love affair with Rochdale.'

Andrew signed a two-year deal with the newly promoted League One club and immediately felt at home.

'I've been at so many clubs but there was something different about Rochdale,' he says. 'It's a small club, but it was the most together club I've been at, if that makes sense? Just turning up every day to see everyone had a smile on their face – from the secretaries to the kit man. Everyone was so happy and positive. On the pitch, we had a good squad of players too, and all of us got on with each other. I know it's cliched to say, but we really did have a strong camaraderie. We didn't just train together, we did stuff after training too, or after a game. I still talk to them all to this day now. I can't say that about all of the clubs I've been at. It wasn't just the players though – Keith Hill and his assistant Chris Beech, Andy Thorpe, the physio, and the doctor, Wes Tensel, were all brilliant. That is testament to the type of club Rochdale was.'

It was Rochdale's most efficacious manager who had the biggest influence on Andrew, however.

'Keith Hill is one of the most genuine people you will meet,' he enthuses. 'Just like I said about Neil Warnock earlier on, in football, genuine people are very few and far between. You respect managers like that more because of it and you then end up giving them more. I know it sounds bad, but there are times in football when you might be tired or injured, and you hold back. But when it's someone like Keith, you think, "I don't want to let him down. He's invested so much in me, I'm going to run an extra ten yards." Now, you should always do that for yourself, but you don't. A good manager will get you doing it, though.'

And while Andrew loved his role in a progressive Rochdale side, it wasn't always appreciated by onlookers.

'I always put pressure on myself to score goals, but Keith never did,' he says. 'He understood that what I brought to the team was more than just goals. In his words, "I had a role in the squad which you couldn't teach or replace." It was difficult, because I always wanted to score goals, but it was something I never really had the knack of. As I said, growing up, I was a winger, a provider. I became a centre-forward, but I never had that magic touch of arriving in the right place at the right time. I was always outside the box, putting it in for the likes of Ian Henderson, or heading it down for Peter Vincenti. Keith understood that, the team understood that, but people outside the dressing room didn't always. Some people didn't watch or understand the game.

'I still hear, "You were a centre-forward, but didn't score a lot of goals." A lot of the time I wasn't playing as a centre-forward though, so people weren't paying attention. I was out in wide areas where Keith would put me, with a specific function of attack and defence. I was there to create more than to score. Keith knew if I did my function correctly then the players around me, Ian Henderson or Nathaniel Mendez-Laing, would get the goals. Often in games, you'll probably have noticed, I got marked by two people most of the time. Well, it may have been frustrating for me, but it left someone else free to get the goals. So, yes, I wanted to score goals, but the game and the team are bigger than just me. If I had a bit more of a selfish mentality, maybe I would have scored a couple more goals, but it's just not who I am, simple as that.'

One of Andrew's favourite memories from his spell at Spotland was his injury-time winner against Port Vale to keep Rochdale in the hunt for a League One play-off place in 2015.

'I think I'd just come off the bench, Callum Camps is on the ball in the far-right corner of the pitch and he just stands it up brilliantly in the box. I think everyone in the ground knew I was going to eat it up. I climbed highest and headed it down into the bottom corner. I ran straight to the crowd. I remember Beechy [Chris Beech] running down the touchline to join in. It was amazing. The ref blew his whistle at that point and we'd won it. Everyone was ecstatic in the dressing room. We still had a shot at the play-offs. Sadly, we didn't make them in the end, but we did secure the club's highest ever finish in the football pyramid. It didn't get that good again, unfortunately.'

His other cherished moment came at the other end of the table. Local lad Joe Thompson, who had returned to playing after recovering from cancer, capped off an emotional 12 months by scoring the only goal of the game against Charlton Athletic to help Dale avoid relegation at Oldham Athletic's expense in 2018.

'I assisted that goal but never get the credit for it,' Andrew laughs. 'No one ever mentions my assist apart from Joe himself. With everything he had been through, beating cancer, for him to get the winner that kept us in League One – you can't write it. Some of the lads were crying, I won't mention any names, but the overriding feeling among everyone was that it was just meant to happen.'

While he says his time at Rochdale is littered with 'too many fond memories to mention', there is one incident that Andrew would sooner forget. In 2016, he was given a 12-match ban after elbowing Peter Clarke in the face during a 1-0 victory over Oldham.

The incident, which took place in the 77th minute of the game, went unseen by officials at the time, but was caught on video, which was quickly circulated on social media. The shock among the Rochdale support, who knew Andrew's good character, was palpable. Many fought his corner on many platforms, as calls for him to be sacked and prosecuted escalated.

'I can't go into too much detail about this because it went to court and there were certain things that were agreed,' Andrew says. 'Needless to say, though, these things go on in football. People try to throw you off your game. It just went too far that day. I saw the red mist. I've never been a guy to take disrespect from people, but I went about it the wrong way that day. I should not have dealt with it that way. Me and Peter are friends now, but we always had a confrontation like that every time we played against each other. He's a fantastic competitor. He's the kind of guy you'd want on your team, actually. He's always had that in him, but we both went too far that day. It's something I don't condone and I do regret it. Credit to the club, who stood by me. Other clubs could quite easily have disposed of me after that. I remember feeling quite worried about my job after it happened. There was a whole big deal about it in the media and so on. Keith Hill reassured me, so did the chairman [Chris Dunphy]. That's what Rochdale is about right there. In my darkest hour, the club crowded round me to protect me.'

The ban was reduced on appeal, too.

'The ban was nothing short of ridiculous, to be honest with you,' Andrew shrugs. 'We went to court and it got reduced down to nine games. But there were two other Premier League players who had done something worse than I had done that week and they both got three-game bans. So, you can see how things are very different depending on who you are and what league you play in.'

Andrew finally left Rochdale at the end of the 2019/20 season. He said he felt his exit was a protracted and uncomfortable process and he cites the departure of Hill as manager, in March 2019, as being the catalyst.

'The club just changed after Keith left,' he says. 'He had such a big influence on everything that went on at the club, after he left, the club's focus changed from being a football club to more of a business. The lads all felt it. People may have said we were overachieving, but we were a football club with aspirations of getting as high up the Football League as possible. Around the time Keith left, other high-profile people left, such as the chairman, and different people were now sitting in senior positions. You felt the difference, literally the day after he left – it felt different. There was less emphasis on what was going on on the pitch and more emphasis on the background. It may have been something the club had to do, I genuinely don't know, but it was definitely more about "Who can we sell?" rather than "Who can we bring in?"

'In the end, nine of us left at the end of that season. I had a bad season performance-wise, but I didn't get an opportunity to play properly under Brian Barry-Murphy, who took over from Keith. It was doubly hard because he's a good friend of mine. It was as hard on him as it was on me, but it put a strain on our relationship when he took over from Keith. The only time I played was when we had defensive injuries and I was put in at centre-half. It's a gift and a curse that I am so willing to play the game that I'll play anywhere. You end up getting used as the utility guy, which definitely happened to me towards the end of my Rochdale career. Under Brian Barry-Murphy, I played 18 games and 15 of them were in defence. The season after, I'm left trying to find a club, pitching myself as a striker. People then look at my scoring record, and the games I played, and look at me funny. I then have to explain, "I didn't play up front last season." So, it doesn't always work out for you, being that person, you know? Looking back, though, I would have done it no other way.

'Still, I felt I was being pushed out. It's hard then to bring a performance to the table when you know everything is against you. It was difficult. It's a shame things ended the way they did, because I had such a good time at Rochdale. All good things must come to end though, I guess.

'I've been to so many clubs in my career and learned so many things – taking a little bit from each. It's a game full of politics. You'll hear people say that but, when you're in it, you really do understand the depths it goes to. It's not always the best 11 out on the pitch because of stuff that goes on behind closed doors, for example. Sometimes it's not the manager's fault, sometimes his hands are tied, but not always. It's things like that which toughen you up as you go on. You learn not to take things as personally. I still maintain those years at Rochdale under Keith Hill are the best I had. There were no agendas, no politics – it was just a case of doing the best you could for a common cause.'

Epilogue

WITH THE last of the personnel to be featured in this book departed from the club, something of a tumultuous period would follow for Rochdale AFC. Dark clouds gathered over the Pennines and brought with them not just a global pandemic, but relegation and opportunism too.

Keith Hill was removed as manager in March 2019 and his understudy, Brian Barry-Murphy, took over with 11 games remaining of the 2018/19 season. He just about managed to keep the club in League One. A steely resolve was evident – a must-not-lose-at-all-costs mentality that saw the side eke out four vital 1-0 victories, among other notable results, on the road to safety.

Installed as permanent manager for 2019/20, Barry-Murphy outlined his vision for the future. There was a realisation that the style of football needed to keep Rochdale in League One in those final 11 games was not his preferred modus operandi. Instead he would want to play a possession-based passing game that should be both pleasing on the eye and allow the youth academy graduates to develop into saleable assets to teams higher up the football pyramid. This business model was not a new one. It was definitely the way former chairman Chris Dunphy wanted the club to operate during his time, albeit the execution may have been different.

With Barry-Murphy's permanent appointment, the atmosphere around the club initially felt good, too. No game better exemplified his preferred style of play as an away trip to Southend United in August 2019. Yes, the hosts had lost all of their opening league fixtures and would eventually be relegated, but the old adage 'you can only play what's in front of you' rings true here. Barry-Murphy's Dale put on a masterclass of champagne football, of which one of the goals in the 3-0 victory became a viral social media clip drawing comparison with Barcelona or Brazil.

Then there were the cup games against Premier League opposition: a magnificent home FA Cup tie against Newcastle United, which earned a replay, and a phenomenal display against Manchester United in the Carabao Cup at Old Trafford, which ended only after defeat on penalties.

The issue was, however, to use those above examples again, that they were performances in isolation. The brand of football just wasn't consistent enough to ensure long-term success or even safety.

As the global Covid-19 pandemic struck in March 2020, and football was suspended, Rochdale achieved League One survival thanks to a points-per-game calculation. However, Barry-Murphy's approach proved unsustainable over a full campaign next time around and Rochdale paid with their place in League One. A return to League Two was confirmed in May 2021.

This relegation came with some unwanted records, too. Seventeen home league games without a win was chief among them. If you add to that the cup tie, it was 18 at home without a win, exceeding the previous record of 16 from November 1931 to September 1932.

Relegation was not to be the sole concern to trouble Rochdale supporters. Sadly, there was a much greater threat to the club's existence brewing in the background. New chairman Andrew Kilpatrick resigned unexpectedly in February 2021 citing 'personal reasons', and there then followed an extraordinary fans' forum where it was revealed Barry-Murphy had had his contract extended without any communication to the supporters and, it appeared, most of the board also.

The relationship between fans and the board was now being sorely tested, but it was to reach a higher peak of despair.

In April 2021, the board had proposed resolutions for releasing new shares in the club and claimed to have already identified preferred investors, who intended to acquire a 51 per cent stake. The identities of these investors were not declared due to the board claiming these parties had signed Non-Disclosure Agreements. In protest at the unexplained contract extension of Barry-Murphy, and the issuing of shares to an unknown party, the Rochdale Supporters' Trust proposed its own EGM, with motions to remove chief executive David Bottomley and director Graham Rawlinson from the board.

During an historic night, the board withdrew its proposals after intense scrutiny from shareholders and the supporters' trust – proposals that would have ultimately awarded an unknown party a controlling stake in the club.

The trust motions were passed by a majority of shareholders too, and saw Bottomley and Rawlinson removed by a democratic vote. This was hailed a victory for supporter power, with new board members put forward from a cohort of long-time fans. Chief among those was Simon Gauge, who was swiftly appointed the club's new chairman. His vision was to unify the club and supporters once again.

However, almost immediately he faced a massive challenge.

Morton House MGT, a payroll company with no prior experience in the football industry, claimed to the EFL in the summer of 2021 to have purchased 42 per cent of all available shares in Rochdale AFC, directly from a small number of individual holders.

This attempted takeover of the club made national news and became the subject of an English Football League (EFL) investigation, as it transpired the private acquisition of shares had not conformed to the EFL's Owners' and Directors' Test. The EFL said it had launched an investigation into 'multiple individuals', demonstrating the depth and complexity of the issue.

Despite it then telling the EFL in August that it planned to withdraw and divest from Rochdale AFC, Morton House lodged a High Court petition, alleging that the supporters' trust and the board had unlawfully caused prejudice to Morton House as a shareholder in the football club – something which the trust and the directors strenuously denied.

The trust was subsequently forced to launch a crowdfunding campaign in a bid to combat the legal action.

It was widely reported in the media that the Morton House takeover was led by an Andrew Curran and Darrell Rose, along with their intermediary Alex Jarvis.

In October 2021, Curran was charged by the Football Association with an aggravated breach of rule E3 after being accused of calling members of the board 'nancy boys' and the people of Rochdale 'small-minded'. Curran was found guilty by the FA in January 2022 and suspended from all football activity, which included a ground ban up to and including Wednesday, 14 March 2022. Curran was also ordered to complete a mandatory face-to-face education programme.

Both Curran and Rose subsequently relinquished their involvement with Morton House, as did Jarvis, leaving only Faical Safouane and Denise Valerie Courtnell listed as directors. It then emerged that former Charlton Athletic chairman Matt Southall was acting as an intermediary and spokesperson for the company.

The EFL announced in March 2022 that it had gathered 'sufficient evidence' from its investigation to go ahead and charge multiple individuals. At the time of publication, the EFL's verdict was still pending, as was Morton House's legal action against the trust and directors.

Despite this, while Rochdale are now back in the 'Rochdale Division', and Brian Barry-Murphy has walked away to join the Manchester City under-23 setup, the future looks bright because the people who make the club what it is are right behind it. There are many fables in football, most of which relate to events that have unfolded on the pitch. This one, however, will long be remembered and used as an example of what supporters can achieve at a club if they work together collectively. Rochdale is a town famous for founding the co-operative movement. Never has it felt more apparent since, than right here and right now.

Acknowledgements

IN ADDITION to all of those interviewed, I would like to extend a special thanks to the following, without the help of whom I would not have been able to complete this book: Mark Wilbraham, Matt Smith, Dan Youngs, Colin Cavanah, Roisin Eadie, Ed Jones, Dany Robson, Derby County Football Club, Mel Booth, Doug Thomson, Gareth Howe, Stuart Niven, Mark Harrison, Craig G. Telfer, Paul Berry, Colin Tatum, Max Fitzgerald, David Charles, Martin Swain, Darren Bentley, Ed Smith, Leighanne Coyle, Ian 'Roccydaleian' Wright, Will Moorcroft, Lawrence Moore.